LIVE & WORK IN
ITALY

Victoria Pybus
Huw Francis

SERIES EDITORS VICTORIA PYBUS & DAVID WOODWORTH

Published by Vacation Work, 9 Park End Street, Oxford
www.vacationwork.co.uk

LIVE & WORK IN

ITALY

LIVE AND WORK IN ITALY

First edition 1992 Victoria Pybus & Rachel Robinson
Second edition 1998 Victoria Pybus
Third edition 2002 Victoria Pybus & Huw Francis

ISBN 1-85458-287-9

Publicity: Roger Musker

Cover design by Miller Craig & Cocking Design Partnership

Text design and typesetting by Brendan Cole

Printed and bound by Legoprint SpA, Trento

Contents

– SECTION I –
LIVING IN ITALY

– SECTION II –
WORKING IN ITALY

ACKNOWLEDGMENTS

The author and publisher would like to thank the following, in no particular order, for their invaluable help in compiling this book: Fabio Ausenda of Green Volunteers, Alessandra Dolloy of Fondazione CENSIS Rome, Barry Walker of the Italian Chamber of Commerce in London, Francesca Piovano of FILEF, Linda Travella of Casa Travella, Morfa Downs of The British Chamber of Commerce in Milan, the Reverend Richard Major of St Mark's, Florence, Angelika Smith-Aichbichler of Piedmont Properties and Joel Tortolero of www.recruitaly.com. Also, Maria Makepeace, Georgina Gordon-Ham, John Matta, Roger Warwick and Sarah Rasmer for providing us with histories of their own experiences of living and working in Italy.

Special thanks are due to Joel Tortelero, Business Development Manager of CESOP Communications for his extensive help with the *Employment* chapter.

We are also grateful to Dott. Paulo di Filippo LL.M, Managing Director of the Internet Group for his invaluable help with the chapter on *Starting a Business*.

TELEPHONE NUMBERS

Please note that the telephone numbers in this book are written as needed to call that number from inside the same country. To call these numbers from outside the country you will need to know the relevant international access code; these are currently 00 from the UK and Italy and 011 from the USA.

To call Italy: dial the international access code + 39 + the complete number as given in this book.

To call the UK: international access code +44 + the complete number as given in this book – *but omitting the first 0 in the British number.*

To call the USA: international access code +1 + the complete number as given in this book.

FOREWORD

*L*IVE AND WORK IN ITALY is part of a successful series of books providing information and advice for those thinking of moving abroad, planning to move abroad or already living abroad. The country specific guides cover the personal aspects of living in each country, as well as work opportunities for foreigners, information on starting a business, buying a business or retirement there. *Live and Work in Italy* is divided into two sections, *Living in Italy* and *Working in Italy* respectively. These two sections cover all aspects of moving to Italy, including how and where to open a bank account, how to arrange a mortgage, how to rent an apartment or house, local employment regulations and opportunities, advice and ideas for setting up a small business and the finer points of Italian etiquette, language and culture.

Over 90,000 Britons live in Italy, of whom around two thirds are homeowners there. The majority of homeowners have set up home in the rolling hills of Tuscany and Umbria, and increasingly, Le Marche and there are others to be found in less publicised regions like Liguria, Piedmont and Puglia. Their rural lifestyles contrast greatly with the urban ones led by expatriates who live in the big cities of Milan, Turin, Ferrara and the capital Rome.

It is not just the climate that attracts foreigners to Italy – the reasons for moving there are as varied as the regions of Italy itself. Some will be posted there by international companies, some have a deep-seated love of the country and wish to immerse themselves in Italian culture, and some will have spotted a gap in the commercial market and a way to make a living and who knows, even a fortune.

Despite its disorganised and notoriously corrupt state bureaucracy, Italy boasts one of the most dynamic and efficient business areas of Europe, mostly in northern Italy; it also has friendly and hospitable host nationals, and a cultural heritage that is the cornerstone of Western civilization. Rewards, both financial and personal, await the diligent and the entrepreneurial.

The cost of property in northern Italy and the popular, idyllic regions of Tuscany and Umbria equates to the UK, though will be cheaper than in the big cities of North America. However, there are still bargains to be found in Le Marche, Abruzzo, Puglia, etc. In the cities property prices can be much higher than rural areas, especially in popular areas of the major cities of the north. When renting accommodation, prices in Naples will be much less than Florence and Rome. The cost of living is higher in Italian cities e.g. Rome, Milan, Bologna etc. than in the UK and North America, but so is the quality of life.

Until 1990, Italy's economy was one of the fastest growing in Europe. This was followed by several years of recession, and political upheaval as corruption scandals swept away the Christian Democrat party, which had held the balance of power for nearly fifty years. By all accounts, particularly her own, Italy has put the traditional political and economic problems behind her and thanks to a Euro tax in 1997 and a 1998 budget designed to get her economy in shape, she met the convergence criteria for European Monetary Union in January 1999. In 2000 the Italian economy grew by 2.9%, only slightly slower than France and Germany.

The split between north and south is still marked, though there are areas of the south that are doing well economically. Unemployment in the north is as low as 5%, while it is still over 20% in the south.

The election of May 2001 swept Silvio Berlusconi and his *Forza Italia* party into power. Berlusconi, Italy's richest man, is a man on of action who will do things his own way. Despite judicial concerns about his business dealings, he is facing a number of bribery, accounting and tax avoidance investigations, most Italians seem not to care – possibly a reflection of Italian lack of faith in the system.

Although known for their parochial outlook, the continued growth of their export economy, closer ties with Europe and a relaxation of currency restrictions has woken Italians up to the potential of international investments and there is a huge market for international consultants. Other areas of particular demand for foreign expertise include teachers of English language, medical and dental practitioners, estate agents and financial services providers, particularly of insurance and pensions.

The European Union has made significant progress towards its goal of a United States of Europe and the single currency is now a reality for Austria, Belgium, Finland, France, Germany, Greece, Ireland, Italy, Luxembourg, Holland, Portugal & Spain. Euro (Euro)notes were introduced on January 1, 2002 and the lira will cease to be legal tender within six months, as will the eleven other currencies. As the EU fosters greater integration, the Italian economy will continue to open to outside investment and increase its own outward growth. There is no doubt that opportunities will continue to increase for foreigners wishing to live and work in Italy, while media and modern communications will enable them to keep in touch more easily with friends and family at home. Italy is one of the keenest players in the European Union as it perceives its own economy will be boosted by close links with stable and strong economies such as Germany's. There is a wide range of opportunities, both professional and personal, for those foreigners who are aware of them and this book will help you learn how, where and why you can go for the best and most appropriate Italian experience for you.

Live and Work Abroad: A Guide for Modern Nomads, also published by Vacation Work Publications, compliments the country specific guides in the *Live & Work* series and covers the personal and family aspects of expatriate assignments and international living and offers advice and information on how to make the most of living in any foreign country. The aim of these publications is to provide an information base concerning the many and various regulations and practicalities involved in moving abroad. The books are applicable and useful to all nationalities of international residents, whether they are from inside the EU, or without. There are complications inherent in setting up a new home and starting a new job and/or life simultaneously in a country which has very different laws and procedures to those with which you are familiar. However, we hope that by using *Live and Work in Italy* and *Live and Work Abroad: A Guide for Modern Nomads* as reference manuals, you will be able to take this giant step briefed with the knowledge of what to expect. This knowledge should make the process of moving internationally much smoother and less stressful for you and your family.

Victoria Pybus
Huw Francis
March 2002

THE EURO

On January 1st 2002 the Euro became the legal currency in Italy, replacing the lire at the unromantic rate of 1936.27 lire to the Euro. The value of the Euro against the UK £ and the US $ varies from day to day: at the time of going to press one Euro is worth UK £0.62 or US $0.87.

Section 1

LIVING IN ITALY

GENERAL INTRODUCTION

RESIDENCE AND ENTRY REGULATIONS

SETTING UP HOME

DAILY LIFE

RETIREMENT

GENERAL INTRODUCTION

CHAPTER SUMMARY

- Italy has only existed as a unified country since 1861, and most Italians feel a loyalty to their region rather than their nation.

- There are marked differences between the more prosperous industrial north and the less affluent agricultural south of the country, but the Italian government offers incentives to attract foreign investment into the south.

- The climate is marvellous and there is a rich artistic and archaeological heritage.

- **The way of life:** Italians have a relaxed approach to doing business and frequently mix business with pleasure, with working suppers and weekend meetings.

- English is not widely spoken so a knowledge of Italian is near essential, especially when tackling the Byzantine bureacracy.

- **Politics**Italian politics is confusing, with a large number of parties broadly divided into two coalitions.

  - Silvio Berlusconi's *Casa delle Liberta* (House of Freedoms) coalition was voted into power in 2001.

- **Geography**: The European fault line runs through Italy north-south and 70% of central and southern Italy is susceptible to earthquakes.

  - Italy has a population of 58 million, and for administrative purposes it is divided into twenty regions and ninety six provinces.

  - Winters can be cold in the north but are generally mild in the south; however, the far south and Sicily can be uncomfortably hot in summer.

DESTINATION ITALY

AS THE EUROPEAN UNION increasingly dismantles economic and trade
borders between its member states, an increasing number of EU citizens are
contemplating joining thousands of their counterparts already living and working
in another member country. Now that the Euro is in people's pockets it is even
easier to cross from one country to another. The Schengen Agreement means that
border posts between Austria, Belgium, Denmark, France, Germany, Greece,
Italy, Luxembourg, Netherlands, Norway, Spain, Sweden and Portugal have been
removed and those allowed to enter the thirteen countries listed above can also
enter Iceland without requiring a visa or passing through customs checks. With
the planned expansion of the EU, more people will move between countries to
work and companies will increasingly look to hire staff from anywhere within
Europe.

As the European economy becomes increasingly united it also becomes more
attractive to non-EU companies and greater numbers of organisations from
North America, South America and the Asia Pacific Rim will send staff to
Europe. As Italy has historically had one of the lowest rates of inward investment
within the EU, it is going to become an increasingly popular target for take-overs
and exports as organisations turn to less saturated markets, resulting in more
expatriates being sent to Italy.

The prospect of being sent abroad is growing for many professionals, though
qualified workers are more likely to be sent than unqualified ones due to the
restrictions placed on unskilled foreign workers by many governments. For EU
nationals, practising their profession or skills anywhere in the European Union
is possible through a comparison system for different national qualifications,
which is becoming more familiar to employers. The EU directives concerning the
recognition of most academic and professional qualifications gained within the
EU have been in place since 1993. Likewise, prospects for setting up a business
abroad are expanding enormously as the governments of EU nations vie with
each other to offer the most attractive incentive packages to foreign investors.

As a country in which to live and work, Italy is considerably more complex, and
is probably less well understood than many other European countries. Italy as a
unified country did not exist until 1861 and most Italians have a regional loyalty
before a national one. Long-established stereotypes of Italians are, as stereotypes
usually are, mostly wrong, but they have had a trivialising and/or damaging
effect on the world's view of Italy and Italians. According to popular caricature
Italians eat vast quantities of pasta, and (if they are male) worship their mothers,
pinch bottoms and sing Verdi in the street. The Mafia is also considered to
run everything. The reality is somewhat different, not least because there are
many different kinds of Italians. Although the sinister brotherhood's influence is
pervasive in politics and commerce, the Mafia does not actually run Italy. Mafia
influence is, however, distinctly powerful in its traditional fiefdoms of Calabria,
Naples and much of the island of Sicily. The Mafia indirectly makes it presence
felt in other parts of Italy too, though to a much lesser extent.

The perception of Italy as a country of two parts has been enhanced in recent
years by the leader of the Northern League (*Lega Nord*), Umberto Bossi, who

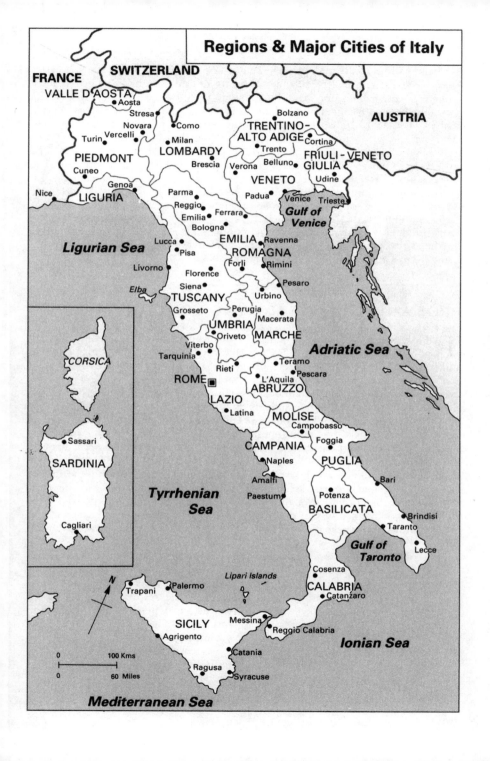

Regions & Major Cities of Italy

FRANCE

SWITZERLAND

AUSTRIA

VALLE D'AOSTA
• Aosta
Stresa
Novara
Como
Turin Vercelli
Milan
PIEDMONT
Brescia
Cuneo
Genoa
Nice
LIGURIA

Bolzano
TRENTINO-
ALTO ADIGE
Cortina
Trento
FRIULI-VENETO
Belluno GIULIA
Verona
VENETO
Udine
Padua
Venice Trieste
Parma
Reggio
Emilia Ferrara
Bologna
Gulf of
Venice

Ligurian Sea

Lucca
Pisa
Livorno
Florence
Siena
Elba
TUSCANY
Grosseto

EMILIA
ROMAGNA Ravenna
Forli Rimini
Pesaro
Urbino
Perugia
UMBRIA Macerata
Oriveto MARCHE

Adriatic Sea

Viterbo
Tarquinia
ROME
LAZIO
Latina

Rieti Teramo
L'Aquila Pescara
ABRUZZO

MOLISE
Campobasso
CAMPANIA Foggia
Naples PUGLIA
Amalfi
Paestum
Potenza
BASILICATA Bari
Brindisi
Taranto
Gulf of
Taranto
Lecce

CORSICA

• Sassari

SARDINIA

Cagliari

Tyrrhenian
Sea

Lipari Islands
Cosenza
CALABRIA
Catanzaro

N

Palermo
Trapani
SICILY
Agrigento
Messina
Reggio Calabria
Ionian Sea

Catania
Ragusa
Syracuse

0   100 Kms
0   60 Miles

Mediterranean Sea

has been calling for an independent state to be created in the north. The Lega Nord has gained up to 10% of the vote elections and even had two government ministers for a while, until the inevitable collapse of the coalition in place at the time. Though the likelihood of a split is remote, the differences between the north and south of Italy are marked. In the north the inhabitants are generally, more serious, industrious and prosperous, while the south, the *Mezzogiorno*, is traditionally poor, violent and ruled by the Mafia. However, it would be an error to write off the *Mezzogiorno* as an area in which to live and work, since the Italian government is offering huge financial incentives for foreign business interests investing in certain areas like Puglia, Molise and Abruzzi where in consequence, prosperity is increasing. SviluppoItalia (Agency for Economic and Entrepreneurial Development, ☎06 421 60939-43-45; investinitaly@sviluppoitalia.it;www.sviluppoitalia.it) now run adverts highlighting the tax breaks and incentives available for investors in magazines like *The Economist* to attract new foreign investment.

PROS AND CONS OF MOVING TO ITALY

THOSE SEEKING EMPLOYMENT or business opportunities in Italy will find that the country has much to offer: the presence of many major Italian and international companies offers a huge range of possibilities for employment and also opportunities for consultancy and other freelance work. There is a dynamism about northern Italian business people which puts some of their fellow Europeans to shame. However, Italians do not like to be hustled and will strictly observe the necessary social and business etiquette before clinching a deal. Italians work late but quite often mix commerce with pleasure: a working supper or weekend meetings with business colleagues being common occurrences. Though different to UK and North American business practices, many expatriates find that they adapt quickly to this style of business and find they enjoy the Italian working style when compared to those of other countries and enjoy working with Italians more than other nationalities. However, many will find the laid back style and apparently relaxed way of doing business frustrating, especially when it eats into evenings and weekends that are usually thought of as free time or family time.

Those who might be concerned that they are moving to a country where living standards and infrastructures leave a lot to be desired and where the government is inherently unstable will find only a few of their worst fears justified. Generally, Italy is a highly developed country where even the farmers have the latest model Lancia or Audi tucked away in a barn, and where workers know the exact market value of their skills in the work place. The Italian postal system, especially for internal services, is probably the most inefficient in Europe, but the telephone system which until recently was comparable with the post, has undergone complete modernisation, and the Italians have embraced the mobile phone like no other nation. The road system which owes much to the Romans, Mussolini and the charging of staggeringly high tolls, is one of the best in Europe.

PROS:

- There are favourable employment prospects for skilled workers and professionals.
- Industry is very advanced and successful, particularly in the north of Italy.
- The Italians have a strong economy that is paying dividends to foreign investors: many of the most profitable companies in Italy are foreign owned.
- Housing and public transport are considerably cheaper than in the UK.
- Managerial salaries are around 30-35% higher in Italy than in the UK.
- The climate in most regions is marvelous and Italy has some of the most beautiful landscapes in Europe.
- Italy has by far the greatest art and architectural heritage of any European country.
- Italy has much to offer by way of lifestyle and living standards.
- Italians are extremely receptive to foreigners.

CONS:

- Knowledge of Italian is essential to conduct business in Italy as state bureaucrats and most Italian business people speak virtually no English.
- Large parts of southern Italy are unsuitable for foreign business ventures thanks to the influence of the Mafia.
- There are enormous differences in business practices between northern and southern Italy.
- Italy has a Byzantine bureaucracy that is notorious for being oiled by the proffering of *bustarelle* (little envelopes), i.e. bribes (a.k.a. *costi aggiunti* – added costs).
- Start up costs for businesses in northern Italy can be horrendously high.
- Employers pay very high employee social security contributions (as they do in much of Europe when compared to the USA and the UK).
- Italian social behaviour and customs can seem totally at odds with the British and American way of doing things.

The much publicised fifty plus changes of government since the end of the Second World War, amount to little more than reshuffles as Italy was dominated by the same political party, the Christian Democrats, for fifty years. Ironically, this made Italy one of the more politically stable countries in Europe.

Italy has made well-advertised efforts to clean up politics in recent years by weeding out the corruptors and corrupted and prosecuting them where necessary and/or possible. Similarly, there has been a concerted move to bring the big Mafia bosses to trial and bang them up for long jail sentences. It remains to be seen how effective this will prove: apparently in some cases, Mafia women have been running things while the men folk are in jail.

One of the disadvantages for foreigners wishing to set up businesses, especially in northern Italy, is that costs are extremely high: office space and service costs etc. seem disproportionate to other factors, including official salary levels which are lower than in the UK and much lower than in the US. Actual levels of individual income are, however, virtually impossible to assess, as nowhere in Europe is the pastime of tax evasion practised with such verve as in Italy. In the 1990's the Italian Inland Revenue estimated that nine out of ten taxpayers were dodging at least some of their dues. In part, such large-scale evasion derives from the fact that many Italians have second or even third jobs. So while the level of salaries does not correspond to the otherwise obvious prosperity of many Italians, the fact is, they manage have more spending money than their counterparts in France and the UK. Admittedly, some aspects of life in Italy are cheaper than in the UK, notably public transport and housing (especially for the many Italians who live in large family groups).

Italy has a marvellous climate, which is a distinct advantage in the eyes of Britons contemplating setting up home there. However, the glorious cities which are a main attraction for tourists and foreign residents alike, often seem to be cared for indifferently by their citizens: traffic problems, pollution and a shortage of funds have all conspired to make many cities, even the historic ones, look dilapidated. Though with such an enormous heritage of art and architecture it is perhaps hardly surprising that there is insufficient money to cover the maintenance of all such treasures.

Moving from the UK to Italy inevitably involves some language problems. Unless you are already proficient in Italian it is essential to take an Italian course as otherwise you will be at a disadvantage in a country where business and social life are virtually intertwined. Furthermore, unlike some Europeans, notably the Scandinavians and Germans, Italians are not noted for their fluent grasp of English. While this situation has been remedied to certain extent by the inclusion of English in the school curriculum, it should nevertheless be unthinkable for foreigners to live in Italy without learning Italian.

HISTORY, POLITICS AND ECONOMIC STRUCTURE

History

THERE IS NOT SPACE HERE to do justice to Italian history, which is, in effect, the history of the former kingdoms, states and duchies that now make up Italy. However, it is necessary to have a basic knowledge of the country's recent past including *Il Risorgimento* (The Unification), in order to understand Italy and Italians today. It could be argued that the first proponent of a unified Italy was Napoleon I who, during the years of French occupation from 1796 to 1814, managed to set up a modern, meritocratic civil service regulated by the Code Napoléon. Unification proper took place in stages beginning with the annexation by Count Camillo Cavour (Italy's answer to Bismarck) of most of northern and central Italy during 1859 and 1860. Meanwhile the popular hero and guerrilla fighter, Giuseppe Garibaldi (1807-82) joined Cavour's Piedmontese northern alliance and conquered the entire south of Italy, which was then united with the north under the Piedmontese king, Vittorio Emanuele II. The remaining pieces of the Italian jigsaw, Veneto (the region around Venice) and Lazio (the region around Rome) were added in 1866 and 1870 respectively. During the process of Risorgimento the seat of government moved three times: until 1865 it was in Turin, followed by a six-year sojourn in Florence before finally settling in Rome in 1871.

In the aftermath of the First World War Italy was in a demoralised and confused state beset by crippling strikes which were accompanied by a breakdown of law and order. There was the very real possibility of a communist revolution until Benito Mussolini rallied the wealthy and middle classes to oppose communism. A former journalist, he managed to exploit fear of the communists on the part of the wealthy and the middle-classes sufficiently to win himself and his Fascist Party 35 seats in the 1921 Parliament. Later the same year the government collapsed and Mussolini staged his famous 'March on Rome' when, accompanied by 30,000 *camicie nere* (the 'Black Shirts') he entered Parliament and convinced the government and the King that in the absence of any other competent powers he should be awarded outright dictatorship. The King and parliament agreed, initially for a one-year period, which in the event extended to 21 years of Fascist rule – much the same as the dictator Sulla did in Roman times. Under Mussolini the Italians were probably more organised than they have ever been since the Romans – an era constantly evoked in Mussolini's military iconography.

At home, Mussolini drained the Pontine Marshes, made the trains run on time, and instigated the Lateran Pact with the Vatican, thus creating a workable relationship between Church and State for the first time in Italian history. Abroad, the Italian Empire of East Africa was created following the shockingly brutal take over of Abyssinia in 1935. Mussolini contributed greatly to the restoration of national pride, at the expense of almost all civil liberties, but he managed to avoid most of the unspeakable excesses of the parallel regime in Germany. In 1939 Mussolini allied Italy to Germany when he signed the Pact of Steel with Hitler.

Following the collapse of his regime towards the end of the Second World War, Mussolini and the die-hard remnant of his supporters fled Rome, which fell to the Allies in 1943, and set up the Independent Republic of Salèo in the north east corner of Italy. The Mussolini era was brought to an ignominious end on April 28, 1945 when 'Il Duce' was captured and executed by partisans and hung upside down alongside his mistress, Claretta Petacci, and his leading supporters from a lamp post in Milan's busiest square, the *Piazza Loreto*.

In May 1946 Italy held a national referendum to decide whether to retain the monarchy or institute a republic. The republic won and the last king of Italy, Umberto II, went submissively into exile. Elections followed for the Constituent Assembly whose function was to decide what kind of constitution Italy would have, and then draw it up. Two years later, in 1948, the first parliamentary elections of the new republic saw the Christian Democrats romp home to victory and begin their lengthy domination of parliament which lasted for almost 50 years until their demise, mainly through corruption scandals, in 1994. Their attempts at rebuilding the party and making a comeback suffered a major setback when it emerged that the Christian Democrats had used their influence to cover up a massacre of an entire Italian village by SS troops in 1944. Allegedly the cover-up was a favour for their counterparts in Germany.

POLITICAL STRUCTURE

AT THE PINNACLE of the state is the President of the Republic who also controls the armed forces and the Judiciary and is elected for a seven-year term by both chambers, plus 58 regional representatives. Next in the hierarchy is the President of the Senate and third comes the President of the Chamber of Deputies. The powers of the President correspond approximately to those of the British monarch, i.e. they are mainly ceremonial and include dissolving parliaments, approving or vetoing the appointing of Prime Ministers and the signing or vetoing of new laws. The seat of government is in Rome, the capital of Italy. Parliament is made up of two chambers, the *Camera dei Deputati* (Chamber of Deputies) and the *Senato* (Senate). Since neither of these chambers takes precedence over the other, frequent conflicts over parliamentary bills are the norm. The *Camera dei Deputati* comprises 630 members housed in the *Palazzo Montecitorio*. The *Senato* meanwhile occupies another building, the *Palazzo Madama*, and has around 326 members some of whom are elected for life. Proceedings in both chambers are generally conducted less boisterously than in the notoriously noisy House of Commons in the UK. Women made up 9.2% of members in both houses after the 2001 election, which is less than after the 1996 election.

The Italian voting system is immensely complicated, involving hundreds of candidates per electoral region. Since most of the candidates are unknown to the voters, a system has evolved whereby major political figures put forward their names for several constituencies simultaneously and then stand down in favour of lesser-known candidates allowing them to sail home on their votes. This is perfectly legal and readily employed.

The proportional representation system has been gradually reduced so that nowadays, three quarters of candidates are chosen on a first past the post system and the rest by proportional representation. In the past, proportional representation has meant an average of around twenty-five parties being represented in Parliament, so Italy can only be ruled by a coalition of parties who are broadly banded into centre-left or centre-right groupings. After the 2001 election 15 parties were elected to the senate and chamber of deputies. They were mainly grouped into two coalitions, The House of Freedoms (*Casa delle Liberta*) and Olive Tree (*L'Ulivo*).

The fashion of adopting celebrity candidates is, like many things Italian, done more flamboyantly than elsewhere, for example the election of the porno-actress Ilona Staller ('*La Cicciolina*') – somehow Glenda Jackson and Clint Eastwood do not have quite the same ring! Alessandra Mussolini, a former glamour girl and actress and granddaughter of Benito Mussolini, was elected as an MP for Naples and Ischia in 1992. She is now a force in the *Alleanza Nationale*, which was part of the briefly lived Berlusconi administration in 1994. As well as flamboyant candidates, Italy also has extreme left and right wing parties which are basically communist and fascist; these parties (e.g. the neo-Fascist *Alleanza Nationale*) are sometimes part of the government.

Italy changes Prime Minister approximately once every nine months. After the 2001 election Silvio Berlusconi, who leads the Forza Italia, gained power and looks likely to last longer than any of his predecessors have done.

Political Parties

Foreign observers of Italian politics may find themselves hard pressed to spot any discernible differences between many of the political parties. In common with many First World countries, Italy has experienced the increasing prosperity of the once poorer classes, which has resulted in a corresponding decrease in extremism that once characterised the leftist parties. In Italy this means that even the *Partito Comunista Italiano* (Italian Communist Party) is broadly comparable to New Labour in Britain. Italian political parties tend to splinter into *correnti* (factions) which gravitate around the more powerful political leaders. Therefore, to achieve any kind of political power, tactical manoeuvring of the most Machiavellian kind is required. Strategic alliances are formed and broken on purely opportunistic grounds. The lengths to which party leaders will go to win the loyalty of the local electorate deepens the imperspicuity of Italian politics.

Italian political parties are funded to a staggering extent by the state. In 1999 the Italian parliament voted in a new law that provides a subsidy of approximately US$2 per voter, that is divided among political parties who received more than 1% of the vote in the last election. With such funds the political support of whole villages and communities can be bought on the promise of extra jobs through the creation of an entirely useless state office or wing of a hospital for which fictitious wages and even false pensions will be paid. After the 2001 election, two main coalitions were elected:

The House of Freedoms (Casa delle Liberta) Coalition: led by Silvio Berlusconi and his *Forza Italia* party, it gained 177 seats in the senate and 368 seats in the Chamber of deputies. The coalition included the following parties:

Forza Italia (Forwards Italy). As a young party, with a businessman as its leader, it remains to be seen how *Forza Italia* will develop. In its own words *Forza Italia* is: '...a party with a very simple name. Its substance is to be 'the people's party', the party of those with goodwill and common sense, the party of the Italians who love other people as well as their own country, the party of the Italians who love freedom. *Forza Italia*: force of freedom.

Alleanza Nazionale (National Alliance). Formed when the *Movimento Sociale Italiano* (MSI) was dismantled in 1994. The MSI was a Neo-Fascist party founded just after the Second World War. There has always been a certain amount of nostalgia for Il Duce (Mussolini) and the recruitment of Alessandra Mussolini, his granddaughter, to party ranks helped turn the fortunes of the MSI around as did its new name the *Alleanza Nazionale*. The old MSI-DS also included sympathisers of the deposed Bourbon royal dynasty and some right-wing thuggery in the form of extremist youth movements. They now have a credible leader in the smooth-talking Gianfranco Fini. The Alleanza Nazionale is trying to drop its neo-fascist image – difficult when you have a Mussolini on board who is determined to wow the neo-fascist voters.

Lega Nord (Northern League). In the May 1990 local elections, a new political party of the right, the Lega Lombarda was voted in. Other similar regional parties in northern Italy, notably the Lega Veneta, did not do as well but these two have now combined into the Lega Nord. The Lega Nord and other right wing political organisations throughout Europe attract a disproportionate amount of publicity and probably does not represent a marked increase in extreme right wing support. In the 2001 elections *Lega Nord* did not reach the 4% nationawide threshold to gain seats in parliament through proportional representation.

Centro Cristiano Democratico (Christian Democratic Center). Formed by splitting away from the old Christian Democrat party just as it was crumbling in the wake of the massive corruption scandals in the early 1990's. Nominally a Catholic party, the Christian Democrats took a hard line on abortion and divorce but a liberal line on most other issues including the treatment of terrorists.

Cristiani Democratici Uniti (Christian Democratic Union). Rose out of the demise of the Christian Democrats in 1995, the CDU is conservative and has allied itself with the CCD.

Partito Socialista Italiano (Socialist Party). The Socialist Party is no such thing, being vehemently right wing and incorrigibly corrupt. When he was leader of the party, Bettino Craxi was Prime Minister for four years. The SPI has historically received about 14% of the national vote but a disproportionate share (30%) of the administration. Therefore it was able to manipulate the Christian Democrats which needed the co-operation of the PSI to stay in power.

The Olive Tree (L'Ulivo) Coalition: led by Francesco Rutelli, this main opposition grouping gained 125 seats in the senate and 242 in the Chamber of Deputies. The coalition included the following parties:

Partito Democratico della Sinistra (Democrats of the Left). This is the former *Partito Comunista Italiano* (Italian Communist Party). The PDS was the traditional main opposition party, but during the years of Italian prosperity has become the virtual equivalent of the Christian Democrats except that it portrays itself as the (only) party free from corruption. Its main base and spiritual home is the supremely wealthy city of Bologna. The PDS won 34% of the votes in 1976 and in 1997 was the single biggest party in the 'Ulivo' (Olive Tree) government of Romano Prodi. In the 2001 election their percentage of the vote dropped to 16.6% – the second largest percentage in the election.

La Margherita is a grouping of four centre left parties, which are: *Partito Popolare Italiano* (Italian People's Party), *I Democratici* (Democrats), *Rinnovamento Italiano* (Italian Renovation) and *Unione Democratici per l'Europa* (Democratic Union for Europe). These parties themselves are made up of separate groups from various cities around Italy.

Partito dei Comunisti Italiani (Italian Communists Party). Founded on October 11, 1998, the party is made up of members who split from the *Rifondazione Comunista* for ideological and political reasons.

I Verdi (Greens). The Greens and the Rainbow Greens (*Verdi-Arcobaleno*) merged to form the Federazione dei Verde and have seats in both the Italian Parliament and the European Parliament. The Greens are gaining popularity in Europe, especially Italy and Germany where they have been part of both governments.

Partito Socialdemocratico Italiano (Italian Democratic Socialists). With very little going for them political, the party is, however, notoriously adept at buying votes – to the tune of 3% of the electorate.

Outside of the two coalitions, the Communist Refocundation Party (PRC), led by Fausto Bertinotti also won 3 seats in the Senate and 11 in the Chamber of Deputies. The *Rifondazione Communista* is a hard line leftist party which formed part of the centre-left coalition of Romano Prodi's 'Ulivo' government elected in the early summer of 1996. *The Radical Party*, led by Emma Bonino lost the one seat they held in the senate as did the *Fiamma Tricolore* led by Pino Rauti.

ECONOMY

ITALY'S POST-WAR economic aims are to a large extent responsible for today's massive division between north and south. The powers of the time decided to open up Italy's economy and go for an international export market rather than concentrate on restructuring production for self-sufficiency at home. This was about the extent to which the Italians went to plan a post-war economy and up until quite recently policy in this area can best be summed up as *laissez-faire*. In other words, production was allowed to rally to the demands of the open market with virtually no controls or restraints. Such an economic 'policy' was to a great extent dictated by circumstance, namely that Italy possessed few of the resources (e.g. iron, coal & oil) essential for most industrial processes. Italy's main markets have traditionally been Western Europe and North America. Rather than pour money into quickly modernising agricultural production methods, which would have resulted in mass unemployment in the south, most resources were directed into expanding the industries of the north. As agriculture slowly modernised and therefore required a smaller labour force, the unemployed farm-workers of the south were used as a cheap source of labour for the expanding factories of the north – which helped offset the cost of importing the resources necessary for the manufacturing processes.

The years between 1958 and 1962 were years of thriving economic growth for Italy. However, with their economy so closely linked with the USA, the lira, which was pegged at 625 per dollar until 1971, collapsed along with the whole system of fixed exchange rates when America devalued the dollar. Italy's economy stayed weak up to the beginning of the 1980's and Italy was well known as the poorest of Western European countries. In the 1980's the economy took off again at breakneck speed. However, there was a downside to the rapid economic growth. As a result of having had no clear discernible economic policy for years, the national debt had now grown to the extent that it exceeded Gross Domestic Product and stood at 123% of GDP. By raising VAT (sales tax) rates in 1997 and exercising great budget discipline, which verged on austerity measures, the budget deficit, which was running at 6%, was reduced to 2.8% and Italy managed to meet the strict requirements of the European Union for entry into European Monetary Union.

Italy's economy grew faster than most others in Europe in 2000 and early 2001, but its growth had stopped by the middle of 2001. The growth in the economy has raised the per capita GDP to around US$21,000, but this figure is misleading as to the general wealth of the country because of the disparity between the north and south of the country. This slowdown, coupled with increased public spending (big pay rises for public servants), means that the budget deficit for 2001 is likely to be greater than EU guidelines for Eurozone members. Berlusconi's government has provided few details on how they will fulfil their election promises and it remains to be seen how the Italian economy will cope with the world economic slowdown that began in 2001.

If stringent budgets are the solution to one of Italy's economic problems the other one still remains. The workforce of the north is highly motivated (some say by runaway hedonism) which makes it an excellent area of Europe for those thinking of living and working abroad. In economic terms, Italy claims to have done better at reducing its budget deficit than either France or Germany – though this seems to be an optimistic claim. If it is true about the budget deficit, then it means that Italy is in a better state to succeed in the single currency than either France or Germany, which does not bode well for the Euro. However, such a claim is belied by the enormous national debt, 9% unemployment and the enormous drain on government resources caused by the demands of welfare system. Also, in the ten years to 2000 the Italian GDP was the slowest growing (in percentage terms) when compared to the USA, UK, Spain, France and Germany. The only good news was that Italy reduced inflation from double figures at the end of 1980s to around 2% in the mid 1990s, though it is now back up to 2.8% – higher then the EU average.

One factor that is not usually taken into account when assessing the state of the Italian economy is the mind-boggling amount of revenue lost through tax evasion. This is despite the fact that taxation accounts for approximately 43% of GDP – second only to France at 46% and compared to the US at 29%. There are signs that the government is at last making some catches in these teeming waters to the extent that tax revenues have shown progressive increases since 1988. The current target is Italians living abroad who are suspected of fiddling the residence criteria to avoid paying their motherland's taxes. The Italian tax authorities can also levy taxes on perceived wealth – such as the Ferrari parked in the garage of an impoverished builder.

Milan is the home of the Italian stock market (Consiglio Di Borsa, Plazza degli Affari 6, Milan, Italy 21033; ☎39-2-724-26-336; fax 39-2-724-26-336; www.borsaitalia.it) and therefore Italy's financial capital. The Milan stock market (*la borsa*) is small, with only 299 companies listed in 2001, compared with 2,500 in London and over 3,000 in New York (including 400 non-US companies). The Italian *borsa* has been run for decades by the same families and insider dealing was legal until quite recently. Italian stockbrokers are doubtful that recent legislation against insider dealing will be effective against a practice that is so engrained and difficult to prove. Italian companies also tend to be much smaller than their European and US counterparts – of the top 500 European companies only 7% are Italian.

The 'borsa' was privatised in 1997 under Italy's big sell off of state assets and from 1998 the government attempted to entice small companies to be quoted by offering generous tax incentives, as well as encouraging larger companies to reinvest profits in the market by cutting tax on them by nearly 50%.

Securities trading companies are known as *Societa di Intermediadiazone Mobiliare* (SIM) and are the sole stock market intermediaries.

Italy in the Future

Despite the difficulties with its economy already mentioned above, Italians are optimistic about the future and the country continues to attract a steady amount of foreign investment – though the amounts are miniscule compared to the UK which attracts around 30% of all inward EU investment. Italian economists have traditionally been pessimistic; in their view the economy was like the Titanic – heading full steam toward disaster. This is probably why the Italians are so keen on European Monetary Union and the stabilising effect of the European Union generally. There is no doubt that government faces economic problems including a large amount of debt and the fact that one mainstay of the economy, the Italian fashion industry, has been greatly undermined by the upsurge of designers in countries which have traditionally bought Italian clothes (i.e. Germany). The undercutting of the fashion market by designers who have clothes made up in the Far East will continue to be problematic for the Italian economy. But some of the old problems are being tackled as determined government policy has shoe-horned Italy into meeting the criteria for monetary union and the problems of corruption, lack of transparency and the massive bureaucracy are at least being considered with a view to being remedied. However, Italy still imports 80% of its oil while having voted in a national referendum to phase out the entire Italian nuclear power programme. Also, the separation between the highly developed north and the poor south will continue to be exacerbated by the ongoing economic success of the north at the expense of the south, unless greater action is taken to encourage investors (both foreign and domestic) to look at areas they have previously discounted.

GEOGRAPHICAL INFORMATION

Mainland and Offshore Italy

ITALY OCCUPIES AN AREA OF 116,000 SQUARE MILES (301,278 sq km). As well as the long peninsula which, as most schoolchildren learn, is shaped like a boot, Italy's offshore elements include the island of Sicily situated off the toe of the boot across the Strait of Messina, the islands of Pantelleria, Linosa and Lampedusa which lie between Sicily and Tunisia, the island of Elba located off Tuscany, and the rocky, barren island of Sardinia which lies west of Rome and south of Corsica. The Tyrrhenian Sea bounds the south west of the peninsula, with the Ionian Sea under the sole of the boot. The Adriatic Sea lies on the eastern side between Italy and former-Yugoslavia. Italy shares borders with France, Switzerland, Austria and Slovenia.

Main physical features include the Alps, which form much of the the northern border with Slovenia, Austria, Switzerland and France. Also in the north are Italy's main lakes: Guarda, Maggiore and Como. An offshoot of the Alps curves round the Gulf of Genoa and runs spine-like down the peninsula to form the Appenines. The longest river, the Po, lies in the north and flows from west to

TABLE 1	AUTONOMOUS REGIONS
5 regions with special autonomy	
FRIULI-VENEZIA GIULIA	Gorizia, Pordenone, Trieste, Udine.
TRENTINO-ALTO ADIGE	Bolzano, Trento.
VALLE D'AOSTA	Aosta.
SARDEGNA (SARDINIA)	Cagliari, Nuoro, Oristano, Sassari.
SICILIA (SICILY)	Agrigento, Caltanissetta, Catania, Enna, Messina, Palermo, Ragusa, Siracusa (Syracuse), Trapini.
15 regions with standard autonomy	
ABRUZZO	Chieti, L'Aquila, Pescara, Teramo.
BASILICATA (LUCANIA)	Matera, Potenza.
CALABRIA	Cantazaro, Cosenza, Reggio di Calabria.
CAMPANIA	Avellino, Benevento, Caserta, Napoli (Naples), Salerno.
EMILIA ROMAGNA	Bologna, Ferrara, Forli, Modena, Piacenza, Parma, Ravenna, Regio Emilia.
LAZIO	Frosinone, Latina, Rieti, Roma, Viterbo.
LIGURIA	Genova, Imperia, La Spezia, Savona.
LOMBARDIA (LOMBARDY)	Bergamo, Brescia, Como, Cremona, Mantova (Mantua), Milano, Pavia, Sondrio, Varese.
MARCHE	Ancona, Ascoli Piceno, Macerata, Pesaro.
MOLISE	Campobasso, Isernia.
PIEMONTE (PIEDMONT)	Alessandria, Asti, Cuneo, Novara, Torino (Turin), Vercelli.
PUGLIA (APULIA)	Bari, Brindisi, Foggia, Lecce, Taranto.
TOSCANA (TUSCANY)	Arezzo, Firenze (Florence), Grosseto, Livorno (Leghorn), Lucca, Massa Carrara, Pisa, Pistoia, Siena.
UMBRIA	Perugia, Terni.
VENETO	Belluno, Padova (Padua), Rovigno, Treviso, Venezia (Venice), Verona, Vicenza.

east across the plain of Lombardy and into the Adriatic. On Sicily, the still active volcano, Mount Etna rises to 10,741 feet (3,274 m). Etna has been very active during 2001 and some experts were predicting a major eruption.

Earthquakes & Volcanoes The European fault line runs right through Italy from north to south. The main risk areas for quakes are central and southern Italy where about 70% of the region is susceptible. Tremors are quite common in Umbria and the Appenines. Seismologists claim that the number, strength and frequency of quakes hitting central Italy is increasing, which has led to a drop in tourism and house buying by foreigners. Italy's last big disastrous earthquake flattened Messina in 1908, killing 84,000 people and causing the shoreline to sink by half a metre overnight. Other serious ones were Friuli (1976), Irpinia (1980), and Umbria (1997) – the most memorable recent quake caused severe damage to

TABLE 2	THE POPULATIONS OF THE OTHER LARGEST ITALIAN CITIES
City	**Population**
Milano	1,724,557,
Napoli (Naples)	1,214,775.
Torino (Turin)	1,181,698,
Palermo	996,000,
Genova (Genoa)	787,011,
Bologna	493,282,
Firenze (Florence)	441,654,
Venice	305,000,
Verona	255,000

the Church of Asissi in front of the television cameras.

As if this were not excitement enough, Italy has three active volcanoes. The most infamous of these is Vesuvius near Naples, which buried 2,000 inhabitants in their hedonistic city of Pompeii in AD79. These days the volcano's rumblings are under continuous monitoring so there should be plenty of warning before it pops again. The other volcanoes are comfortingly offshore (unless you live there): Etna on Sicily and Stromboli on a small island off the western coast of southern Italy.

Regional Divisions

For administrative purposes Italy is divided into twenty regions, five of which have special autonomy, ninety-six provinces and more than 8000 comunes. The regions and their respective provinces are as follows:

Population

Italy's population numbers approximately 58 million, a little more than that of the UK and approximately a third of that in the US. However, the Italians have more elbow room than Britons with 190 persons per square km compared with 232 in the UK. Surprisingly for a country associated with large families, Italy has the lowest birth rate in Europe with many couples choosing not to have children and those that do having a single child. This low birth rate has led to fears that the population will shrink so much that there will be severe labour shortage in the future that will ruin the economy.

The population includes a large number of immigrants from ex-colonies, including Somalia, Libya and Eritrea. Most of the immigrants have arrived within the last fifteen years as a result of Italy's liberal entry regulations. These have, however, been tightened up under the Schengen Agreement because of fears from other EU countries that Italy would become a stepping stone for massive numbers of immigrants. There are also significant numbers of Eastern Europeans, Filipinos and Brazilians in the country. There is no official census of the number of immigrants, though around half a million have arrived through official channels. The majority of immigrants remain illegal (aided by Italy's 8000 km long and difficult to patrol coastline) and the total number is believed to exceed two million. Naples now has a large African population while Rome has become home to a wide variety of ethnological backgrounds amongst its population of nearly four million. The most recent influx of immigrants and refugees to Italy has come from the stricken country of Albania. An estimated 80,000 Albanians have entered Italy both legally and illegally, amongst them a ruthless criminal element who are rumoured to be more deadly than the Mafia whom they are replacing in some areas, particularly Milan.

States within the State

Within its borders Italy contains three micro sovereign states, the most famous of which is the Vatican City; no less arcane, but wielding considerably less temporal power, are San Marino and the Knights of Malta. Each of these three states has its own government, head of state and car licence plates:

The Vatican City: The Vatican City (area: 116 acres; population: 730), became a sovereign state in 1929 and is located within the boundaries of Rome. Its high walls enclose all the apparatus of a mini-state: the secret archives, Radio Vatican, Vatican Television, the Vatican bank, the Vatican Museums, the Vatican Newspaper (*L'Osservatore Romano*) and a legion of staff including accountants, Swiss Guards, Vatican Police, the Palatine Guard and even its own football league made up of teams from each of these. It is small wonder that the Vatican is considered to be less of a spiritual entity than a political one, the Catholic Church being as faction ridden as any Italian political party. During a period of liberalisation in the sixties and seventies under popes John XXIII and Paul VI many intellectuals of a progressive outlook were elected to positions of power in the Church and its associated lay organisations such as the *Azione Cattolica*. The retrogressive tendencies of the present incumbent 'Papa Wojtyla' and his 'presage-of-doom' view of mankind's future need no further elaboration here. For the effect of Wojtyla's conservatism on the Italian church see Chapter Four, *Daily Life*.

Saint Peter's Church and parts of the Papal Palace designated as The Vatican Museums are open to the public.

San Marino: The largest of the micro states, San Marino covers an area of 24 square miles (61 square kilometres) and has a population of 22,000. It is well-known for its large and colourful postage stamps and big losses in international football matches. San Marino lies between the regions of Emilia Romagna and Marche about fifteen miles inland from Rimini and has been in existence since the Middle Ages.

The Knights of Malta: The Knights have several enclaves which, like the Vatican City, are located within the boundaries of Rome. The venerable Knights are an international brotherhood led by a Grand Master who is seventy-eighth in a line dating back to the Middle Ages.

TABLE 3	AVERAGE TEMPERATURES			
City & Province	**Jan** °F/°C	**Apr** °F/°C	**July** °F/°C	**Nov** °F/°C
Ancona (Marche)	42/6	56/14	77/25	55/13
Bari(Puglia)	46/8	57/14	77/25	59/15
Bologna (Emilia Romagna)	37/3	56/15	78/26	50/10
Florence (Tuscany)	42/6	55/13	77/25	52/11
Genova (Liguria)	46/8	56/14	77/25	55f/13
Milan (Lombardy)	36/2	55/13	77/25	48/9
Naples (Campania)	48/9	56/14	77/25	59/15
Palermo(Sicily)	50/10	61/16	77/25	50/16
Rome (Latium)	45/7	57/14	78/26	55/13
Trieste (Friuli-Venezia)	41/5	55/13	75/25	52/11
Venice (Venetia)	39/4	55/13	75/24	52/10

Climatic Zones

The climate of Italy shows the kind of regional variation one would expect from a country with its head in the Alps and its toe in the Mediterranean. At the foot of the Alps in the north is the flat and fertile Plain of Lombardy, which is also one of the main industrial areas. Cold and wet in winter, those who find themselves living and working in the north can escape to different climatic regions to rejuvenate themselves. There are the cold, dry Alps further northwards for winter sports. The Italian Riviera (Liguria), which is pleasantly mild in winter. Or there is the south, including Sicily, where the winters are even milder and typically Mediterranean. In summer and winter, the middle regions of Tuscany and Umbria, which are home to many expatriates, have the best of both worlds: neither too cold in winter nor too parched in summer. However, the higher areas of even these favoured regions can be cold and snowbound in winter. The far south and Sicily are generally considered too hot for comfort in summer.

REGIONAL GUIDE

HISTORICALLY, Italy as a unified country has existed for little more than a hundred and thirty-seven years. Before the *Risorgimento* (unification) the whole region was a collection of city-states, kingdoms, duchies and the republics of Venice, Naples, Lombardy, Florence, Piedmont and Sicily. The result of such a relatively recent union is that Italians have not really had time to adjust to the concept of national identity and instead consider themselves Neapolitan, Piedmontese etc., and only Italian as an afterthought. This regionalism is expressed by the word *campanilismo*, from the word for a bell-tower (i.e. a village). Thus, in a slightly derogatory way, Italians express their obsession with discussing the finer points of the differences in character and culture of the inhabitants of the many different regions that make up the country.

In view of the separate historical development of the Italian regions it comes as little surprise that not only do the customs and outlook vary considerably amongst them, but also the language spoken. Dialects abound in every province and are a source of pride to Italians as a way of defining their identity. Italians from almost every area are able to speak their local dialect and make themselves incomprehensible not only to those struggling to get by with evening-class Italian, but also other Italians.

In France and Spain there are areas favoured by expatriates who are looking to set up a second home or a permanent one if they are retired. This is no less true of Italy where hilltop dwellings in Tuscany and more recently Umbria, have been selling steadily to the Brits, the Dutch and the Germans, among others. Professional expatriates with full-time jobs are, on the other hand, more likely to find themselves based in the bigger cities: Milan, Florence, Genoa, Turin, Naples or the capital, Rome. It is, however, becoming more common for expatriates to find themselves in almost any city from Como to Cagliari.

Information Sources

An excellent starting point for information is the Italian State Tourist Board – ENIT, which supplies free maps and brochures as well as the invaluable, annually updated *Travellers Handbook* packed with useful information on everything from how to get an audience with the Pope to where to go for Italian courses. The ENIT website (www.enit.it) also provides much information, in a number of languages. In Italy itself every regional capital city has its own tourist board called either: *Ente Provincial Turismo* or *Azienda Promozione Turistica*. For specialist maps such as the large-scale road maps or maps for hiking, contact Stanfords (address below).

Useful Addresses

Italian State Tourist Board (ENIT): 1 Princes Street, London W1R 8AY; ☎020-7408 1254; fax 020-7493 6695; www.enit.it.

Italian State Tourist Board (ENIT): 212-245-496; www.italiantourism.com.

Stanfords: 12 Long Acre, Covent Garden, London WC2E 9LP; ☎020-7836 1321; fax 020-7836 0189; www.stanfords.co.uk. Perhaps the best known map shop in London. Large Italian section including regional Italian driving maps and town plans of all major towns and cities of Italy. Also has branches at the British Airways Travel Shop, 156 Regent Street W1B 5SN; ☎020-7434 4744 and 29 Corn Street, Bristol BS1 1HT, UK; ☎0117-929 9966; fax 0117-927 7232.

THE NORTH WEST

Regions: Piedmont, Lombardy, Liguria, Val d'Aosta.
Main cities: Turin, Genoa, Aosta, Milan.

In the north west corner of Italy the two regions of Piedmont (Piemonte) and Val d'Aosta are probably the two least Italianate regions of Italy. Tiny Val d'Aosta is wedged between France and Switzerland and is a mountainous, bilingual (in French and Italian) area. Peaks picturesquely ring the regional capital, Aosta, and as you would expect ski resorts are plentiful.

Until the end of the nineteenth century the Piedmontese were also French speaking. In the eleventh century Umberto Bianca-mano founded the kingdom of Savoy-Piedmont, which included the Val d'Aosta. Unfortunately situated on the invasion route from France, the kingdom suffered its fair share of intrusions over the years. However, a successful swipe at the French on their way to Lombardy to fight the War of the Spanish succession enhanced the prestige of Duke Vittorio Amadeo II of Savoy-Piedmont, who not only gained Sicily but was also elevated to kingship at the Treaty of Utrecht (1714). Turin (Torino), the main regional city, has the distinction of being at the centre of the drive for Italian unity and was home to the first Italian Parliament in 1861 when unification of the greater part of Italy had been achieved. The giant corporation FIAT (*Fabbrica Italiana di Automobili Torino*) and Olivetti have their headquarters in Turin; the former company since its founding in 1899. The Turin area is also famous for its good quality wines particularly Barolo and Barbera, and the internationally known aperitifs Cinzano and Martini, which are produced there. Wealthy Turin is not immediately attractive as a place to live and work, but it is handy for the Alps, France and the Italian Riviera and much less atmospherically polluted than Milan.

Throughout history Lombardy has dominated northern Italy and continues to do so. Not only is it the most commercially and industrially successful area but it is also the country's financial powerhouse. It is the most heavily populated region of the country with an estimated eight million inhabitants, many of them workers from the south. The heavily industrialised area around Milan produces around 40% of Italy's GNP and Milan is easily the most expensive and luxurious city in the country. Historically, Lombardy is one of the great battlefields of Europe – most noticeably perhaps during the Thirty Years War (1618-48), when the French, Spanish and Austrians were simultaneously rampaging over the landscape in a dispute over Valtellina. The resulting privations led to a long period of economic decline in Lombardy, which was reversed in the more constructive period of the eighteenth century. This welcome respite from war lasted until the return of the French under Bonaparte in 1796, which culminated in his coronation as King of Italy in Milan (1805). Following Napoleon's defeat, the Kingdom of Lombardy-Venetia was absorbed into the Austrian Empire until the unification of the greater part of Italy with Piedmont was achieved in 1861.

The Liguria region, also called the Italian Riviera is a coastal strip that follows on eastwards from the French Riviera and is centred on the ancient trading port of Genova (Genoa) which was one of the five great maritime republics of Italy in the thirteenth century. Successively invaded by the French and the Austrians during the seventeenth and eighteenth centuries, the port of Genoa suffered progressive economic decline. During the period leading up to the Unification, the area became a haven for political refugees and the popular hero of the Italian liberation movement, Garibaldi (1807-82), came from the region. In the nineteenth and twentieth centuries an economic resurgence in the form of heavy industry made Genoa Italy's third most important industrial centre. Its fortunes have since taken a nosedive with the decline of heavy industries like steel production, thus forcing many of the region's one million, seven hundred thousand inhabitants to move to other areas of Italy in search of work.

The majority of the foreign business community in Italy are based in the north, particularly Milan, rather than Rome as one might expect. Though there is a large expatriate community in Rome, including many diplomats, as can be seen from the number of International schools there. Those who live in the north and can afford it may have a city flat and a weekend house at one of the nearby lakes.

THE NORTH EAST

Regions: Trentino Alto-Adige, Veneto, Friuli-Veneto-Giulia, Emilia Romagna.
Main Towns: Bolzano, Trent, Udine, Trieste, Cortina, Verona, Venice, Parma, Ferrara, Bologna, Ravenna.

The first three of these regions contain the beautiful scenery of the Dolomite mountains, which run along the north-eastern edge of Italy and form a natural border with Austria. Justly famed for its wine producing qualities, this landscape is usually only visited by foreigners in search of mountain holidays, notably winter sports. Trentino-Alto Adige was part of the Austrian Empire until 1918 and German is still spoken there. In fact, linguistic squabbling between German and Italian speakers in the region is an on-going source of tension there. Ethnic Germans claim they were 'Italianised' by Mussolini and want to revert place names to their German versions, while rival factions like the Ladins, who claim their origins and language go back to the Romans, want their Italian language rights protected. The region is a semi-autonomous section of the Veneto region and has a population of around 800,000.

Friuli-Veneto Giulia, which has a population of just over a million, also came within the ambit of the Hapsburgs in the nineteenth century. Later, in the chaotic aftermath of the Second World War it was partitioned between Italy and Yugoslavia. The last dispute between the two countries over the area was not settled until the 1970's. As a legacy of its turbulent history the region is ethnically mixed and more eastern European than typically Italian. Trieste is the regional capital and projects into Slovenia – it used to be part of Slovenia and does not have the appearance of an Italian city at all. Historically, Trieste was one of three great cities of the Austro-Hungarian Empire – Vienna and Prague being the other two. These days it is being revitalised by a more open Europe and is being increasingly used as a base within the EU to do business with Slovenia, Croatia and the Czech and Slovak Republics which are outside of the European Union. When these countries join the EU Trieste will once again have to reinvent itself.

The Veneto region is one of the undisputed treasure houses of Europe. In addition to Venice, the cities of Verona, Vicenza and Padua are also of great cultural interest. By the year 1000, Venice had become powerful in the region through commerce and maritime prowess, which enabled her to be the main conduit for trade between Europe and the Orient. This supremacy lasted until the mid-thirteenth century when the Black Death swept across Europe. In the twelfth century, when the German Kings were making unrealisitic claims to the Veneto, the first Hohenstaufen Emperor, Barbarossa (red beard) had already conquered Milan. Then the Trevisan League of cities, with Venice at their head, routed his army and negotiated with Barbarossa to be the sole supplier of the imperial armies on their future sorties in Italy. During the fifteenth century, the existence of Venice was threatened by the rival state of Genoa. These being two great maritime republics, the contest naturally took place on the seas and resulted in victory for the Venetians. Venice reached its *terra firma* limits with the conquests of Brescia and Bergamo in the first half of the fifteenth century. The long decline of Venetian greatness was heralded by the fall of Constantinople (1453) with whose fortunes those of Venice were inextricably linked. During the sixteenth century the policy of the Venetian Republic proceeded along defensive lines, treading a delicate path of diplomacy amongst the expansionist powers of the time – the Hapsburg Empire and France. There was also the added irritant of political interference by the Pope. However, by far the main threat to the Venetians were the Turks, who were in the process of usurping the supremacy of Venetian trading interests. It was this struggle, principally a maritime one, which gradually enfeebled Venice and left a vacuum for the ascendancy of the old archival, Genoa. In 1797 Venice took up Bonaparte's unrefusable offer to become part of the Austrian Empire. After crowning himself Emperor of France in 1804, Bonaparte returned to Italy to organise its reconstruction. The result was a kingdom of Italy, which included Lombardy and Venice. Having more pressing matters to attend to, Napoleon left his stepson, Eugéne Beauharnais, in charge of the Kingdom as its Viceroy. After Napoleon's defeat, Venice returned to independent status, which lasted until 1849.

For all its incomparable glories, Venice is notoriously foggy in winter and smelly in summer which may be a reason, along with the high prices and excess of tourists, why its native population has shrunk by two thirds in the last 20 years. Within the same period the prosperity of the Venetian hinterland has been considerably revived with the creation of many new companies producing small, high-quality goods including shoes, medical equipment, spectacle frames and machine components. Treviso is also host to the headquarters of the Benetton group. If it were not for the dismal winters many more foreigners would probably choose to settle in this commercially upbeat region – though expatriates will continue to be sent there and be able to enjoy the aesthetic beauty if not the weather and the aroma.

Emilia Romagna takes its name from the ancient Roman road to Rome, the Via Emilia, and Romagna, the name of the former Papal State which covered the area of what are now the provinces of Forli and Ravenna. The northern part of the region is characterised by a flat and featureless wheat prairie, while the south takes in the foothills of the Appenines. An extremely prosperous region, its main town, Bologna experienced an economic boom in the eighties largely through the development of high-tech industries. As a place in which to live and work, Emilia Romagna has obvious attractions, especially its beautiful towns and a rich gastronomic heritage; Bologna is also the seat of Europe's oldest university. However the main problem for foreign residents is the expense: the cost of daily living in Bologna matches, if not exceeds, that of Milan or Florence. Properties in the region are, however, reasonably priced but are not much sought after by either foreigners or Italians and so foreign residents can feel isolated unless they like peace and quiet, or are near enough to Bologna to make use of the social life there. There is a small community of foreigners in Bologna who speak highly of their adopted home and find it lively, congenial, cultivated and relatively tourist free. There are also possibilities for teaching English as a foreign language in the region (see the chapter *Employment*).

THE UPPER CENTRE

Regions: Toscana (Tuscany), Umbria, Marche.
Main cities: Pisa, Florence, Siena, Orvieto, Perugia, Urbino.

Of all the regions of Italy, Tuscany and Umbria continue to attract the most foreign residents who are looking to buy property and/or live in Italy, but who do not require employment. The superlatives of best climate, best scenery, best cultural heritage, etc. continue to draw foreigners looking for archetypal Italy. The region is so popular that the International School in Florence receives thousands of unsolicited applications from foreign teachers every year, despite the relatively few vacancies that occur. Parts of the western, central region of Tuscany are now 'colonised' by foreigners including Britons, Northern Europeans, and Irish. While the Brits continue to flock to Tuscany (there are currently around 8,000 permanent residents and many more holiday-home owners), the Italians are streaming out. The two trends are not necessarily connected. The departure of the Italians has more to do with the economic depression of the area than a wish to flee from the delights of 'Chianti-shire'. Even this beloved region of hilltop villages, vineyards and files of cypress trees is not without its drawbacks: water and electricity supplies are a problem in the remoter regions and tourists overrun the principal attractions, Florence, Siena, Pisa and the coast, for six months of the year. Originally a marquisate under Matilda of Tuscany, the area became prosperous through the woollen and cloth industries in the fourteenth centuries. The history of the region is essentially centred on Florence, which was the focus of the Renaissance and existed as a republic under the Medicis in the fifteenth and sixteenth centuries. Cosimo Medici then made himself the first Grand-Duke of Tuscany in 1570. During the eighteenth century Tuscany became part of Austria until 1859 when the Risorgimento was in process. There was, however, a brief fifteen-year interlude under French rule during the Napoleonic era.

Despite its propensity for earthquakes, the landlocked region of Umbria has become the other 'in-place' for foreign residents to set up home – though property sales slump after every reported tremor. With a smaller population than Tuscany, and somewhat overshadowed by the spectacular glories of that region, Umbria nevertheless has some lures for the prospective foreign resident. Most attractive of these are the property prices, which are about half those of Tuscany. However, the rapidly growing popularity of the region with both foreigners and Romans means that this financial advantage may quite soon evaporate. The main problem for foreign residents appears to be that communications are not brilliant. Rome airport is reasonably convenient for those living in the southern part of Umbria: Rome to Perugia takes about three hours by road. For those in the north coming from Pisa airport, it takes considerably longer.

The region's attractions include Assisi, an important destination for pilgrimages dedicated to Italy's patron saint, St Francis, and the walled town of Spoleto. Sadly, the earthquake that hit the region in 1997 destroyed much of the renowned frescoes in Assisi's Basilica of St Francis and highlighted the fact that Europe's fault line runs down almost throughout the centre of Italy. Restoration of the frescoes was begun with a grant from the Vatican while many local residents still lived in temporary accommodation after their homes were destroyed in the earthquake – prompting a debate as to whether it was more important to bring the tourists back, or to provide new housing. The Umbrian city of Foligno was also badly hit by the quake which bought down the cathedral's bell tower. Umbria also has a Foreigners' University (*Universita italiana per gli stranieri*) based in Perugia, to which students from all over the world come to take courses on Italian art, culture and language. This institution would be extremely useful for foreign residents keen to absorb Italian culture and make the most of their stay in the country.

Marche, situated between Umbria and the Adriatic, is a mountainous but varied region almost unknown to foreigners. Not many expatriates will be posted to the region either, as there are few large cities that play host to international organisations in the region. Italians flock to its coastal strip where resorts such as Rimini (popular in the days before Queen Victoria began frequenting Nice) and Riccione are the playgrounds of northern Italians throughout the summer. As a result, property prices on the coast are pushed high by the demand for summer flats. The hinterland is just beginning to attract foreign buyers but the remoteness of the region is regarded as something of a drawback. Communications with the north are excellent from the coast and once the region opens up, are likely to improve in the hinterland. The southern part of Marche used to be regarded as part of the Mezzogiorno but owing to increasing prosperity it has now had its financial benefits withdrawn by the government. Historically, Marche made a major contribution to civilisation through Frederico da Montefeltro, whose patronage of some of the greatest artists and architects to build and embellish his palace at Urbino, made it one of the most aristocratic and civilised courts of the Renaissance period. Ascoli Piceno is another large town that flourished in the same period.

THE LOWER CENTRE AND SARDINIA

Regions: Lazio (Latium), Abruzzo, Molise.
Main cities: Rome, L'Aquila, Isernia.
The region of Lazio encompasses Rome, the Italian capital, which as the centre

of the former Roman Empire shaped much of Western civilisation. However it seems more through geography than suitability that Rome found itself the capital of modern Italy. Following full unification in 1871, Rome appeared ideally situated between northern and southern Italy. She was however far from being the largest or most important city of the time: the claims of Milan, Turin and Naples were greater since they had been administrative centres or capitals for centuries. In contrast, Rome had nothing to offer but glorious and symbolic antiquity and the Vatican. The ruinous expense of building her up into a capital city of appropriate grandeur lasted well into Mussolini's time. Nowadays Rome is notorious amongst other things for being the headquarters of the state apparatus whose thousands of functionaries drive anyone who has dealings with them to distraction with their legendary inefficiency and corruption – the predominant characteristics of the national administration. Many of these state employees are from the south of Italy, which aggravates the northerners' contempt for Rome and the south. The perception is of Rome squandering the hard-earned wealth of the north on the lazy and unproductive south. Since the 1980's Rome's slightly backward reputation has diminished thanks to industrial expansion particularly in the high technology field; the reality is however that it still lags behind Milan and Turin in the league table of industrial cities.

However exciting the prospect of living and working in Rome and its environs may seem, there are considerable drawbacks in doing so. These include the difficulty of finding accommodation and the traffic congestion, which has reached unendurable limits while it fills the narrow, high-sided streets with noxious fumes that cannot disperse. To reduce both the atmospheric pollution and noise pollution of Rome, the traditional two-stroke mopeds (including the Vespas made famous in numerous movies) will be banned from 2002. However, for all its faults and frustrations Rome is a city that fosters deep fascination, not the least of which is the pleasure of living in an atmosphere created by two thousand years of occupation, power, wealth and history.

After Milan, Rome has the second largest community of foreigners living and working in the city and its environs. Formerly the Abruzzi, the region east and south of Rome was partitioned into the two regions of Abruzzo and Molise in 1963. Both areas are mountainous and sparsely populated and to many foreigners they seem wild and forbidding. Folk traditions, which have faded out in the more developed areas of Italy, survive here among the hilltop villages along with witches and wolves. The latter can be found in the Parco Nazionale dell'Abruzzo along with brown bears and chamois. In recent years Abruzzo has grown wealthier than poverty-stricken Molise by taking full advantage of government incentive schemes for businesses and proving that factories in Abruzzo can operate as efficiently and productively as anywhere in the north of Italy. The Abruzzese have also been quick to develop the potential of their Adriatic seaboard and in particular Pescara, which has become a popular holiday spot for Italians. The main town of Abruzzo, L'Aquila (eagle), has a 99-spout fountain (one for every village from which the city's original population is reputed to have been formed), and a brooding sixteenth century castle built by the Spaniards during their 150 year period of influence in Italy.

Poor and backward Molise, which is about half the area of Abruzzo, is where the south really begins. The entire Abruzzi area is an earthquake zone that places a dampener on the real estate market there, while the main town of Molise, Isernia, is still propped up by scaffolding from the quake of 1984. It is not too far across the Adriatic to Albania and Croatia and the connections between the regions are evident in the customs and dialect of the region. There is a young coastal resort at Termoli.

Sardegna (Sardinia)

Sardinia, the Mediterranean's second largest island after Sicily, has long been on the periphery of Italian affairs. At one time in the possession of the Spanish, the Dukes of Savoy took it over in 1718. The barren and harsh landscape of the island is capable only of subsistence agriculture. The islanders speak Sardo (see *The Italian Language, Daily Life*). A small community, which speaks undiluted fifteenth century Catalan, is an even more curious linguistic anachronism. The available options for working in Sardinia are mostly limited to tourism-related jobs and English language teaching. The island's main town is Cagliari and there is also millionaires' row on the Costa Smerelda in the north-east. For retiring to the island has its charms, notably some incredible scenery, though it may be too quiet for many people outside of the holiday season when considering the legendary insularity of the Sardi.

THE SOUTH AND SICILY

Regions: Campania, Apulia (Puglia), Basilicata, Calabria.
Main cities: Naples, Amalfi, Lecce (Lucca), Bari, Brindisi, Reggio.

It is a widely-held belief that the South of Italy is penurious throughout and crawling with gun-toting mafiosi who will knee-cap or assassinate anyone who seems to threaten their interests. If this were the case, the possibility of any normal business activity would be nil. In fact there are pockets of wealth and industry in the south, e.g. in Puglia and Sicily, which rival anything in the north. Such development has been greatly encouraged by enormous financial incentives offered by the Italian government (see the Chapter, *Starting a Business*). However there are areas where the risk of Mafia interference should be taken extremely seriously: these include virtually the whole of Campania, the toe of Calabria and much of Sicily. As the home ground of the various brotherhoods: the *camorra*, 'ndrangheta' (the Calabrian Mafia), and the Sicilian Mafia (*Cosa Nostra*), these are regarded as virtual no go areas, particularly for small businesses which are less resilient to threats than the large corporations which can hope to shrug them off. It is estimated that 80% of shops in Palermo and Catania pay protection money.

The crackdown on Mafia activity paid dividends in the late 1980s and early 1990s. However, it seems that Mafia activity is again on the increase despite Silvio Berlusconi's party winning most of the Sicilian parliamentary seats in the 2001 election where Mafia controlled candidates usually win.

Campania

Campania is dominated by the city of Naples which represents the south in much the same way that Milan represents the north. The region was called *Campania Felix* by the Romans, whose elite built their palatial villas along the Riviera of the bay of Naples. The Roman idyll is in stark contrast to the Naples coastline of today, which is blotted with the smokestacks and industrial installations of the city's more recent heritage. Naples is largely neglected by foreigners who perhaps fear the reputation of its pickpockets, its *bassi* (slums), and its notorious rubbish disposal problem – the result of the chronic inefficiency of the local council. Naples' tourism heyday was probably the eighteenth century when it was an obligatory stop on the English gentleman's Grand Tour of Europe. Influenced by the Spanish for 300 years, it passed to the Bourbon French in 1734. Famed for its Roman ruins, in particular nearby Pompeii and Herculaneum in the shadow of Vesuvius, Naples acquired a reputation for its courtesans when ruled by the French. The city remained a hit with the British until the killjoy Victorians denounced it as a latter day version of Sodom and Gomorrah. After the end of the Kingdom of Naples in 1860 the city became rapidly provincialised, a process which was accelerated when Rome became the capital of a united Italy.

Foreigners are unlikely to choose Naples as a place to live unless they are offered employment there, though Positano and Amalfi are very desirable places to live. The endemic problems include extreme poverty, and the petty crime and organised criminal activity that go with it. Naples comes under the domain of the *camorra* (the Neapolitan version of the Mafia). Neapolitans and Italians in general are reputed to be anarchic drivers who are oblivious to all road signs and traffic signals, but expatriates with experience of driving in parts of the world away from Europe and North America may find the roads quite civilised. However, for those driving abroad for the first time the dictum 'see Naples and die' can become a real possibility.

Property on the three islands in the Bay of Naples – Ischia, Capri and Procida – rarely comes on the market and is reputed to be fabulously expensive. On the mainland the most attractive coastal areas are Sorrento, Amalfi, Positano and Ravello, but one has to run the gauntlet of Neapolitan motorists on the precipitous cliff roads to get to them. Inland, property prices fall dramatically. However, there is an inherent danger in the area from earthquakes – the earthquake of 1980 devastated the area behind Salerno. In acknowledgement of the poverty of the extreme south, all the *autostrade* south of Salerno are toll free.

Despite the infamous poverty and high unemployment in the city, Naples is Italy's largest trading port and commerce is very important for the local economy. As an industrial city, Naples is home to engineering, petrochemical, shipbuilding and other heavy industries; the fashion industry is, however, also present too.

Apulia (Puglia)

The olive and wine-producing area of Puglia is a long strip that stretches for over 250 miles (400 km) along the heel of Italy. The Normans invaded Southern Italy, including Puglia, in the eleventh century (thus ousting the Ottoman armies). The

Normans left behind many fine cathedrals including those at Trani, Barletta, Bitonto, Ruvo di Puglia and Bari. The main city, Bari, is situated about halfway down the Adriatic coast of Puglia, and is one of the showcases of the south owing to an economic boom from high tech and service industries. The other main industrial area is located around the ancient port of Taranto, which has long been given over to steel production. The upper part of the region, *il Promontario del Gargano* (the Gargano Promontory), which juts into the Adriatic is considered one of the most attractive parts of Puglia with its wooded hills and stunning views of the sea. The area was once rich with religious sanctuaries and Monte Sant'Angelo, where the archangel Michael put in an 'appearance' in AD490, has long been a point of pilgrimage. Between Taranto and Bari are numerous *trulli* (circular, dry-stone built houses with conical roofs) and you can see a whole town of them at Alberobello. While you may hear that they were prehistoric dwellings, it is generally accepted that they represent an early form of tax evasion from the Spanish invaders' tax on bricks and mortar in the 16th century. Lecce, in the far corner of Puglia is usually regarded as the architectural gem of southern Italy – it is built in a particularly refined baroque style. Galatina is the home of the dance *tarantella* that is celebrated annually in a medieval festival. The dance, named from the tarantula spider, is supposed to reflect the writhing of those bitten by the deadly arachnid. The Isole Tremiti (Tremiti islands) 25 miles off Gargano, were once the Devil's Islands of Italy. The presence of prisoners has long since been replaced by that of tourists (an estimated 100,000 in August).

A number of foreigners have found the charms of Gargano irresistible and made their homes in these pleasant surroundings. Anyone thinking of retiring there could probably rent a holiday villa in the area while they carry out a reconnaissance. Unlike Campania, there is little organised crime in Puglia. From the ports of Otranto and Brindisi there are ferries to the former Yugoslavia, and Greece.

Baslicata (Lucania) and Calabria

The two most southerly regions of Baslicata and Calabria are the poorest and most underdeveloped in Italy and best epitomise the plight of the Mezzogiorno. The traditional migration of southerners from these regions to the north in search of jobs continues apace, despite government efforts to bring industrial development to the south. In an effort to deal with the prosperity imbalance between north and south the Italian government set up a development fund, *La Cassa del Mezzogiorno* in the 1950's, which has since been superseded by various other bodies with specialised responsibilities. Massive government resources have been poured into the south to fund irrigation projects, an improved infrastructure, modern communications and industrial and tourism development. However, the area has suffered from corruption on an unprecedented scale and this, coupled with gross inefficiency and the lack of an overall investment plan, has resulted in most of the money being squandered on political patronage. Much of the money has thus ended up in private bank accounts and the coffers of the 'ndrangheta'. From 1992, the EU Regional Investment Fund took over the organising of funding the Mezzogiorno.

The dramatic decline of the populations of Basilicata and Calabria is the result of the constant migration of those desperate to escape poverty. Add to this the mountainous and inhospitable landscape and the undercurrent of criminality, and there does not seem to be much here to appeal to many foreign residents. Basilicata's main city is Matera. Prominent features of the landscape in the region are the *Sassi* cave dwellings, where until very recently peasants slept with their animals.

Calabria, which forms the 'toe' of Italy, has the attraction of its beautiful Tyrrenhian coastline, which draws a regular summer tourist trade boosted by the elimination of the Malarial mosquitoes that were a problem in the area up to the twentieth century. Towns like Crotone and Reggio Calabria still have a pretty evil reputation for their current crop of mosquitoes. In the sixth century the Greeks flourished in Calabria and this was probably the high point of Calabrian history. From the promontory of Tropea in the south west of Calabria you can see the Lipari islands and even Stromboli (whose last reported bout of volcanic eruption was in 1971). The main problem for anyone thinking of living in Calabria is the risk of kidnapping. Calabria is notorious for the practice and it is estimated that only one in ten victims are ever located by the *carabinieri* owing, it is said, to a combination of their incompetence and the difficulty of searching the terrain. It is reported that local shepherds have to be sent into the mountains to locate carabinieri who have become lost while attempting to perform their duties. Owing to a dearth of Calabrian industrialists, the kidnappers prey on the professional classes and their offspring. The kidnappings tend to be family affairs and well organised. Ransoms are likely to end up in the pockets of the local drug barons or the construction industry, which is known to be rife with *malavita* throughout most of southern Italy. There is even a rather macabre custom in Calabria of nicknaming hotels and apartment blocks after those whose ransom money has paid for them. Foreigners are not generally regarded as prime targets since the ensuing publicity in the foreign media would put the Italian government in a position of ridicule and expose their incompetence at combating the problem and draw unwanted international attention on the kidnappers. Furthermore, such goings on would have a devastating effect on much-needed tourism in Calabria. Even so, hill walking and child rearing are not recommended pursuits for the area.

SICILY (SICILIA)

Main towns: Palermo, Messina, Catania, Syracuse.
Population: Five million.
The island of Sicily which lies off the toe of Italy is a *regioni a statuto speciale* meaning that it has a greater degree of autonomy than most of the other twenty regions. This status has less to do with the fact that Sicily is the home of the *Cosa Nostra* (Mafia) who are a law unto themselves, and more to do with historical and ethnic differences. Nonetheless, to many people the name of Sicily is synonymous with the dark force of the Mafia. The origins of this brutal brotherhood are obscure; some claim that the Mafia have existed for two thousand years as a kind of freemason organisation. It is evident, however, that the end of the nineteenth

century marked the onset of their notoriety. During the 1920's the fascists under Mussolini lost no time in stamping out such an undesirable phenomenon – they were competition in the quest for power and wealth. The responsibility for their revival in Sicily after the Second World War can be laid at the door of the American military and the predecessor of the CIA. Having successfully invaded Italy during the Second World War, they implanted several veteran Mafiosi from New York to counteract and combat the spread of Communism that they feared would take over Italy. Unfortunately, the preventative medicine turned out to be much more deadly than the disease.

There is no way of estimating the Mafia's clandestine wealth world-wide, but in Italy their turnover is estimated to be 12% of the GNP. Until the 1960's the Mafia area of operations was largely confined to Sicily, since then there are few areas of Italian commercial life which it has not penetrated and its multinational operations have made it probably the richest and most powerful criminal organisation in the world. The Mafia was turning guns into ploughshares long before the Cold War ended by investing their ill-gotten wealth in legal enterprises.

Palermo, Sicily's main city, has the infamous distinction of being a world centre of the illegal drugs and armaments trade. With this awesome power over life, death and the economy it comes as little surprise that there are few who will stand up to the Mafia, though there are some notable exceptions among the judicial profession. One example of those who stood up to the Mafia was the young Sicilian judge Giovanni Falcone who conducted the much publicised *maxi-processi* (mega-trials) of Mafia luminaries, which put several, including Michele Greco the leader, behind bars. The price Falcone paid for his courage was to be the Salman Rushdie of Sicily, guarded round the clock by twenty-five armed bodyguards. These were not sufficient protection from the (some say inevitable) assassination that ended his life in 1992. The Mafia, like the Mounties it seems, always get their man. However, there was such an outcry over the murder of Falcone and another judge, Paola Borsellini, that the Mafia went quiet for a while and began working in a much more unobtrusive way. The man reputedly responsible for the murder of the two judges, Benedetto Spera, was eventually captured just outside Palermo in 2001.

Sicily is slowly modernising itself; there is even a Europe Office in Palermo offering information in English. It is perfectly feasible to buy a house in Sicily, and many foreigners do have holiday homes there. Despite unemployment of 23% amongst the local population, it is possible for foreigners to find work on the island: there are opportunities for English teaching in Messina and Siracuse and there are foreigners working for the oil companies at Gela. There is also the American Air Force base on the island, which has a school that employs teachers with American citizenship and certification. The island has many attractions including beautiful scenery and Greek ruins (Siracuse was the second largest city of ancient Greece). Trampled by other invaders, including Roman, Ottoman, Norman, French and Spanish, the island of Sicily is a fascinating mixture of styles as is the capital Palermo, where Arab architecture meets Baroque. Another of the island's famous sights is Mount Etna, which lies in the north-east between Messina and Catania. Etna erupted in 1983 and again in 2001, when it threatened a number of villages and the experts forecast an even bigger eruption to come.

The railway from Palermo to the other major town, Catania, remains single track though the new motorway from Messina to Palermo will make that journey quicker. Silvio Berlusconi says he will build the long talked about bridge linking Sicily to the mainland, but many other governments have said that before and Sicily is still an island. Work has been about to start on the bridge for over thirty years, but successive governments have never quite managed to get things moving. Stretching across the Straits of Messina from Villa San Giovanni to Messina, the planned road and rail bridge will be two miles long, 195 feet wide and building it will take many years. The designers claim it will withstand winds of over 200 m.p.h and more importantly that it will be earthquake proof. The straits are one of Italy's seismic hotspots, most notably when the town of Messina was flattened by the big quake of 1908. The bridge will be funded internationally and it is expected to pay for itself in tolls after ten years.

GETTING TO ITALY

HIGH STREET TRAVEL AGENTS and the travel pages of most national newspapers are obvious sources of discounted fares to Italy and there is plenty of choice. Non-stop flights are available from the UK to about 20 Italian cities. If you change to a domestic flight at Milan or Rome, you can reach still more. Due to the state of crisis in the airline industry at the time of writing, it is possible that flight schedules, routes and even airlines listed here may disappear by the time you read this. Therefore the information below is for guidance only and should be checked with your travel agent well in advance of your departure and before you make concrete travel plans. The Austrian Airlines website has a comprehensive interactive flight planner that allows travellers to find details of most scheduled flights, on any airline, in the world: www.aua.com. Most of the airlines listed below allow passengers to book flights online.

Travel agents specialising in offering discount fares to Italy can be found in the Travel sections of newspapers such as *The Sunday Times*, *The Sunday Telegraph* and *The Mail on Sunday*. Many agencies and budget airlines now also have websites offering special deals and discounts and special offers change frequently. It is worth looking at the following websites:

Lupus Travel: www.lupustravel.com
Orbitz: www.orbitz.com
Holiday Choice: www.holidaychoice.co.uk

Airlines offering direct flights from the UK:

Alitalia: ☎020-8745 8200.
British Airways:☎ 0845-7733377; www.britishairways.com.
British Midland: ☎0870-6070 555 (UK Only) ☎01332-854854 (international); www.flybmi.com.
RyanAir: Online booking www.ryanair.co.uk;
Virgin Express: ☎020-7744 0004 (in the UK), ☎02-482 96 000 (Milan),

☎ 800-097 097 (Rome & other areas), www.virgin-express.com.

Airlines offering direct flights from the USA and Canada:

NorthWest: ☎ 800-447 4747 (US – international reservations), www.nwa.com

Delta: ☎ 800-221 1212 (in USA and Canada) ☎ 800-864 114 (in Italy), www.delta.com;

Alitalia: ☎ 800-223 5730; www.alitaliausa.com.

Air Canada: www.aircanada.ca.

RESIDENCE AND ENTRY REGULATIONS

CHAPTER SUMMARY

○ Any non-Italian – even a national of another EU country – planning to stay in Italy for over 90 days must apply for a *permesso di soggiorno* (permit to stay).

○ Those not from EU countries must apply for the *permesso di soggiorno* and a work visa before they enter Italy.

○ All those planning to take up employment – including EU nationals – also need to obtain a *libretto di lavoro* (worker registration card) from the town hall; this will be held by your employer.

○ Once you have the *permesso di soggiorno* and have moved into an Italian address you should obtain a residence permit (*certificato di residenza*): this is not compulsory for EU nationals, but has several uses as proof that you have settled in Italy.

○ All Italian residents, whether native or foreign, must carry an identity card (*Carta d'Identità*) with them at all times.

○ Italy is currently tightening its immigration laws to combat a rising flood of illegal immigrants (*clandestini*) from eastern Europe and Africa.

THE SCHENGEN ACCORD

BEFORE DISCUSSING THE VISA REGULATIONS for Italy, it is important to understand the implications of the Schengen Accord. The introduction of new immigration laws (see below) and the extra vigilance at vulnerable border areas in Italy is not unrelated to the Schengen Accord – introduced in Italy in

October 1997. At the time of writing there are fifteen countries in the Schengen group: Austria, Belgium, Denmark, Finland, France, Germany, Greece, Iceland, Italy, Luxembourg, Netherlands, Norway, Portugal, Spain and Sweden. The United Kingdom and Ireland, who have limited border controls between their two countries, have declined to participate in the Accord because they (especially the UK) believe that they are the final targets of most illegal immigrants and so wish to maintain border controls.

The Schengen countries have generally eliminated passport and baggage controls except for general airport and airline safety in the airports of their countries. In some cases this has meant modification of existing airports like the Malpensa 2000 airport in Milan to accommodate increased traffic. It is now possible to travel around much of Europe and only be aware that a border has been crossed when the street signs change language and car number plates change style.

The main fear of other Schengen countries, particularly France and Germany, has been that illegal immigrants will still find it easier to enter Italy, which has 8000 miles of coastline, than other countries and will then pass through Italy to the other European countries. The Schengen agreement has been suspended once and temporary border controls implemented because of fears of a sudden major increase in illegal immigrants from Italy.

The Schengen agreement also allows nationals of countries from outside the EU to enter a member country through the normal passport controls on a visa issued by that country and then move around the Schengen Accord countries freely without further passport checks. To counteract possible abuse by the criminal fraternity and those that have been deported from one country and try to return through another, the member countries came up with the 'Schengen Information System' (SIS). This will connect Consulates and Embassies worldwide to a centralised data' bank in Strasbourg where the names and details of all known criminals will be stored. Apart from at Embassies and Consulates, the information can be accessed from terminals at first points of entry to the Schengen Area. Under the protection of personal data regulations, private citizens are allowed to check information relating to them that is stored in the system.

VISA INFORMATION

All Nationalities

FOR STAYS of longer than 90 days all nationalities of visitor require a *permesso di soggiorno* (permit to stay), which must be applied for within eight days of arrival. EU nationals whose passports will not be stamped on arrival will not have to worry quite so much about this timescale as non-EU visitors whose visas will be checked and their passport stamped at the port of entry. With the Schengen Accord in place, passports of non-EU nationals will only be checked when they first enter Schengen area and the Italian authorities may use this date when calculating the 90 days.

Citizens of the following countries do not require visas for Schengen area countries when visiting for business or tourism, though technically they need to register for the residency permit (*permesso di soggiorno*) within eight days of arrival in Italy: Andorra, Argentina, Australia, Brazil, Canada, Chile, Cyprus, Czech Republic, Ecuador, Estonia, Hungary, Israel, Japan, Latvia, Lichtenstein, Lithuania, Malta, Mexico, Monaco, New Zealand, Paraguay, Poland, San Marino, Singapore, Slovakia, Slovenia, South Korea, Switzerland, USA, Uruguay, Vatican City.

Citizens of the following countries do not require visas when entering Italy for business or tourism for 90 days or less: Bolivia, Bulgaria, Costa Rica, Croatia, El Salvador, Guatemala, Honduras, Malaysia, Nicaragua, Panama, Venezuela.

Up to date visa information can be found on the Italian Embassy in Washington website (www.italyemb.org), though visa applications must be made to the consular office whose jurisdiction covers the region or country in which the applicant lives (see end of this chapter for contact details).

Applications for all visas must be made in person and the length of time that the application takes to be processed ranges from twenty-four hours to five weeks. It is usually best to assume the longer timescale to ensure your visa arrives in time for your departure, especially during the busy summer months. The visa itself currently costs about US$30.

European Union Nationals

In theory the creation of the European Union is supposed to mean that European Union nationals can live and work anywhere they want inside the European Union borders. However, there is still a lot of red tape for those who wish to relocate within it for a long-term stay and obtain a residence permit that entitles them to public services as if they were a local national. Although all EU nationals are entitled to live and work in Italy, the bureaucratic rigmarole involved with taking up residence there can be complex and time consuming. The regulations concerning residence permits are dealt with in detail below and, in theory, the procedure for obtaining them should be the same everywhere in the country. In practice there may well be differences depending on the *comune* in which you are living and your particular circumstances. The main thing to bear in mind is that Italy is excessively bureaucratic and the bureaucracy is as much a bugbear for the Italians themselves as it is for foreigners.

Non-European Union Nationals

For non-European Union nationals the process is much more involved. For a start, a non-EU national must apply for their work visa and visitors visa before they enter Italy. For some nationalities it is also necessary to apply for and receive the visas through the Italian embassy in their home country, though it will often be possible to apply for a visa in the area where you are permanently resident. For long-term expatriates this usually means that they can apply for their visa in the country where they are currently living, especially if they have a residence permit or other official documentation to prove they live there full time. It is also necessary to have employment before applying for the visas. Work permits for non-EU nationals will be issued only to people outside Italy, and only for jobs where the provincial Office of the Ministry of Labour is satisfied that no Italian can do the job.

The Italian employer must apply for an *Autorizzazione al Lavoro* which must then be presented by prospective employee at the Italian Embassy in the applicant's home country or place of residence. In recent years large numbers of non-EU citizens have been given work permits, mainly because of the skills shortage in the north created by the booming economy in the area. Skilled workers, especially in electronics and other high-tech industries, and those looking for work in an area where a skill such as native English ability or a skill only possible to obtain on another country is necessary will be most likely to secure a work permit. It is not possible to convert a tourist visa to an employment visa inside Italy – i.e. tourists must leave the country, apply for a work permit and then return once they have it. For those who want to try and work illegally, renewal of a tourist visa is possible, but not guaranteed. Proof of funds and a good reason for the extension (other than a nice job) are essential if one is to be obtained.

The Permesso di Soggiorno

EU Nationals: EU nationals who arrive in Italy without a job, but hoping to find one, must apply at the police station for a *Ricevuta di Segnalazione di Soggiorno*, which entitles them to stay for up to three months looking for a job. The only document required to obtain *Ricevuta di Segnalazione di Soggiorno* is a passport. In order to obtain a *Permesso di Soggiorno* the *Ricevuta* together with a letter from an employer confirming employment must be taken back to the police station.

EU nationals who arrive in Italy with a job already arranged must apply at the *questura*, or the police station in smaller towns, for their *Permesso di Soggiorno* (sometimes also known as a *Carte di Soggiorno*), within eight days of arrival. Reports vary as to how long it takes for the *Permesso di Soggiorno* to be issued, but three months is the official delay.

Requirements for the *permesso di soggiorno* may vary. In many cases you will be required to produce proof of financial solvency, of having some kind of income and be able to name your intended profession while in Italy, if this is relevant. The soggiorno is free of charge and issued initially for three months and then either every two years or five years. Note that failure to renew the document can result in a substantial fine. Renewals are made through the *comune*, or the *questura* in large towns and cities. The *Permesso di Soggiorno* has to be renewed every five years, no matter how long you live in Italy. All renewals must be made on special document paper, *carta bollata*, which can be purchased from most tobacconists (*tabaccherie*). Depending on your status, the *permesso di soggiorno* will have a different suffix, for example: employee, student, tourist, student, spouse, foreign spouse of an Italian, etc.

Non-EU Nationals: All non-EU nationals intending to live in the country must have received the necessary visas before arrival. Within eight days of their arrival they need to apply for their *permesso di soggiorno* to the *questura*, or the police station in smaller towns.

All Nationalities: When making an application for *permesso di soggiorno* it is advisable to take every document required at the time of application to make a return visit unnecessary, or worse, prevent having to repeat the entire process of waiting and aggravation. The list below is guide to what many people have been requested to present, though the list should be checked at the office you will apply to as local requirements may vary, especially between EU and non-EU nationals.

- A valid passport. Most countries require your passport to be valid for six months or more beyond your intended stay and Italy is no exception. A photocopy of the relevant information pages, including your visa, will also be required.
- Up to four black and white passport sized photos.
- A tax stamp (marca da bollo) of the correct value (check what is required at the local *questura*).
- For employees, a letter of employment is necessary.
- For the self-employed, proof of registration with the Chamber of Commerce and VAT certificate (or exemption) is required.
- For students a letter from their institution is required.
- For retired/non-working people proof of financial resources is needed.
- Proof of health insurance or coverage by social security system of Italy or another country.
- Marriage/divorce certificate.
- Passports of children to be included on the *permesso di soggiorno*, if the children are not on the parents passport, plus the birth certificates of the children.

It is necessary to have notarised translations of certain documents and have others provided in Italian – check with the office where the application will be made for current requirements. Official translations of the marriage, divorce and birth certificates, as well as the letter of employment in Italian will probably be required. Translations should be done by an official translator and enquiries should be made at an Italian Embassy or at the *questura* where an application is to be made.

Libretto di Lavoro

Many employees, including EU citizens, are also required to apply for a worker registration card (*libretto di lavoro*). This is obtained after the *Permesso di Soggiorno*, at the town hall (*municipio*). The *libretto di lavoro* is valid for ten years and once obtained will be held by the employer. During any periods of unemployment it will be kept by the equivalent of the job centre (*Ufficio di Collocamento*).

Certificato di Residenza

Once you have obtained a *permesso di soggiorno* and moved into your new Italian home, you will find it to your advantage to apply for a residence certificate, *certificato di residenza*. For non-EU citizens it is mandatory and should be applied for within 20 days of receipt of the *permesso di soggiorno*. Applications should be made at the Vital Statistics Bureau (*Anagrafe*) of the *Comune*.

The *certificato di residenza* entitles the holder to many vital privileges. The *residenza* is also proof that you are no longer resident in another country and can have tax advantages for UK citizens and other nationalities who need to demonstrate that they are living abroad. The *residenza* also enables the holder to numerous other benefits, e.g. to ship your personal effects to Italy, apply for a driving licence, open a bank account, claim health care and send children to local schools. The number of certificates which you are required to obtain once in Italy for other, more obscure reasons, will vary greatly depending largely on the commune in question and on the nature of the local *maresciallo* (head of the commune).

The *comune* of Rome has a web page that lists, in English, the current application requirements for a residence permit: www.comune.roma.it/info-cittadino/schede/stranieri/inglese/ss-im-ps.htm

Entering to Start a Business

EU Nationals. Those EU nationals who wish to enter Italy to start up a business are free to do so and no prior authorisation is required (further information is given on this in Chapter Seven, *Starting a Business*). Anyone in this category should apply for a *permesso di soggiorno* in just the way described above. However, if you have received a *permesso* as an employee it is necessary to have it amended to reflect your change in circumstances. Proven experience of three years in the field of the intended business and registration with the Chamber of Commerce is necessary as is obtaining a VAT number, or an exemption. Registration with the Chamber of Commerce is relatively simple, though obtaining the tax papers can be more difficult and many expatriates employ a specialist company to help them through the process. Starting work before completing the registration process is not recommended as it is technically against the law and can lead to fines and confiscation of equipment. There are a number of incentive programmes available in Italy that include low-interest loans and tax rebates.

Non-European Union Nationals: For those without right of abode in the EU who wish to enter and start a business a visa is necessary, for which proof of qualification to do so to do so in Italy is required. To obtaining the visa it may be necessary to obtain documentation from Italian organisations in Italy (e.g. Chamber of Commerce), sometimes it is necessary to obtain the documentation from the local of office in the area where the business will be located. Advice should be sought from an Italian Embassy and other Italian oriented trade organisations.

Entering with Retirement Status

Anyone intending to retire to Italy must be able to show proof of funds with which to support themselves in order to obtain their *permesso di soggiorno*. Depending on nationality, the residence permit must be renewed at varying intervals from one to five years and continuing proof of funds must be provided each time. Non-EU nationals must also furnish proof of health insurance that covers them in Italy.

Further information regarding residence regulations for those retiring to Italy is given in the *Retirement* chapter.

The Carta d'Identità

All residents, native and foreign, are required to carry an identity card (*Carta d'Identità* with them at all times. This is a regulation that the majority of Italians comply with, without feeling that it is any kind of infringement of their personal liberty. Outside of the UK, most European countries require people to carry some form of identity at all times, as do the majority of countries around the world – the premise being that if you have nothing to hide why should you worry if the police want to know who you are. Permanent residents are issued with an identity card that includes the holder's nationality and passport number. The card should be bought from the *comune*. However, only Italian nationals can use their Italian identity card as a travel document in lieu of their passport.

Registering with the Embassy

Expatriates are advised to register with their Embassy or Consulate in Italy – US, Canadian and British offices are listed below. This registration enables the Embassy to keep their nationals up to date with any information they need to be aware of and also enables the Embassy to trace individuals in the event of an emergency. The Consulates can also help with information regarding their nationals' status overseas and advise with any diplomatic or passport problems. They may also be able to help in an emergency such as the unfortunate event of the death of a relative. However, the Consulates do not function as a source of general help and advice, nor act as an employment bureau and they make this quite obvious in response to any such appeals. Some embassies run social clubs for their nationals and the nationals of friendly countries may be allowed to join too. Apart from being a good place to meet fellow nationals and other expatriates, these social clubs can be useful places to network for employment and business opportunities.

Italian Citizenship

Residency is not synonymous with citizenship and those who wish to be adopted as a citizen of Italy may find that they have some difficulty in doing so. There are however various ways to gain Italian citizenship, some of which are easier to complete than others, these include:

- By descent (if one or more parent or grandparent were Italian).
- By marriage to an Italian, after six months of residency in Italy or three years of marriage.
- Through residency of more than two years in Italy (see www.escapeartist.com/efan/living-in-italy.htm or www.lainet.com for the story of a US national trying to obtain Italian citizenship).

However, for EU nationals it should be no inconvenience to retain your current nationality, as you will have most of the rights, and also obligations, of an Italian national – expatriates can even vote in local elections. However, non-Italian males resident in Italy are not liable to perform military service (*il servizio militare*) – probably something most people would want to avoid anyway. However, from 2005 compulsory National Service will finish and Italy will have an entirely voluntary armed forces.

Immigration

Italy is currently tightening its immigration laws in an effort to restrict the flood of immigrants (legal and illegal) from Eastern Europe, particularly Albania, the numbers from North Africa and the sub-Sahara are also causing concern. These immigrants form Italy's 'underclass' and are the main pillar of Italy's flourishing black economy. The *clandestini* as they are known, work without being registered, so apart from being able to pay lower wages, their employers save up to 50% of their usual labour costs as there are no social security or holiday benefit payments to be made. Although the official immigration figure for Italy currently stands at around a million, the true figure is probably double that. To combat this problem, immigration legislation has been introduced, visa controls are being imposed and large numbers of police and military units have been deployed along the country's massive land frontiers and coastline in a concerted effort to repel the swelling ranks of Italy's illegal immigrants. Most recently there has been an influx of Kurdish refugees from Turkey and Iraq. Areas where vigilance has been especially concentrated are Sicily, Calabria and Puglia in the south and Friuli in the north.

The problems of illegal immigration are not limited to volume, but include organised crime. Either the illegal immigrants end up working for the Mafia or, as in the case of Albanians, they turn out to be more deadly than the local Mafia whom they have managed to intimidate and supplant in northern cities like Milan.

One of the new Immigration Laws enables the Italian state to deport any *clandestino* found guilty of committing a crime on Italian territory. The same applies if they are found to have a previous criminal record, or they refuse to produce proper identification. If a *clandestino* is unable to produce identification, he or she can be held at a detention centre for a maximum of 30 days while identification is being sought.

On a number of occasions Italy has allowed *clandestini* already living in the country without valid documents to apply for their situation to be regularised. If they can show good reason why they should be allowed to stay, they are almost always allowed to do so.

Sources of Information

Before getting too far into planning any move to Italy all and every piece of information should be checked and double checked – including information in this book. Italian Embassies and Consulates in whose jurisdiction you live and your own Embassy in Italy are the best places to get information, though they might not always respond quickly.

Inhabitants of Rome, its province or region, who are floundering helplessly in a sea of incomprehensible bureaucracy can call an emergency telephone line (06-884 8484). The helpline dispenses invaluable advice on where to go, what you will need to take with you and what the cost is of all of the *certificati* and *permessi*, which you now find you need. This is a free public service known as Socialtel, provided by a local government, university, trade union and telephone company amalgamation, formed in response to the numerous calls incited by the Italian bureaucratic system. The helpline also provides helpful advice about finding work in Italy and information about medical treatment.

Useful Addresses

Italian Embassies and Consulates in the United Kingdom:

Italian Embassy: 14 Three Kings Yard, Davies Street, London W1Y 2EH; ☎020-7312 2200; fax 020-7499 2283; www.embitaly.org.uk.

Italian Consulate General: 38 Eaton Place, London SW1; ☎020-7235 9371.

Italian Consulate General: Rodwell Tower, 111 Piccadilly, Manchester M1 2HY; ☎0161-236 9024. Easier to get through to than the London Consulate. For latest regulations send a request and a stamped addressed envelope to the Visa Department.

Italian Consulate General: 32 Melville Street, Edinburgh EH3 7HW; ☎0131-226 3631; 0131-220 3695.

Italian Vice Consulate: 7-9 Greyfriars, Bedford MK40 1HJ; ☎01234-356647. Operates 9.30am-12.30pm Monday to Friday.

Italian Embassies and Consulates in the United States of America:

Italian Embassy: 3000 Whitehaven Street NW, Washington DC 20008; ☎202-612-4400; fax 202-518-2154; www.italyemb.org.

Italian Consul General: 690 Park Avenue, New York, NY 10021, USA; ☎737-9100 or 439-8600; www.italyconsulnyc.org.

Italian Consul: 2590 Webster Street, angolo Broadway, San Francisco; ☎415-931 49224/5/6; visa enquiries visa@italcons-sf.org; www.italcons-sf.org.

Italian Consul: Boston www.italcons boston.org.

Italian Consul: www.italconschicago.org.

Other Italian Embassies and Consulates:

Italian Embassy: 21st Floor, 275 Slater Street, Ottawa, Ontario, K1P 5H9; ☎613-232240; fax 613-233 1484; www.italyincanada.com.

Italian Consul General: 136 Beverley Street, Toronto (ON) M5T 1Y5, Canada; ☎416-977 1566; fax 416-977 1119; www.italconsulate.org.

Embassy of Italy: 12 Grey Street, Deakin A.C.T. 2600, Australia, ☎621-6273 3333; fax 612-6273 4233; www.ambitalia.org.au.

Embassy of Italy: 63 Northumberland Road, Dublin, Eire; ☎031-6601744; fax 031-6682759; http://homepage.eircom.net/italianembassy/

British Embassies and Consulates in Italy:

British Embassy: Via XX Settembre 80a (Porta Pia), 00187 Rome, Italy; ☎064-220 0001 (8am-1pm & 2-4pm); www.britain.it.

British Consulate General: via S. Paolo 7, 20121 Milano, Italy; ☎02 723001; fax 02-864 65081.

British Consulate: Viale Colombo 160, 09045 Quartu SF, Cagliari, Sardinia; ☎070-828628; fax 070-862293.

British Consulate: Palazzo Castelbarco, Lungarno Corsini 2, 50123 Firenze; ☎055-284133; fax 055-219112.

British Consulate: Piazza della Vittoria 15/16, Third Floor, Genoa; ☎10-564833; fax 10-5531516.

British Consulate-General: Via dei Mille 40, 80121 Napoli; ☎081-423 8911; fax 081-422 434.

British Consulate: via Saluzzo 60, 10125 Torino, Italy; ☎011-650 9202; fax 011-669 6982.

British Consulate: Vicolo delle Ville 16, 34124 Trieste; ☎040-764752.

British Consulate: Accademia Dorsoduro 1051, 30123 Venezia; ☎041-522 7207; fax 041-522 2617.

Other Consulates are listed on the UK Embassy website www.britain.it.

United States Embassies and Consulates in Italy:

Embassy of the United States of America: via Vittorio Venetto 119/A, 00187 Roma Italy; ☎06-467 1; fax 06-4882 672 or 06-4674 2356; www.usembassy.it.

US Consulate General: Lungarno Vespucci, 38, 50123 Firenze, Italy; ☎055-239 8276; 055-284 088.

US Consulate General: Via Principe Amedeo, 2/10 – 20121 Milano, Italy; ☎02-290 351; fax 02-2900 1165.

US Consulate General: Piazza della Repubblica – 80122 Napoli, Italy; ☎081-5838 111; fax 081-7611 869.

American Embassy to the Holy See: via dell Terme Deciane 26, 00162 Rome, Italy; ☎06-4674 3428; fax 06-575 8346.

Canadian Embassy and Consul in Italy:

Canadian Embassy: Consular Section, Via Zara, 30, 00198 Rome, Italy; ☎06-445 981; fax 06-445 98 912; www.canada.it.

Canadian Consulate General: Consular Section, Via Vittor Pisani, 19, 20124 Milan, Italy; ☎02-67581; fax 02-6758 3900.

SETTING UP HOME

CHAPTER SUMMARY

O Tuscany, Umbria and, increasingly, Le Marche are the favoured regions for British expatriates wanting to settle in Italy.

O **Property prices:** Away from Tuscany and Umbria property is generally cheaper, but there will be fewer other expatriates to socialize with.

O **The Italians and housing.** There is not a large supply of single accommodation as Italians tend to live in large family groups so it can be hard to find.

   O Italians themselves tend not to use estate agents, preferring to buy privately from vendors.

   O Those letting out property back home may find employing a letting agent a worthwhile investment.

O **Buying property.** Italian banks move slowly, and it can take a month to get a mortgage approved.

   O British mortgage lenders will not normally lend money to buy property in Italy, but you may be able to raise money by re-mortgaging your UK property.

   O Foreigners not familiar with Italian property buying procedures may find it useful to employ an *avvocato* (lawyer) to represent them.

   O Surveys are not compulsory but are advisable, especially for older property.

O **Renting Property.** Renting an apartment can provide a base from which to try the way of life of a region while you look for your ideal home.

O **Utilities.** Before moving in you should always check that the electricity, gas and telephone are connected before as getting reconnected can take time.

ITALY WAS AMONG the first group of countries to use the Euro in January 2002, along with Austria, Belgium, Finland, France, Germany, Ireland, Luxembourg, The Netherlands, Portugal and Spain. Denmark, Greece, Sweden and the United Kingdom have not yet joined and it is unclear at this point whether/when they will join the club.

As the European nations continue their relentless progress towards political and economic union, thousands of Europeans are relocating to new jobs, homes and countries to set up home. France, Italy, Spain, Greece and Portugal are the most popular destinations for UK citizens moving abroad, and Italy has long been a favourite of North Americans, as can be seen from the number of American schools in Rome and other Italian cities. Over the past three decades Italy has been the dream destination of thousands of Europeans wishing to escape the temperate northern European winters and who also have a passion for Italian landscape and culture.

Those who do not need to work have set up home in assorted properties including converted convents, shepherds' cottages, farmhouses, seaside flats, Renaissance villas and 18th century *palazzi*, with the favoured regions being the picturesque provinces of Tuscany and Umbria and increasingly Le Marche. The number of British expatriates resident in Italy is in the tens of thousands with many thousands more owning holiday homes there. With British Prime Minister, Tony Blair, holidaying in Chiantishire too, the regions popularity is sure to grow further. However France and Spain each have more than twice as many British foreign residents as Italy does; some might say this shows the exclusivity of Italy, while others would point to the potential risks to property that may be subject to whims of the European fault line that runs through the country. The fault line causes reasonably frequent tremors to occur in Umbria, Tuscany and elsewhere and serious damage does occur at not too lengthy intervals, as shown by the 1997 earthquake in Umbria.

For working expatriates the north of the country is most likely to be their destination, especially Milan and Bologna. Rome is, of course, home to many expats. There is no disputing that Italy has glorious scenery, an impressive cultural heritage, and a relaxed lifestyle. In theory it is of course possible to live anywhere in the country, but in reality, it will depend on commuting times, Italian language ability (or the availability of English-speaking estate agents and other expats to socialise with), budget limitations and how discouraging is the prospect of living in an earthquake zone.

When buying property, Umbria and Tuscany have been popular with overseas house buyers for so long it is probably easier to find an English-speaking estate agent in those areas. However, it may be possible to find English speaking agents in other areas.

For expats who have been posted to a city by their employer, or have secured a job with a new employer, there is no choice but to buy or rent somewhere close enough to the office that commuting times are acceptable. There are also local weather conditions to consider too; Bologna and Ferrara suffer from fog during the four months from November to February, so it can be better to live closer to work and avoid the inevitable accidents and delays of commuting.

BUYING PROPERTY

A WAY FROM UMBRIA and Tuscany there are other parts of Italy where the aesthetic attractions are equally as good; these include Le Marche (pronounced markay) and north-eastern Puglia (pronounced poolia), Piedmont and Calabria. British-based estate agents barely cover these other regions, with the exception of Brian A. French and Associates (☎ 0870 7301910; fax 0870 7301911; louise.talbot@brianfrench.com; www.brianfrench.com: Italian office 075 9600024 or mobile 340 341 5667, Mr. Steve Emmett), Liguria specialist, Casa Travella (www.casatravella.com) and Piedmont Properties (www.piedmontproperties.com). Another source of property for sale is the Internet and a search using any of the leading search engines will find numerous online agencies. There is also the Shop Casa section on the home page of Yahoo! Italia – where property in most regions is advertised. If you cannot find a property you want in the area of your choice through an international estate agent or the Internet, you will have no option but to make several trips to the region to find an agent in the locality of your choice or to deal directly with a vendor. Unless you have a thorough knowledge of the region in which you are interested, have Italian friends and contacts, and/or you speak fluent Italian, the latter option would be like jumping overboard at shark feeding time. In other words, getting through the buying procedure in one piece would be *un miracolo* and this is not the recommended way to buy Italian property. Properties are advertised for sale in all the main Italian newspapers, but they tend to be city properties. Few expatriates are interested in city properties as short term residents would be unlikely to find it financially worthwhile to buy property whose value rises slowly and costs a lot to buy in bureaucratic charges.

For a large company that expects to send a steady stream of expatriates to Italy a purchase may be worthwhile as it will save the repeated charges of estate agents when the new expat rents an apartment upon arrival. It will also save the initial hotel bills while the new expat is searching for somewhere to live. On the downside, successive expats may not find the accommodation suitable for their varying family circumstances, i.e garden, parking, location of schools, etc.

Buying property in a foreign country is always different to doing it in your home country. Therefore, unless you have the money to pay for the best legal advice and have someone else take responsibility for buying a property that matches your requirements and produces no surprises after the purchase, it will take a lot of effort on your part to complete a satisfactory purchase. Although this chapter explains the main processes involved, it is essential that professional advice applicable to both your home country and Italy be taken before any financial commitments are made. It is necessary to seek legal advice both at home and abroad as property purchase and setting up home in a foreign country often affects your residency and tax situation. Such advice is easily obtainable from property agents and lawyers in the UK, US, Canada and Italy, and personal recommendations can be obtained from those who have already set up home in Italy. However, it is important to make sure that advice is taken from a reputable and reliable expert with specialist knowledge of Italy and your home country – most embassies hold lists of local lawyers who also speak the language of their country.

The Price of Property

In the popular region of Tuscany price-tags can start at around £60,000 (approximately US$84,000) for a derelict farm house requiring three times that amount to restore it. However, more typical prices are £200,000+ (US$280,000) for a farmhouse ready for occupation with 30 acres of land, and up to £1,300,000 (US$1,872,000) for a dilapidated eighteenth century villa with twenty-five bedrooms and 350 hectares of land. Properties in need of restoration and those located far from the telephone, gas and electricity mains are always cheaper. Umbria is slightly cheaper than Tuscany and some say, just as beautiful. Properties in Le Marche are cheaper all round: a habitable, three-bedroomed house could cost about £38,000 (US$54,000) and a typical farm house with a little land and in need of restoration would be in the region of £80,000 (US$115,000) to £100,000 (US$144,000) – though as little as £19,000 (US$27,000) is possible for something that needs a lot of work. Away from Tuscany and Umbria country purchases are cheaper, but there are fewer foreigners for expat retirees to socialise with, which can mean life is lonely for non-Italian speakers.

How do the Italians Live?

To understand the Italian property market and the availability of certain types of accommodation, it is necessary to understand how Italians live and the sort of accommodation they prefer. The Italian concept of home is virtually inseparable from the family. A high proportion of Italians tend to live in a large family *appartamento* in a *palazzo*, which can mean a palace but is more likely (depending on the circles you move in) to refer to a fairly modest block of flats. Even when children do move out of the parental apartment, usually to get married, they will voluntarily take a flat in the same block as their parents and continue to live as part of the family. Despite families living on top of each other in this fashion, there are surprisingly few social problems, which may come as a surprise to Anglo-Saxons and many North Americans with their cherished belief that everyone needs their own personal space in which to develop and relax.

However, in some areas this family proximity reaches extremes. In Naples, for instance, overcrowding resulting from poverty and an acute housing shortage means that sprawling families live in large single-room apartments, the notorious slums (*i bassi*) of that city. As a result of the way Italians live, irremediably bonded in tight family units, bachelor apartments or single accommodation (i.e. small flats) can be extremely difficult to find.

Another aspect of Italian life that is liable to come as a shock to an unsuspecting foreigner is the noise level in and around apartment blocks and other residences. Italians do not live quietly and though a lively and vibrant city can be exciting and enjoyable when on holiday, living in a traditional Mediterranean country, with its late nights and voluble people, can take a lot of getting used to for quieter Northern Europeans and North Americans.

Italians, and Europeans in general, take much longer than North Americans to become friends with someone – though they will be very friendly and polite to newly arrived expatriates. It can take quite a while before new friends are invited to visit the home, as this is an honour reserved for family and close friends. Just because you work with someone does not mean they consider you their friend. Initial socialising is likely to be done in restaurants and bars, until Italians consider they know you well enough or like you enough, to invite you to their home.

Owing to the ever-worsening traffic and public transport problems, there is a trend towards city-centre dwelling, usually in the old part (*centro storico*) which most Italian cities of any note possess. Thirty years ago the old quarters in many European cities were invariably overcrowded, rundown or plain slum areas. Nowadays they are turning into chic residential districts popular with the young, trendy and artistic members of the community. In Italy the areas just outside the centre are known as *il semicentro*, where most of the purpose-built palazzi are located. The suburbs, (*periferia*) are where the least well off generally live, though new American-style housing estates, sporting detached homes and gardens are appearing – Silvio Berlusconi made a fortune by building one of the first in Italy.

Council accommodation (*le case popolari*) does exist in Italy but it is an administrative disaster area and is nowhere near as widespread as in the UK or other EU countries. Council tenants are charged *equo canone* (fair rents) which is an understatement, since many have not been increased since the 1960s. In any case the question of council rents is an academic one since an estimated 80% of tenants have not paid any rent at all for the last decade. Around 78% of Italian families are owner-occupiers, one of the highest rates in Europe; the rest live in the limited rented accommodation (*un appartamento in affitto*) that most working expatriates will have to compete for.

Rich Italians looking for a second or holiday home in their own country rarely go for the type of quaint, rustic property favoured by foreign retirees and those dreaming of moving to a life of ease in the Italian countryside. Italians are more likely to buy or rent a luxury seaside flat or a house in the mountains.

Estate Agents and Other Property Advisors

Whenever there is a boom in demand for Italian property, estate agents seem to leap out of nowhere, hit the ground running and then disappear or switch to another area of Europe when things go quiet. The real Italy specialists are likely to manage the leaner years by letting out Italian property, and improving their contacts ready for when the next boomlet occurs. They may be based in Italy or have long-standing contacts based there. The Federation of Overseas Property Developers and Consultants – FOPDAC (3rd Floor, 95 Aldwych, London WC2B 4JF; ☎020-8941 5588; fax 020-8941 0202; www.fopdac.com; info@fopdac.com) is an association of English speaking estate agents, lawyers and other specialists in the property field who work with people looking to buy European property in a country other than their own – companies must meet very strict criteria for membership.

Italian estate agents (*agenzie immobiliari*) are not as numerous as you might expect as Italian buyers tend to buy privately from the vendor, thus saving the large agency fees. The profession has developed in Italy to the extent that all estate agents, whether Italian or foreign, must be registered and have a document from the *comunale* (borough) attesting to their legality. The Italian association of real estate consultants is the AICI (Via Nerino 5, 20123 Milan; ☎02-725291; fax 02-86452597).

Foreign estate agents selling property in Italy usually operate in conjunction with local associates in Italy who may be either English or Italian.

Useful Addresses

Estate agents in the UK & FOPDAC:

Brian A. French and Associates: ☎0870-7301910; fax 0870-7301911; louise.talbot@brianfrench.com; www.brianfrench.com: Italian office 075-9600024 or mobile 340-341 5667, Mr. Steve Emmett). Offers the widest range of areas of any of the British agents including Tuscany, Umbria, Le Marche, Abruzzo and Calabria.

Babet Ltd: 6 North Street Farm Workshops, Stoke-sub-Hamdon, Somerset TA14 6QR; 01935-825772. Specializes in central and northern Tuscany and Umbria including the popular area of Lake Trasimeno; also Le Marche.

Casa Travella; 65 Birchwood Road, Wilmington, Kent DA2 7HF, England; ☎ 01322-660988; fax 01322-667206; www.casatravella.com. Has agents in Northern and Central Italy and will help with relocation, restoration, etc.

Chalcross: 18 Market Place, Chalfont St. Peter, Bucks SL9 9EA; ☎01753-886335; fax 01753-886336. Will search for requested property on request, through an agent in Italy. Mostly searches for property for sale, particularly around Lucca in Tuscany. Contact: Kenneth Arton.

Eurovillas: 36 East Street, Coggeshall, Essex CO6 1SH; ☎01787-479191. In business for 30-40 years, they are a letting agency for the Lake Garda area and Tuscany around Lucca. They can also provide purchasing contacts

in these areas and can rent accommodation from which to carry out a reconnaissance of likely properties to purchase.

Hello Italy: Woodstock, Forest Road, East Horsley, Surrey KT24 5ES, England; ☎01483-284011. Letting agent for northern Tuscany (about 30 minutes from the Ligurian coast). Can provide introductions to purchasing contacts in the area, help with restoration and building, and sales after care. Many clients who buy, have subsequently used Hello Italy as a letting agent.

Knight Frank; Head Office, 20 Hanover Square, London W1S 1HZ, ☎020-7629 8171; info@knightfrank.com; www.knightfrank.com an international agency with associates in Tuscany and North America (*Grub & Ellis*; 800-877-9066; www.grubbellis.com; with offices across America).

Piedmont Properties: Angelika Smith-Aichbichler, 4 Beechcroft Close, Ascot, Berks SL5 7DB; ☎01344-624096; www.piedmonproperties.com; pp@smithgcb.demon.co.uk. Specialise in marketing villas and vineyards in the Monferrato and Langhe regions of Piedmont (south and west of Asti).

Undiscovered Tuscany: Linda Travella, Woodstock, Forest Road, East Horsley, Surrey KT24 5ES; ☎01483-284011; fax 01483-285264. Started in 1987. Deals with property mainly in the Lake Como area and the lakes region as well as Liguria and Tuscany. Can arrange long and short term rentals and provide full property purchasing service.

Estate agents in Italy: In addition to the addresses listed below, online agencies can be found via websites such as www.findaproperty.com and www.accommodation.com.

Concept Italia: via Vittorio Emmanuelle II 54, 55100 Lucca; ☎0338-7127122; fax 583-32740939. Contact: Sally Adams.

Giorgio Vigano: 003914. Milan estate agent deals with property all over Italy.

La Rocca: Louise Rocca di Vecchi, via Torino 51, 20123 Milan; ☎02-7252141; fax 02-89010909. Covers all regions of Italy.

Michael Goodall: ☎0577-941703. Property agent.

Villaman: Via di Cecina 610, 55029 Ponte a Moriano, Lucca; tel/fax 583-404066.

Useful Publications

Porta Portese: comes out in Rome on Tuesdays and Fridays and contains a useful accommodation section.

Ville & Casali: Edizioni Living International (ELI) SpA, Via Anton Giulio Bragaglia, 33-00123 Rome; ☎ 06-30884122; fax 06-30889944. Ville & Casali is a national property and decoration magazine in Italian, the classified property advertisements are listed in both Italian and English.

HOME SWAPS

IF YOU ARE NOT SURE which region you would like to buy a property in, would like to 'try the region out', or have a base from which to look around for a suitable property, a home swap can be an economic way to do this. There are branches of the main home swap organisations in Italy, which are listed here:

Family Links: Via Brescia 34, Rome; tel/fax 06 85354524.

Green Theme International: Euroculture, Via A Rossi 7, 36100 Vicenza; www.gti-home-exchange.com. Home swaps for those who care about the impact of tourism on the environment and the culture of the country they are visiting who want to swap homes with like-minded travellers.

Homelink International: Casa Vacanze, Campiello del Duomo 7/8 31046 Oderzo (TV); www.homelink.org. Worldwide organisation with branches in 32 countries. Founded in 1952.

Intervac International Home Exchange: www.intervac.com. Private organisation started in 1953 to give people the change of affordable holidays and to enable them to have a true experience of other ways of living.

LETTING PROPERTY IN YOUR HOME COUNTRY

FOR THOSE WHO OWN accommodation in their home country, letting it while they are away can be a good way to maintain a source of income whilst living in Italy. However, it should be born in mind that being an absentee landlord is not always easy and the income not always reliable – tenants do not always pay the rent and it can be hard to find a replacement when living in another country or if your visits home are infrequent. Estate agents often act as letting agents too and will manage property for absentee landlords. For expatriates, utilising a local agent to manage their property, rather than a friend or family member, can be well worth the agency fees. 10% of the income is not much for relieving the stress and worry of managing rental property in another country and lessening the likelihood of falling out with friends or family if the tenant damages the property or skips with the deposit.

Some expats specifically buy property in their home country to rent while they live abroad. This can be to generate income, as a form of investment, or be the intended place of retirement at the end of an international career. Recommended reading on this subject is listed below.

UK publications:

Buy To Let, By Stuart Powers. Covers all aspects of buying and letting and how to choose an agent, available from www.keysteps.co.uk, £4.20.

The Which? Guide to Renting and Letting, £10.99. Peter Wilde/Paul Butt. Covers mainly landlord/tenant issues.

Making Money from Letting, £9.99, Moira Stewart.

US publications:

Every Landlord's Legal Guide: Leases & Rental Agreements, Deposits, Rent Rules, Liability, Discrimination, Property Managers, Privacy, Repairs & Maintenance, Marcia Stewart/Janet Portman/Ralph Warner.

Landlord's Handbook: A Complete Guide to Managing Small Residential Properties, $29.95, by Daniel Goodwin, Richard Rusdorf.

FINANCE

Mortgages with Italian Banks

ITALIANS OFTEN BUY their apartments by outright purchase in one go, though all the family will probably chip in. However, mortgages (*ipoteche*) can be arranged with Italian banks in Italy, but bear in mind that they can be expensive. Also, financial sector services verge on the moribund (see *Banking* in *Daily Life*), though they are improving, and arranging a mortgage with an Italian bank can easily take one to three months – and that's just for the paperwork approving the loan!

Historically Italian banks have granted relatively low percentage mortgages (i.e. around 75% mortgage or less) on a property ready for habitation. This is now changing though as foreign lenders such as Abbey National and Banca Woolwich offer up to 85% on some types of mortgage and local lenders are trying to remain competitive. A few banks offer a *mutuo per ristrutturazione* (a mortgage for properties requiring restoration) of 90%. Most Italian banks offer a choice of fixed or variable interest mortgages, *tasso fisso* and *tasso variabile* respectively. Some banks in the Mezzogiorno and Sardinia offer reduced interest rates (*abbattimento tasso*) in order to attract buyers to certain areas. Such banks include *Banco Sardegna* and the *Cassa Risparmio Calabria*. Most banks do not have an upper limit (*importo massimo*) on the amount of the mortgage.

Specialist mortgage departments in Italian financial institutions have become more common in recent years and can be found at Benetton and the Banca Nationale Agricultura (BNA). These can provide up to 80% mortgages over a fifteen year period, which would be attractive for expatriates earning an Italian salary.

Useful Addresses

Banca Nazione di Lavoro: Direzione Generale, Via Vittorio Veneto 119, 00187 Rome.

Banca Nazionale dell'Agricultura (BNA): Direzione Centrale, Via Salaria 231, 00199 Rome.

Banca Woolwich SpA: Milan Regional Office: Piazza della Repubblica 8, 20121 Milan; ☎02 290401; fax 02 290 40619.

Conti Financial Services: 204 Church Road, Hove, E Sussex BN3 2DJ; ☎0800-018 2811; fax 01273-321269. Conti have many years of experience arranging finance for clients (both UK and non-UK nationals) purchasing properties overseas and is an independent mortgage broker.

Credito Romagnola:Via Zamboni 20, 40126 Bologna.

Istituto Monte dei Paschi di Siena: U.S.I.E. Sett. Serv. V.le Toselli 60, 53100 Siena.

Mortgages With non-Italian Institutions in Italy

Banca Woolwich, which operates in Italy, provides banking services geared to Italians and expatriates living and working in Italy. The Woolwich Bank customer service helpline in the UK (☎0208-298 4400) will provide advice and connect customers and potential customers to the correct department. Banca Woolwich SpA in Milan (☎02-584881; fax 02-58488511) would be more applicable for those already resident in Italy.

The Abbey National has a branch in Florence (☎055-500 1514; fax 055-500 1546) which could be useful for those already living in Tuscany and who speak Italian or have someone willing to translate. If you are arranging a mortgage for an Italian property from outside Italy, you should deal with the Milan branch of Abbey National (☎02 6672910; fax 02 66988955).

Italian banks and financial institutions tend to process mortgage applications more slowly than British and North American ones. For instance, it takes a minimum of five days to get a mortgage approved with a UK building society or bank, compared with a minimum of one month with an Italian bank or financial institution. The main reason for this difference is that the client vetting procedures of the Italian banks are extremely cumbersome. However, increased competition from foreign organisations will undoubtedly compel Italian banks and finance institutions to streamline their procedures.

Useful Addresses

Abbey National Mutui S.p.A: Via Nicolo Putignani, 137, 70122 Bari; ☎080-5237030; fax 08 05237094.

Abbey National Mutui S.p.A: Via Quarenghi, 36, 24122 Bergamo – (Bg); ☎03-5313130; fax 03 5313636.

Abbey National Mutui S.p.A: Via Marconi, 71, 40122 Bologna – (Bo); ☎05-14210028; fax 05 16390361.

Abbey National Mutui S.p.A: Viale G.Matteotti, 33, 50121 Firenze – (Fi); ☎055-5001514; fax 055 5001546.

Abbey National Mutui S.p.A: Via G.Fara 27, 20124 Milan; ☎02-6672906; fax 02-66729247.

Abbey National Mutui S.p.A. Ag. Milano 1, Via Dante 16. Milan; ☎02-86465193; fax 02-86465158.

Abbey National Mutui S.p.A: Via Medina 41/42, 80133 Napoli – (Na); ☎081-2520038; fax 081-5422124.

Abbey National Mutui S.p.A: Via Altinate, 8, 35139 Padova – (Pd); ☎04-98761380; fax 04-98761381:

Abbey National Mutui S.p.A: Ag. Roma 3, Via Cicerone 58, 00198 Rome; ☎06-328061; fax 06-3221536.

Abbey National Mutui S.p.A: Via San Tommaso 24, 10121 Torino; ☎011-542000; fax 011-546110.

Banca Woolwich SpA: Via Pantano 13, 20122 Milano; 20122 Milano; ☎02-584881; fax 02-58488511.

Woolwich Europe Ltd: 30 Erith Road, Bexley Heath, Kent DA7 6BP; ☎020-8298 4771; fax 020-8298 5315.

UK and Offshore Mortgages

It is extremely unusual for a British building society or bank to lend money for the purchase of a property abroad. However, some people have bought a second home abroad by re-mortgaging their UK property in order to pay cash for a new purchase in Italy.

Another option open to expatriates is to take out an offshore mortgage: these work slightly differently to standard mortgages and potential mortgagees should investigate them thoroughly before taking one on. Articles on offshore mortgages and details of providers can be found in expatriate magazines such as *FT Expat* (for contact details see the *Daily Life* chapter).

THE PURCHASING AND CONVEYANCING PROCEDURE

Professional Assistance

THE OFFICIAL USUALLY APPOINTED to handle a property sale is a *notaio* (public notary) who in Italy acts for both the vendor and the purchaser, as they do in other European countries such as France. There are also some lawyers (*avvocati*) who are qualified to handle property transactions. Foreigners, who are generally not versed in Italian property buying procedures, may wish to appoint both a *notaio* and an *avvocato*. This way, an expatriate can have a competent professional who works for them directly explain the process to them fully and completely, and not someone who is supposed to be an impartial administrator. Italian lawyers based in the UK can represent expatriates in Italy (see addresses below) when you are buying Italian property, alternatively your embassy or regional consular office should be able to supply a list of local lawyers who speak your language. The *notaio* is responsible for gathering together all the necessary documents, checking that the title deeds are in order, that the property is legally registered and that it has no illegal buildings on it. Having ascertained that this is the case, the next step is for the purchaser and vendor to sign a preliminary contract of sale.

You may also want to call on the services of a surveyor (*geometra*) to check the soundness of the building, point out any structural defects and estimate the cost of putting them right. Unlike in Britain, however, surveys are not compulsory and many Italians do not bother with them. For foreigners buying older buildings, especially those in need of restoration, a survey is almost certainly essential to prevent post-sale surprises.

A *geometra* can draw up contracts, carry out land searches and also monitor building work and make orders to suppliers if restoration is needed once the sale is completed.

Specialist lawyers based in the UK:
Giovanni Lombardo Dobson & Sinisi, 1 Throgmorton Avenue, London EC2N 2JJ; ☎020-7628 8163; fax 020-7920 0861. No lawyers in the London office but they will provide contact to their Italian office.
Claudio del Giudice: 5-7 Folgate Street, London E1 6BX; ☎020 76132788.
John Howell & Co.: see details above
For Italian lawyers in Italy who are members of the British Chamber of Commerce in Milan, see list of *Major Employers* in the *Employment* chapter.

The Compromesso

The *compromesso* or preliminary sale agreement outlines the conditions of purchase and any get-out clauses for the prospective purchaser, which may be applicable in some circumstances. These may include planning permission not being granted or failure of the purchaser's mortgage application. The *compromesso* also sets a date by which the transfer of property will be completed. Alternatives to the *compromesso*, the *Promessa d'Acquisto* (purchase proposal) or the *Promesso di Vendita* (promise of sale) are sometimes used.

Once one of the above documents has been authenticated, the purchaser then pays a deposit (*caparra*), which is usually about 10% of the sale price but can be up to 30% of the purchase price. The *caparra* is forfeited if the purchaser backs out of the agreement for a reason not covered by the *compromesso*. Likewise, if the vendor backs out of the sale, or does not hand over the property by the date given in the *compromesso*, then he or she is legally obliged to reimburse the vendor with double the amount of the *caparra*. The *caparra* is of course deductible from the purchase when the remainder of the money is paid.

The Rogito *and Under-Declaration of Value*

The *rogito* is a legally binding deed that transfers ownership of the property to the purchaser. Once the conditions of the *promesso* have been fulfilled and the balance has been handed over, the *rogito* can be drawn up by the *notaio*. The *rogito* includes a declaration of the price at which the property changed hands. The price on the *rogito* and the actual price paid can be vastly different. The purpose of this typically Italian wheeze is to avoid paying capital gains tax. By under-declaring the property's price considerable savings can be made on Capital Gains Tax which is charged at between ten and forty per cent. In some areas, property values are well known and to under-declare excessively would be to arouse the suspicion of the tax authorities who are then liable to make their own snap judgement on the property's worth and tax accordingly. In the vicinity of Rome, or big cities in the north, under-declaration is usually a modest 10% to 20%. In less well-documented rural areas such as Umbria, Abruzzo and Calabria under-declarations of up to 60% are commonplace. When negotiating the price to be entered on the *rogito* the purchaser should be aware that the Italian government, in its pursuit of lost revenue, is tightening up its controls, by encouraging local authorities to revise their estimates of local property values to a more realistic level. However, this will almost certainly not result in stamping out the practice. Moreover, if you are perverse enough to insist on declaring the actual price, the Italians are liable to consider you intellectually challenged. However, if you ever do sell the property, then the higher the declared price when you bought it, the less you have to pay in capital gains tax if the price of the property has gone up in value.

Charges for Property Purchase

There are a number of charges payable by new purchasers of property. These include the notary's fees which are usually 2-3% of the amount shown on the *rogito*, the estate agent's commission (usually 3% of the actual purchase price) and the fees of any other professionals (e.g. lawyer, accountant, surveyor, etc.), whose services have been engaged by the purchaser. In addition, new owners pay land registration fees (stamp duties), which vary according to the type of property involved. The highest fees are for agricultural land (17%) and the lowest for new properties purchased from the developer (4%); on other houses and apartments the rate is 11%. If you are buying new property, IVA (Italian VAT) is payable at 10% of the value. All rates are calculated on the price declared on the *rogito*.

Typically, total charges come to around 12% of the purchase price compared with about 2% in the UK, 10% in Spain and Portugal and up to 15% in France.

Ownership of Property and Land

Normally sane foreigners looking for land or property abroad can sometimes develop a sense of light-headedness in the Tuscan or Umbrian air. This dangerous condition apparently causes them to abandon any caution that they would normally exercise when buying a house or land in their home country. Having appointed a representative to handle a property transaction it is essential that the buyer ensures that the title deeds to the property are in order. It is also a good idea to find out whether any major developments are imminent in the immediate vicinity of the property – this can best be done by making local enquiries amongst the inhabitants of the region, but not the seller or his agent. These enquiries also give you a chance to make contact with prospective neighbours. You should also check on the likelihood of a *coltivatore diretto* being exercised (see below).

Coltivatore Diretto

One of the potential hazards lying in wait for the unsuspecting foreigner who is considering buying land and property in Italy is the *coltivatore diretto* (farmer's right). This Italian law enables smallholders to increase the size of their farms by giving them the right to buy land or buildings adjacent to their property for up to two years after it has been sold. The *coltivatore diretto* is dependent upon the farmer being able to pay the price on the *rogito*. If the figure on the *rogito* is a gross under-declaration of the property's value (see details above) the foreign purchaser is liable to be left grossly out of pocket. Meanwhile, the chortling farmer will be gloating and enjoying a luxury villa and swimming pool, which he just obtained at a knockdown price. However, steps can be taken to preclude the possibility of such an occurrence. The best way to do this is for the prospective purchaser's legal representative to furnish the farmer with a Special Delivery document, asking the farmer to confirm within 30 days whether he or she intends to exercise a *coltivatore diretto*. If the farmer has not expressed his intention to claim the land within thirty days of being served the Special Delivery document, he then waives any future right to do so.

The *coltivatore diretto* is only applicable to rural property registered as a *casa rurale*. Houses designated *case urbane* carry no such risk.

The *coltivatore diretto* can also work in favour of the foreign resident who wishes to preserve his or her privacy. In order to qualify for a *coltivatore diretto* you have to earn at least 70% of your income from agriculture or agro-tourism (bed and breakfast, riding holidays, etc.). Not only will foreigners registered as *coltivatore diretto* be able to stop anyone building in uncomfortable proximity, but they may also be eligible for government grants and soft loans (see Chapter Seven, *Starting a Business*).

Obtaining Planning Permission

As with many things in Italy, it can be difficult to perceive any consistency in official procedures, and planning permission is no exception. In some areas, it is obvious by the way monstrous blocks of flats have been built without any regard for their surroundings that they are illegal constructions. However, such is the lack of resources for dealing with the legislation and enforcing it, that the perpetrator usually pays a fine and the building remains. However, areas where planning regulations are pretty rigorously enforced include Tuscany and Le Marche and many see this is a blessing as it has meant that unsightly buildings have never spoiled the landscapes. If you do get permission to put up a building in the Tuscan countryside, it has to be made from local materials. In Le Marche, you are not allowed to build new property in the countryside, (except farm buildings). However, you can restore existing buildings.

Estate agents who deal in land normally do so only for terrain for which planning permission (*permessi communali*) has been granted. If, for some reason, you find yourself interested in a piece of land for which permission has not been granted then you should allow about three months to complete this process. You can find out if planning permission has already been granted by checking with the *comunale* (town hall). You should do this in any case rather than just accept the word of the vendor. One of the main problems for illegal buildings is that they cannot be connected to gas, water, telephone etc.

RENTING PROPERTY

SOME EXPATRIATES have their accommodation arranged for them as part of their job package, though many have to arrange their own accommodation on the spot once they arrive. Finding property to rent in most big Italian cities will be like trying to do so in any other big metropolis around the world – time-consuming, tiring, stressful and requiring large outlays of money. Renting accommodation in a foreign country with its different procedures in a foreign language and in an unfamiliar city adds additional problems. Although not high by British and American standards, rents in Italy can be expensive when measured against Italian salaries. If you decide to do as the Italians do and have three jobs and evade your taxes, then you will probably not find this an undue hardship. As already mentioned, Italians tend to live in large family apartments and so contribute their share to the pot with many contributors. For single foreigners the main difficulty is finding single accommodation, which is comparatively scarce. You can get round this by staying as a lodger with an Italian family. However, this will involve becoming a part of the family, which can be claustrophobic and tiring for those who are used to having peace and quiet in a place of their own – though it will speed up the rate at which language fluency is achieved.

Those intending to buy property in Italy in order to become resident on a long-term or permanent basis will probably want to rent a villa, farmhouse or apartment to use as a base from which to look for a property to buy. This provides the chance to decide which area appeals the most and determine any local conditions that might explain why certain properties are much cheaper than similar ones in the neighbourhood. There are a number of firms offering holiday rentals and a full list may be obtained from the Italian State Tourist Office (see below). Alternatively, websites such as www.estate.net list accommodation for rent in most parts of Italy.

A pre-relocation visit is well worth the effort and cost even if your employer will not pay for it, as accommodation can be arranged to be available when you do actually relocate. It can take some time to find accommodation and it would be advantageous for your employer or a contact to set up estate agents or a relocation agent in advance of your arrival to begin showing you potential accommodation shortly after you arrive in Italy. A translator would also be very useful if you do not speak Italian, as the intricacies of Italian rental contracts can be unfathomable to the uninitiated.

One expat has the following to say on renting an apartment:

> *My husband and I took over an apartment from a couple who were moving back to the U.S. and did not look on our own. The couple we took over the apartment from said that it is better to find a furnished apartment because an unfurnished apartment might not have kitchen cupboards, light fixtures, etc. I know that they also hired a translator to assist them in their search. It is also essential to have the lease agreement translated, before signing it. We did not realise we were supposed to have the furnace inspected each fall (which is required under Italian law) and that we were responsible for paying for the inspection – it was, however, in our lease agreement, in Italian. It is also a good idea to establish up front who will be paying for any maintenance done to the apartment.*

The website www.wantedinrome.com has listings of accommodation for rent and links to relocation agencies in the Rome area.

Useful Addresses

Eurovillas Italy: 36 East Street, Coggeshall, Essex CO6 1SH; ☎01787-479191. Rents property in Tuscany; can also arrange sales.

Hello Italy: Woodstock, Forest Road, East Horsley, Surrey KT24 5ES; ☎01483-284011. Letting agent for Lunigiana, northern Tuscany (about 30 minutes from the Ligurian coast). Can provide introductions to purchasing contacts in the area, help with restoration and building, and sales after care. Many clients who buy, have then used Hello Italy as a letting agent.

Italian State Tourist Office: 1 Princes Street, London W1R 8AY; ☎020-7408 1254.

Studio Papperini: 114 Via Ugo Ojetti, 00137 Roma; ☎06-86895810; fax 06-86896516. A comprehensive relocation service headed by Giovanni Papperini a solicitor specialising in immigration and nationality law. Based in Rome, but operates throughout Italy. Offers a pre-move service and cost effective, tailor-made package to suit employer or employee.

Tailormade-Tours: 22 Church Rise, Forest Hill, London SE23 2UD; ☎020-8291 1450. Holiday properties in Tuscany and Umbria for rent. Does not help arrange sales/purchase.

Vacanze in Italia, Manor Courtyard, Bignor, Pulborough, West Sussex RH20 1QD (01798-869426) has several hundred properties covering most areas of Italy, but concentrated in Tuscany and Umbria.

TABLE 4	USEFUL TERMS

un apartamento ammobiliato: a furnished apartment – more expensive than an unfurnished (*da ammobiliare=*) one, though possibly ending up cheaper and almost certainly more convenient than having to buy a lot of furniture for a short stay.

attico: it may be an attic in the country, but in the city it means a penthouse.

il bagno: bathroom.

il balcone: balcony – also called *la terazza.*

la cucina: kitchen.

la salla da pranzo: dining room.

un giardino: garden. Not many flats or palazzi have these, even on the ground floor.

monolocale con servizi: one-room with kitchen and bathroom. Average price around £400 a month but difficult to find.

piano: floor: *primo/secondo/terzo piano* = first/second/third floor.

il portiere: doorman/janitor in charge of a block of flats.

il salotto: (sitting-room). For many Italian families this doubles as an extra bedroom.

i servizi: kitchen and bathroom. Advertisements do not include these when giving the number of rooms.

stanze: room. un appartamento di due/tre/quattro stanze = a two/three/four-roomed flat.

stanze da letto: bedroom.

terra: ground floor.

un villino: cottage.

Where to Look for Accommodation

Apart from following up *affitasi* (to let) signs outside *palazzi*, the other obvious place to look for accommodation is in the classified sections headed *appartamenti da affittare* (flats to let), of main local papers. There is the daily *Il Messagero* in Rome, the bi-weekly publication *Seconda Mano* (Mondays and Thursdays) in the Milan area and most major cities also have free newspapers. For other papers see the section, *Media and Communications* in Chapter Four, *Daily Life*. You may also wish to consult one of the relocation specialists that offer accommodation services to individuals. Another possible alternative would be to consult university notice boards and even the notice boards of large international companies and organisations, where adverts for accommodation are displayed, primarily for the benefit of staff, but potentially useful to outsiders brazen enough to use them *in extremis*.

Tenancy Laws

Obtaining a tenancy agreement is undoubtedly easier if you are a non-resident since anyone with *residenza* status is protected by state laws from being evicted (*sfrattato*). The length of rental contracts varies but is normally for four years. When the landlord or lady (*padrone/padrona*) wishes to have the property back the tenant (*inquilino*) will be sent a notice to quit.

As a tenant you will also have certain responsibilities, such as obtaining an annual certificate to confirm your central heating boiler and gas heaters conform to EU requirements. The tenant is liable for the cost of the certificate. Check with other expats as well as your landlord exactly what is expected of you and what the landlord is responsible for as local conditions and rental contracts vary – as does the quality of landlord.

Communal Apartment Blocks

In Italy, a communal apartment block is known as a *condominio*. As virtually all Italian property is sold freehold, it is not necessary to pay ground rents to the leaseholder as well as rent to the building landlord who is responsible for the upkeep of the building. In Italy the residents have to make all the decisions regarding the upkeep and repair of the communal parts of the building; the roof, lifts, hallways, central plumbing and heating, etc. and are jointly responsible for the cost. If you are renting a flat in a condo you should have an agreement with the owner about who is going to pay the communal charges set out in the building's covenant. Important decisions concerning the future running of the building are made by the residents at the residents' meetings (*riunione di condominio*), which are held at not less than one year intervals.

In blocks of flats containing five or more apartments it is obligatory for the owners to appoint an agent *amministratore del condominio* to manage the property on behalf of the owners.

Letting Out Italian Property

Once your Italian property is furnished, letting it out can be a useful way of helping to pay off the cost, particularly if it is not occupied by you for much of the year. It is worth remembering that if your property is in a rural area of Tuscany, Umbria etc. the main letting period will be from spring to autumn. The income you can expect will vary according to the degree of luxury offered and whether the let is in high season (July and August), mid-season (June and September) or low (April, May and October). Rentals range from about £200 for a studio apartment to upwards of £1,700 a week for a seaside villa. Rentals are usually a week or longer. In the main season two weeks is usual while out-of-season lets tend to be shorter. It is possible to let to Italians or foreigners; including the British. Of course not everyone relishes the idea of a constant stream of strangers marching through their property inflicting additional wear and tear, but most tenants behave responsibly and you can always stipulate no animals, small children or pop stars if you are particularly fastidious about your furnishings. For those who decide to go ahead and rent out their villa, farmhouse or seaside apartment, there is no shortage of holiday villa rental companies that can be approached – the Italian State Tourist Office can provide a list: see also the list under *Renting Property* above.

INSURANCE

ITALY HAS A BAD REPUTATION for petty crime – burglary, pickpocketing and theft. However, this is much worse in the cities than in country areas and villagers often leave their homes unlocked. The rates of crime detection are appalling – less than 10% of burglaries are solved. As a result, insurance premiums are high and because it is expensive to insure house contents, most Italians do not bother. Foreign residents from Britain will find that insurance quotes from Italian firms are at least double what they would expect to pay in the UK and North America – Turin and Milan, two of the most likely destinations for expatriate workers, also have some of the highest premiums in Italy. Italian insurance companies are also notoriously slow about settling claims.

Estate agents sometimes offer house and contents insurance at competitive rates to their clients and it is worth asking them about this. For owners of second homes, an alternative to an Italian insurer is to use a British company such as those listed below, who will insure rural properties in Italy. Annual rates vary depending on the extent of the cover but are roughly £4.00 per £1,000 of the house value and £9 per £1,000 of the contents value. It is important to note that if you are moving to the earthquake zone, most insurance policies exclude earthquake damage.

Owing to the expense of insuring city apartments, it is prudent to take anti-burglar precautions – multiple locks and bars on ground floor windows are two of the basic requirements and an obvious deterrent to any prospective burglar.

Useful addresses

Barlow Redford & Co: 71a High Street, Harpenden, Herts AL5 2SL, England; ☎01582-761129; fax 01582-462380.

Copeland Insurance: Roy Thomas (Managing Director), 230 Portland Road, London SE25 4SL; ☎020-8656 8435); fax 020-8655 1271; service@andrewcopeland.co.uk; www.andrewcopeland.co.uk. Provides insurance for both holiday homes and permanent residents.

John Holman: Broadway House, 1-7 The Broadway, Wickford, Essex SS11 7AQ; ☎01268-730733; fax 01268-730490. Has overseas house-insurance designed for owners of property in Europe (expatriate and holiday homes).

Jon Wason: 72 South Street, Reading, RG1 4RA, England: ☎01734-568800. Does basic expatriate homes cover. Will also insure holiday homes abroad.

O'Halloran and Co: St James Terrace, 84 Newland, Lincoln LN1 1YA, England; 01522-537491; fax 01522-540 442; tpo@ohal.org. Will arrange cover for holiday homes in Europe.

Property Insurance Abroad: P O Box 150, Rugby CV22 5BR, England; ☎01788-550294; fax 01788-562579. Will provide a free quote.

Woodham Group Ltd.: 17 Fircroft Close, Woking GU22 7LZ, England; ☎ 01483-770787; www.woodhamgroup.com. Insurance Consultants linked to John Holman (above).

WILLS

UNDER ITALIAN LAW a foreigner's will drawn up outside Italy is deemed to be governed by the laws of the foreigner's country. If the will is straightforward, i.e. the property goes directly to the surviving spouse or the children there will be no problem. However, theoretically, problems could occur when English Common Law clashes with Roman Law as practised in Italy. In English law, executors are appointed by the deceased to administer the will according to his or her wishes. Under Italian law the death duties paid on the estate are minimal on bequests to next of kin and swingeing on distant or non-relatives. The concept of intermediary ownership as practised by English executors does not exist and it therefore poses a problem for Italian lawyers who must reach some kind of compromise. In order to keep complications to a minimum it is advisable to have a will drawn up by a lawyer with experience of both the Italian system and the legal system of your country.

UTILITIES

IT IS IMPORTANT for anyone contemplating a move to Italy to be aware that if their property is not already connected to the gas or water mains or is without electricity, they may have a long wait in store before these service are connected. Also, the further away the property is from the nearest telephone line or mains, the greater the cost of linkage. Such costs can add considerably to the price of an Italian property and you should therefore expect to pay a lower price for property without utilities than would be asked for a property with them.

In Italy it is unwise to delay paying your utilities bills. Whereas in many countries it is customary for service providers to send a politely-worded reminder notifying their customers that they have fallen behind with payments, in Italy there is no such finesse and the services of late paying subscribers are liable to be cut off. Conversely, getting reconnected can take an inordinate length of time.

Electricity

The national electricity company is *Ente Nazionale per l'Energia Elettrica* (ENEL). Before you can be plugged into it an ENEL inspector will have to ascertain that the wiring you have had installed meets ENEL specifications. It is important that if your property is being wired for the first time, the electrician is aware that you wish to be connected to the national supply, as some householders prefer to run a private generator and in such cases the wiring may be done to a lower standard. Once the ENEL inspector is satisfied you will be allowed to take out a contract with the electricity company on a non-resident or a resident basis. The latter is preferable as non-residents pay a premium rate. In order to obtain a resident's contract one needs to produce a residence certificate (see *Residence and Entry Regulations* chapter).

In very rural areas where the lines are strung out for miles the power can be feeble or subject to wild fluctuations, which can be damaging to sensitive electronic equipment including televisions. For those who require a reliable electricity supply a backup generator may be a useful purchase. In any case a UPS (uninterruptible power supply) with surge protector for computer equipment can prevent expensive damage to equipment and prevent loss of data when the power goes off.

The easiest way to pay bills is by direct debit from your bank. Like other European countries the electricity company in Italy bases its bills on estimated consumption and biannually adjusts them to the exact amount. The adjusted bills are invariably a bit of a shock.

ENEL was in the process of being privatised by the government but at the time of writing this has been suspended because of a depressed stock market.

Gas

Gas is widely used in northern Italy for central heating and cooking. Most cities and large towns are supplied by the *Societe Italiana per il Gas* (SIG). Unfortunately the SIG network does not penetrate rural areas or much of the south including Tuscany and Umbria where many foreign residents buy homes. For inhabitants of these areas who wish to have central heating, the solution is a gas tank, known rather alarmingly in Italian as a *bombolone*. Gas tanks can be loaned from the larger gas companies and installation is governed by strict regulations. The property owner must provide a concreted site for the tank and a padlocked, metal fence must surround it. The site must also be equipped with a fire extinguisher – a scarcely effective method of controlling the fire, one would imagine, in the event of a *bombolone* igniting. For obvious reasons, the tank should not be immediately adjacent to the house or road, which means that pipes have to be laid to connect the tank to the house. The contract with the gas company supplying the liquid gas will stipulate a minimum annual purchase usually in the region of £800, and additionally, that the gas will only be used for heating and hot water. The size of the tank depends on your needs and the number of deliveries etc. The gas company will provide advice and offer various solutions for your requirements.

Potentially less nerve-racking than living with a *bombolone* is the ubiquitous gas bottle (*bombola*), which is used in rural areas for cooking. It can also be used for heating and in Italy, as in other Continental countries, special heating appliances for use with bottled gas are available. For those who do not wish to go to the bother or expense of arranging connection with mains gas, particularly if their Italian home is only used for holidays, the bombola is a useful alternative to mains gas. Unlike mains gas there is no difference in the rate for residents and non-residents and it can usually be delivered.

Water

Italy's notorious water shortage may not be acute by Saharan standards, but it can still be a possible inconvenience for some people thinking of setting up home in the south of Italy. In summer, the water supply is liable to be cut off during the day and resumed at night. For this reason it is essential for those in rural areas and in the south to have a storage tank (*cassone*) which can be topped up when the water supply is on. For those living in flats in the main cities a 500 litre tank may be sufficient. In isolated dwellings in the rural south it may be necessary to store several months' supply of water in huge underground tanks. If the water in your area is metered (most of northern Italy already is) water may be rationed to a fixed number of litres per house, regardless of the number of occupants.

The water supply is under the control of the local *comune* and there are conditions governing the various uses of this often precious commodity. For instance, if you wish to water a garden, a separate contract from that which deals with household water becomes necessary. With such rigid controls it is perhaps no surprise that swimming pools are out of the question in some areas, which can come as a shock to the sybaritic foreign resident. However, for the clued-up and those with a little ingenuity, there are solutions for both gardeners and swimmers. It is possible to recycle water used for washing and bathing for the garden by draining it into a separate tank. However, water thus recycled should not contain bleach or detergent or the results will be disastrous for the plants subjected to it or dangerous for the swimmers swallowing it. Pure soapsuds on the other hand are harmless to plants, though they may make swimming pools frothy. The way round the swimming pool ban is to build what is a called a *vasca*. A *vasca* is an artificial water basin common in rural areas and ostensibly for domestic use when the mains water is cut off. The idea is that it fills up during the winter when rain is plentiful; it may also be fed by a spring or well. With a proper lining and some kind of filtering system to keep the water pure, a *vasca* could be used as a swimming pool, the less obviously, the better.

Nothing beats having mains water for convenience, and for peace of mind a contingency plan (ie. storage tank) for when the supply is cut off. If you are lucky enough to have a well (*pozzo*) on your land, so much the better as this will make life a great deal easier. When looking for property to buy, it is advisable to take into account the water situation in the locality. You may even wish to call in the services of a water-diviner (*rabdomante*). Probably the most inconvenient position for anyone living in Italy is to be marooned in an isolated house in the dry south, with no mains water and no well. In such cases it is possible to have water delivered by tanker as happens in Portugal and Spain. However, this service does not come cheaply and is far from convenient.

Telephones

A decade or so of modernisation has transformed the Italian telephone service from one that inflicted daily outrages on its subscribers and made new ones liable to scandalous delays for a telephone installation, to a thoroughly modern telecommunications system. In 1997, Telecom Italia was privatised and in 1998 deregulation meant competition was introduced. This is not to say that there may not be problems for those living in rustic isolation who want to be connected – the cost of erecting a line of telegraph poles as well as the installation charges may still be prohibitive.

With the opening up of Italy's telecommunications to international consortia comes the end of the monopoly of Telecom Italia (the state telephone company). STET the Italian state telecommunications giant was merged with its subsidiary

Telecom Italia, which became the overall name in 1997. No longer are subscribers told which gadgets they may or may not plug into their line. Cordless telephones, faxes and answering machines are offered in a profusion of choice, which brings its own irritations in terms of having to change provider frequently as better and better deals come along.

Bills, though they may be coming down if you choose wisely, may still inflict some nasty surprises as wild inaccuracies in the company's favour are not uncommon; a problem for which there is very little remedy. You could try installing a metering device (*indicatore di conteggio*), but should you ever convince the company of your right to a rebate, it is doubtful whether you would ever manage to obtain it. Bills are usually paid by banker's order and you should note that as in the UK and other Europena countries, directory enquiries are chargeable to your account if you call from home – though the service is not always chargeable if you call from a public payphone.

The Italians have taken to mobiles (*telefonini*) in a big way and the number of providers is growing as is the quality and coverage of the services. For more information see *Media and Communications* in *Daily Life*.

Yellow Pages (*pagine gialle*) and White Pages directories are issued on a regional basis, free of charge. They are also available online, Yellow Pages: www.paginegialle.it and White Pages: www.paginebianche.it. Infobel also provides online telephone search facilities at: www.teldir.com/eng/euro/it. There is also the *Into Italy* information website (www.eypdaily.it) aimed at English speaking residents of Italy.

REMOVALS

THE AMOUNT OF POSSESSIONS that an expatriate will take with them to Italy is likely to vary considerably. Generally speaking, however, anyone moving to a new home in Italy for their retirement and families moving there on an expatriate employment contract will want to export a large enough quantity of bulky possessions to require the service of a professional removal company with international expertise. Being Italy there are a number of bureaucratic formalities to be dealt with before the shipping company can deliver your possessions. If you live outside the EU the first step before you leave for Italy is to submit a list of the items you wish to import into Italy to the nearest Italian Consulate (see Chapter Two, *Residence and Entry Regulations* for addresses), who will officially stamp it. All nationalities must also apply for their *permesso di soggiorno* (permit to stay – see *Residence and Entry Regulations*) from the *questura* (police station) in Italy once you have arrived. Once the permit is issued you can then import your belongings.

The removal firm will require both the list stamped by the Consulate, the *permesso* and copies of documents relating to your ownership of property in Italy or proof of address. If you have not been resident in Italy long enough to have obtained the *permesso* you can obtain an attestation from the *commune* to the effect that you have purchased or leased accommodation in the area. This should allow the shipping company to import your belongings successfully.

Shipping personal belongings internationally is always best done by a professional and reputable company that has, most importantly, experience in dealing with the system of the country you are going to. When leaving Italy it is also important to make sure you use a company that is experienced in that process too, as there are procedures such as cancelling your residence permit to be undertaken so that you can export your possessions again.

General Import Conditions

The good news for those importing household goods into Italy is that there are no regulations about how long they must have been in your possession. However, a large selection of expensive, pristine equipment would undoubtedly arouse the avaricious instincts of the customs officers. It is advisable that any new items show a few obvious signs of wear and tear in order not to attract import duty and VAT – another way to lessen the interest of customs officials is to make sure that the items are not perfectly wrapped in their factory packaging.

The most important regulation regarding the import of personal possessions is that the items must be imported within six months of taking up residence in Italy. Excess Baggage Co lists current import regulations on their website: www.excessbaggage.co.uk.

If you decide to take a loaded van of furniture and other items for your home from one European Union country to Italy, you should have no problems, especially if the country is inside the Schengen area. If you are driving from an EU country through Switzerland to get to Italy (which is not strictly necessary) and you are stopped by Swiss customs, you should inform the Swiss customs that you are in transit to another EU country. An employment contract, rental agreement or ownership document would undoubtedly help convince the Swiss officials of your legitimacy.

If you are going to drive your possessions from a non-EU country into Italy you should have your consul stamp and *permesso di soggiorno* in your possession at the point of entry. However, you should also ensure that you have the necessary paperwork required to transit through any country *en route*.

Removal Firms

There are a number of large firms that specialise in international removals and it makes sense to consult one of these. UK residents can obtain a list of such companies from The British Association of Removers (3 Churchill Court, 58 Stations Road, North Harrow, Middlesex HA2 7SA) in return for a stamped addressed envelope. Be sure to ask for a list of international movers as these are a subgroup of the association's members. The BAR also publishes a free leaflet of handy hints for those contemplating removals overseas, available from the same address.

Residents of other countries should consult the membership directories of the international associations listed below. Most of the organisations also maintain their directories online.

Household Goods Forwarders Association of America: www.hhgfaa.org
International Federation of International Movers (FIDI): www.fidi.com
Overseas Moving Network International: www.omnimoving.com

Useful addresses

Baxter's International Removers: Brunel Road, off Rabans Lane, Aylesbury HP19 3SS; ☎01296-393335. Specializes in removals to Italy and Germany.

Interdean: Worldwide removals (UK 020 8961 4141; USA Headquarters , 55 Hunter Lane, Elmsford, New York 10523-1317; ☎ 914-347 6600; fax: 914-347 0129; Chicago 630-752 8990, fax 630-752 9087; Dallas 817-354 6683, fax 817-354 5570; Houston 281-469 7733, fax: 281-469 9426; Los Angeles 562-921 0939, fax 562-926 0918; Raleigh/Durham 919-969 1661, fax 919-969 1663; San Francisco 510-266 5660, fax 510-266 5665; www.interdean.com). Interdean have offices in a number of European countries (including Italy) and the Far East, which can be found via the website. They also offer relocation services.

IMPORTING A CAR

WHEREAS NON-RESIDENTS may freely drive back and forth between the UK and their Italian holiday home with British car registration documents and an EU or International Driving Licence, residents are obliged to either officially import their British registered vehicle or buy one in Italy. For drivers moving to Italy who are already resident in Europe (except UK and Irish residents who will have right hand drive cars), taking their own car with them is often a good idea. This is because you have to be a resident before you can buy an Italian car and therefore have to manage without private transport for a number of months, unless you can afford a rental car for that length of time. UK and Irish residents, who know far enough in advance that they are moving to Italy, may want to buy a left hand drive car in preparation for their relocation. Second hand left hand drive cars for sale in the UK can found online on the Exchange and Mart website (www.exchangeandmart.co.uk).

When taking a UK registered car to Italy it will be necessary to ensure that the insurance cover purchased in the UK will be applicable for a long stay abroad. In the past, failing to notify the insurance company that the car will be used predominantly outside the UK for an extended period has been grounds to refuse an insurance claim. 12 month Europe-wide car insurance can be secured through *Stuart Collins & Co.*, 114 Walter Road, Swansea SA1 5QQ; ☎01792-655562; fax 01792-651126.

On arrival at customs, the owner must present the registration documents, proof of insurance and a certificate of residence. After checking the vehicle against the documents the customs will issue a customs receipt (*bolleta doganale*). The owner may then drive the car with foreign plates for up to six months before the car has to be registered in Italy. There is no duty or VAT levied on cars imported in this manner, but it is a once in a lifetime concession. The problem with this procedure is that now the Schengen agreement has been implemented there are, often as not, no customs officers present at the point of entry into

Italy. In this case it will be necessary to find a customs office and apply for your customs certificate soon after your arrival in Italy.

To register a foreign vehicle in Italy it must first pass a *collaudo*, the Italian equivalent of an MOT. From then on the process becomes the usual Italian, time-consuming rigmarole. No wonder most people are happy enough to call on the services of one of the specialist agencies (*agenzie pratiche auto*) that wade through the necessary procedures on your behalf. Once the *collaudo* has been obtained it must be taken with all the car documents and a residence certificate, to a *notaio* who will apply for the car registration at the local (*Uffizio della Motorizzazione Civile e dei Trasporti in Concessione*) and register the vehicle with the local *Pubblico Registro Automobilistico*. The car will then be issued with a registration certificate (*carta di circolazione*). Licence plates (*foglio di circolazione*) are issued by the *Pubblico Registro Automobilistico*. Registration costs vary according to car size but in any case will not be less than £100.

Following registration you become liable for car tax. Note that since 1998 it has no longer been necessary to display a car tax disk (*bollo*) on the windscreen. You will also need an insurance badge (*contrassegno*). There are additional taxes for diesel driven cars and radios (but not cassette players).

For further information about driving in Italy, the rules of the road, buying or selling a car and insurance see *Daily Life, Cars & Motoring*.

Useful addresses:

Automobile Association (AA): Import Section, Fanum House, Basingstoke Hants RG21 2EA; ☎01256-20123; www.automobileassociation.co.uk. Information is supplied only to members of the AA. Ask for information on the permanent importation of a vehicle into Italy. For membership details contact your nearest AA office.

Automobile Club d'Italia (ACI): Via Marsala 8, 00185 Rome; ☎06-49981; www.aci.it.

IMPORTING PETS

MANY PET OWNERS find the thought of leaving their pets behind when they move overseas heartbreaking. Kids, especially, can find leaving the family pet behind a traumatic experience. However, it is a reasonably straightforward process to transport your dog or cat (and other species not on the endangered species list) with you to your new home in Italy, providing you take care to follow the regulations. To the Italians, though, a dog tends to be more of a fashion accessory than a faithful companion – they reserve all doting pride for their children and grandchildren.

To import domestic pets it is necessary to have a certificate of health issued by a veterinarian registered with the Ministry of Agriculture in the country of origin. A list of vets who have this designation is usually available from the Ministry of Agriculture. However, in some countries it is necessary to visit the local offices of the Ministry of Agriculture to obtain the necessary Health Certificate, or have one issued by a veterinarian stamped and approved by the Ministry of Agriculture. In addition to the Health Certificate, which must be translated into Italian, the animal must have received a rabies inoculation not less than twenty days and not more than eleven months prior to crossing the Italian border – a rabies certificate attesting to this is also required. Finally, the vaccination record (sometimes known as an animal passport) of the animal is required to show that the animal has received the standard vaccinations required for the particular animal – as prescribed by a veterinarian. These vaccinations are usually required to have been administered not less than thirty days prior to entering the country. Always check with Italian embassy to ensure the current requirements as regulations can change suddenly, as was the case following the Foot and Mouth disease outbreak in the UK in 2001; dogs and cats can be carriers of foot and mouth even though they do not display symptoms.

If the animal is to enter the country by air, it can often accompany passengers as excess baggage, though it is necessary to book cargo space in advance as airlines often limit the number of animals to two per flight. Airlines can also advise on the current bureaucratic requirements for importing an animal, as they are responsible for checking the paperwork before accepting the animal on board their aircraft. Taking a dog or cat as excess baggage is often easier than sending the animal as air cargo independently from the owner as customs officials are less worried that the animal is being imported for commercial reasons.

Regulations now in force in most areas of Italy compel owners to have their dogs tattooed on the body as a means of checking their registration. An alternative to the tattoo is for the dog to have a tiny microchip inserted under the skin of the neck. Any loose dog without either a tattoo or microchip is liable to be destroyed. The tattoo/microchip insertion can be done by a vet, or in some areas by the *Unita Sanitaria Locale*. Dog insurance against claims for damages is advisable for those with unpredictable animals and those whose canines have no traffic sense.

Rabies vaccinations have to be given yearly and a log-book will be provided by the vet for the purpose of recording these. Apart from rabies, which is reputedly prevalent in the far north of Italy, hazards further south are more likely to include encounters with porcupines and snakes. For animals (and human beings) it is advisable to keep a supply of venom antidote in the fridge, but make sure that it is regularly renewed before the expiry date has been reached.

UK Pet Passport Programme UK resident pet owners who wish to take their pet back and forth between Italy and the UK and avoid subjecting their animal to quarantine should be aware that the Passport for Pets scheme only applies to cats and dogs. There are also a limited number of entry points where an animal can be returned to the UK as part of the programme. Consult your veterinarian well in advance of departure from the UK as it can take up to six months to fulfil the requirements necessary for your pet to qualify for the scheme. Residents of Italy can take their cat or dog to the UK for a holiday without having to place them in quarantine if they have fulfilled the necessary requirements as outlined below.

In addition to having an up to date pet passport, the animal should also have a microchip inserted under the skin of their shoulder and be vaccinated against rabies. A blood test one month after the vaccination to prove immunity is also required. It is also necessary for the animal to be given anti-parasite medication the day before entering the UK – i.e. when entering by ferry from France. Though the animal does not have to undergo quarantine it can take a number of hours after arrival in the UK for the animal to be cleared through customs.

Current details about the scheme and a number of factsheets can be found on the website of the *Department For Environment, Food and Rural Affairs* that replaced the Ministry of Agriculture and Fisheries in 2001: www.defra.gov.uk/animalh/ quarantine/index.htm. DEFRA also has a PETS helpline: 0870-241 1710 (or +44 20 7904 8057 from outside the UK) – open 8.30am to 5pm, Monday to Friday. Further information about the quarantine rules can be obtained from 020-7904 6221.

Useful Addresses:

Independent Pet and Animal Transportation Association International Inc.: www.ipata.com. A directory of members, as well a advice on transporting pets, is contained on this website.

D.J. Williams: Animal Transport, Littleacre Quarantine Centre, 50 Dunscombes Road, Turves, Nr Whittlesey Cambs PE7 2DS; ☎01733-840291; fax 01733-840348.

International pet collection and delivery service, will deliver overland or arrange air transport. Will collect from your home and arrange all the necessary documentation. For those people whose pet is not covered by the PETS scheme, they also provide quarantine services.

DAILY LIFE

CHAPTER SUMMARY

- To cope successfully with life in Italy the ability to speak the language is essential.

- The Italian state education system is generally good but standards are generally better in the more affluent north of the country: international schools are the best bet for the children of expatriates who do not intend to stay in Italy for too long.

- There are English-language papers and websites to help new arrivals settle down plus English-language tv on satellite and cable.

- Buying a car in Italy is complicated for the foreigner, but the public transport is good with cheap, reliable trains, more buses than any other country in Europe and well-used internal air services.

- The Italian banking and postal systems are among the least efficient in Europe.

- Tax in Italy is complicated and widely evaded by the Italians.

- The state health service should be avoided if possible, so private health cover is recommended.

- Despite the reputation of the Mafia there is generally less street crime than in many other European countries.

- Italians are sociable, tending to stay with their families into adulthood and going out in groups rather than alone or in pairs.

- Over-indulgence in food or drink is frowned upon; on the other hand Italians will spend extravagantly on their appearance.

THE MOSTLY UNCOMPLICATED and mundane rituals of daily existence in your home country are liable to assume a completely bewildering aspect when encountered in the context of a new country with different customs, culture and language. Buying a car, using public transport, opening a bank account can all become frustrating and bewildering tasks when you realise that you do not know whether your driving licence is valid in Italy, you have forgotten the word for season ticket and never even knew the word for banker's draft in Italian.

This chapter deals with all of these issues, and many more everyday concerns. Its aim is to help familiarise you with Italian ways and lessen the headaches that arise with each new and initially daunting task. However, it cannot be overstressed that the key to coping successfully with life in Italy whether domestically, socially or professionally lies in the ability to speak and understand the language with some degree of fluency. Thus, the first section deals with ways of brushing up, or initiating, your knowledge of Italian, either before leaving home, or on arrival in Italy.

Please note that all information provided here is subject to regional variation and that the difference in procedures between the city and country areas of Italy may be particularly striking.

THE ITALIAN LANGUAGE

ITALIAN IS CONSIDERED to be one of the easier European languages to learn, though this is no consolation to a newly posted family who have never met an Italian, let alone considered moving to the country and learning the language. A romance language, Italian shares many features with French and Spanish and anyone who has a knowledge of either of these will find it that much easier to acquire a mastery of Italian. Moreover, in the majority of cases, tortured attempts at pronouncing the most simple of Italian words and sounds will be met with a good humoured and largely enthusiastic response. Always remember that when speaking to strangers, the third person is the polite form and using the second person is a mark of disrespect. An inevitable consequence of Italy's fragmented and internally strife-ridden history (unification, *Risorgimento*, was not achieved until 1861) is that variations in dialect are strong throughout the country. Neapolitan, in particular, can be difficult to understand and the Sicilian dialect is different enough from conventional Italian as to be almost a separate language and to confuse native Italians and struggling foreigners alike. However, people will slip into more orthodox Italian with foreigners – the equivalent of BBC English.

Apart from the variations in Italian spoken around the country, some of the inhabitants of the border and outlying regions do not, in fact, use Italian at all. Various forms of French are spoken by a large percentage of the population in the Val d'Aosta and a strongly Germanic minority in the Trentino-Alto-Adige region uses German. The majority of the island population of Sardinia speaks a mixture of Italian, Latin, Punic and Spanish while in Calabria and Sicily, entire villages still speak Albanian and Greek.

Anyone who moves to Italy assuming that all Italians can speak English will have an unpleasant shock. Italians tend to be only mildly better talented in learning foreign languages than the notoriously monolingual British, and in some of the more remote southern areas you may well find that no English is spoken at all. Not all that much English is regularly spoken by businessmen either, and as Italian business is inextricably mixed with pleasure, fluency in Italian is a must, both professionally and socially, unless you decide to restrict your social and business life to a purely anglophone circle of expatriates. Even then you will miss out on some of the main reasons for moving to Italy – the Italian people themselves and also the culture that is inextricably tied up in their language. In order to avoid feeling inarticulate and alienated it is as well to begin learning Italian as soon as possible, ideally before relocating to Italy. Language schools and organisations in the UK, USA, Canada and numerous other countries offer many types of Italian courses (self-study, conversation, business, etc.) and there are, of course, numerous course available in Italy. Some of the most popular forms of language learning and the organisations which offer them are listed below.

Self-Study Courses

For those who prefer to combine reciting verb endings with cooking the dinner or repeating sentence formations while walking the dog, then self-study is the most suitable option. Various well-known organisation produce whole series of workbooks, CDs, audiocassettes and videos for learning a wide range of foreign languages, including the BBC, Berlitz and Linguaphone. Sample self-study courses are listed below:

Buongiorno Italia! Coursebook, £10.99 (plus three cassettes at £6.99 each). This combination of texts and recordings from the BBC focuses heavily on such aspects of everyday, conversational Italian as finding the way, shopping and understanding numbers and prices. The book contains texts of conversations recorded in Italy, language notes, information about the Italian way of life, exercises and a glossary. The conversations and interviews are on the cassettes. The textbook, teacher's notes and cassettes can all be purchased individually from the BBC online shop: www.bbcshop.com.

Hugo: In Three Months Italian Course Book, £5.95. 253 page book, without cassette or CD Rom; www.hugo.com.

Italianissimo, also from the BBC, has courses ranging in price from £6.99, through to a full course at £42.99. Further details on all BBC courses can be obtained from the BBC Mail Order/Shop in Newcastle (☎0191-222 0381), or online at: www.bbcshop.com.

Italian for Dummies, US$24.99, including CD Rom. Based on the well known Berlitz courses.

In addition, Linguaphone (Carlton Plaza, 111 Upper Richmond Street, London SW15 2TJ; 020-8333 4898; fax 020-8333 4897; www.linguaphone.com) have courses which range from Italian for tourists at £12.99, beginner courses that aim to teach a new language in twelve weeks (from £49.99) to complete course leading to fluency in Italian at £299.90. Linguaphone also have a limited number of online courses, and provide services to customers in a number of countries. Full information can be found on their website listed above.

The book prices listed above reflect their publisher recommended price in the country of publication, however, online bookstores such as www.amazon.com, www.amazon.co.uk and www.bn.com have a wide range of courses, including some of those listed above, at discounted prices on their North American, European and other regional sites.

For those who want to maintain or improve their fluency in Italian *Acquerello Italiano* audio magazine is ideal for anyone interested in Italian language and culture. *Acquerello Italiano* is an hour-long programme on audiocassette with news, features and interviews from Italy. Rather than teaching you to order meals or book a hotel room, the programme is aimed at helping you expand and update your vocabulary. The cassette comes with a magazine that has transcripts, glossary and copious background explanatory notes. There are optional study supplements also available. For six editions annually the subscription is £69 (US$99), the study supplements are an additional £18 (US$30) from *Aquerello Italiano*, UK ☎0117-929 2318; fax 0117-929 2426; USA ☎1-800 824 0829; www.acquerello-italiano.com or www.champs-elysees.com/aihome.php3).

Intensive Language Courses

The Berlitz School of Languages: 321 Oxford Street, London W1A 3BZ; ☎020-7408 2474; fax 020-7493 4429: Berlitz USA – 40 West 51st Street, New York City, NY 10020, USA; ☎212 765 1001; fax 212 307 5336; www.berlitz.com for international centres. One real advantage of an international organisation like Berlitz is that it offers language courses which, begun in your home country, can be completed on arrival in Italy. Each course is specifically tailored to the individual's own requirements as far as the language level and course intensity is concerned and the cost of the courses varies enormously depending on these factors. Further information on Berlitz courses is available from the above address or from any of the other Berlitz branches, located in Birmingham, Manchester, Leeds, Edinburgh and round the world. A full directory of their training offices can be found online at their website.

Inlingua School of Languages, 28 Rotton Park Road, Edgbaston, Birmingham B16 9JL; ☎0121-454 0204; fax 0121-456 3264; www.inlingua.com; for information about US inlingua schools visit www.inlingua.com/usa.html. A worldwide network of privately-owned language schools – there are approximately 280 schools in all, 240 of which are located in Europe, though there are quite a number in the USA and a few in Canada. The schools only employ native-speakers as teachers and tuition is offered on both an individual and a group basis. The cost of a 45-minute session is approximately £26 (US$38). The most intensive course (50 lessons) costs £1,900 (US$2500) for a week including board, lodging and activities. Italian courses can also be arranged at many inlingua centres around the world. In addition to language courses, inlingua also offer translation, cultural training programmes and other services. A full directory of their training offices can be found online at their website.

Linguarama: 7th floor BPP House, 70 Red Lion Street, London WC1R 4NG; ☎020-7405 7557; fax 020-7430 8372; www.linguarama.com. Linguarama offers many different language courses in a number of European countries and caters for a wide range of standards and abilities. Tuition can be given on an individual basis if requested. In the UK Linguarama has branches in Manchester, Winchester, Birmingham and Stratford and their website contains a directory of all their language centres in Europe. Accommodation can be arranged.

Part-time Courses

Part-time courses are ideal for those with domestic or professional commitments and are cheaper compared with the language courses offered by commercial organisations such as Berlitz, inlingua, etc. Local colleges of education and community or adult studies centres are the best option as they often run day and evening courses in a wide and amazing variety of subjects. The courses cater for a variety of standards, ranging from beginners who want to learn Italian for next year's holiday or for general interest, to those who wish to take an exam leading to a qualification at the end of the course. Italian cultural organisations also offer courses and sometimes lessons can be arranged through the Embassy in countries where there is no formal Italian cultural organisation.

Classes often begin in mid-September or the first week in October and run for between two and seven months with a two or three-hour class once a week – though classes do start at other times of the year too. Enquiries about all courses should be made direct to the relevant organisation.

Alternatively, there are often Italian nationals keen to exploit their earning potential as private tutors who can be found through advertisements in local papers, Italian cultural and business organisations and within the Italian expatriate community. In all cases, however, it is just as well to check just how qualified the teacher is, and to pay them an hourly fee that reflects their level of expertise and experience. Even with unqualified teachers you can gain good conversational experience exchange and it is worth remembering that just because someone has a piece of paper saying they have a qualification it does not mean that they are going to be a good teacher.

Cultural Training Courses

Apart from being able to speak the language of the country you are going to, understanding why the host nationals behave the way they do in both a social and a business context can make the difference between loving the country and hating it. A number of organisations offer cultural awareness courses and these can be as valuable as language courses, though they are often expensive. Working through culture shock is an important an unavoidable aspect of living abroad and its importance can not be underestimated and this book will help you through many of the practical aspects of culture shock. However, there are many emotional aspects to culture shock and the subject is discussed in detail in *Live and Work Abroad: A Guide for Modern Nomads*, also published by Vacation Work Publications, along with other non country-specific aspects of living abroad.

In addition to the specific addresses below there are some useful Websites to consult. *Italian Cultural Institutes in the World* is an online directory of Italian associations categorised by region and country; www.italcult.net. There is also an online directory of Italian Cultural organisations, language schools, formal Italian course and Italian related events in the UK: ww.embitaly.org.uk/culture/mainpage.html. For an online directory of Italian institutions in the USA look at www.italyemb.org/ItalianInstitutions.htm.

Useful Addresses

Dante Alighieri Society: is an Italian cultural society based in Siena, Italy, with branches around the world. Their main website (www.dantealighieri.com) provides information on the activities offered in Sienna and allows visitors to contact regional representatives of the Siena institution. The society organises year-round language courses and other events. Other branches around the world can be found at: http://orb.rhodes.edu/encyclop/culture/lit/Italian/da-s.htm.

Federazione Italiana Lavoratori Emigranti e Famiglie (FILEF): (96/98 Central Street, London EC1V 8AJ; ☎020-7608 0125; fax 020-7490 0938). Cultural organisation that runs Italian evening classes for all levels.

The Italian Community Centre: 96-98 Central Street, Islington, London EC1; ☎020-7608 0125. Organises language courses at the Centre.

The Italian Cultural Institute: 39 Belgrave Square, London SW1X 8NX; ☎020-7235 1461; fax 020-7235 4618; www.italcultur.org.uk. Runs courses at the Institute in London. Also, can advise on language courses throughout Italy. Helps undergraduates and postgraduates find out about courses at Italian universities.

Private schools which offer business Italian:

International House: 106 Piccadilly, London W1J 7NL; ☎020 7518 6950; fax 020 7418 6951; main website – www.ihworld.com; USA branches – 2725 Congress Street #2M, San Diego, CA 92110, USA; ☎1 (619) 299 2339; fax 1 (619) 299 0235; www.ih-usa.com.

Language Studies International: Woodstock House, 10-12 James Street, London W1M 5HN; ☎020 7499 9621.

St George's International: Language House, 76 Mortimer Street, London W1N 7DE; ☎020 7299 1700; fax 020 7299 1711.

Business Traveller and Cultural Briefing Courses:

Farnham Castle International Briefing and Conference Centre: Farnham Castle, Farnham, Surrey GU9 OAG; ☎01252-721194; fax 01252-711283; w w w . f a r n h a m c a s t l e . c o m . Programmes are aimed at corporate expatriates and business travellers so prices are high. Intercultural briefings and language course lasting from one to four days. Families can also attend the courses.

inlingua School of Languages, 28 Rotton Park Road, Edgbaston, Birmingham B16 9JL; ☎0121-454 0204; fax 0121-456 3264; www.inlingua.com; for information about US inlingua schools visit www.inlingua.com/usa.html. inlingua offer cultural awareness courses in addition to language courses.

Courses in Italy

In almost all large Italian towns there are facilities for foreigners to learn or improve their Italian at language schools or universities. These courses are aimed at a wide range of standards and abilities and usually run from early April until late August, each course lasting two to four weeks. The better classes are small and ideally have no more than ten to a class. Accommodation is often available, either in dormitories and camp sites or university and hotel accommodation. Some schools also offer classes on Italian history, culture and art in conjunction with the language course. Various leisure time activities are organised for students, e.g. film and slide shows and trips to museums, concerts and theatres. The fortnight-long courses are priced from approximately £300+ (including bed and breakfast) and mostly run throughout the year, although some are only open during the summer months. A limited list of Italian language schools etc. that offer a wide variety of such courses is listed below. Expatriate organisations, embassies and local institutions in Italy will be able to provide further information to expatriates once they are resident in Italy.

Useful addresses

An extensive list of language schools can be found on the *Into Italy* website: www.intoitaly.it.

Carabelli Elena – Italian for Foriegners: Via Moscova 46/1, 20121 Milan (MI); ☎02 6554033; fax 02 6554033; www.carabellilanguage.web.com.

Centro Lingua Italiana Calvino: Viale Fratelli Rosselli 74, 50123 Firenze; ☎055-288081, fax 055-288125; clic.plus@flashnet.it. School open all year. Residential summer courses are organised in Calabria.

The Centro Linguistico Italiano Dante Alighieri: Via dei Bardi 12, Firenze; ☎055-2342984, telex 055-580072, fax 055-2342766; also Via B. Marliano 4, Rome; ☎06-8320184, fax 06-8604203; www.dantealighieri.com.

Centro Educativo Professionale: Viale Regionale Sicilian 279, 90123 Palermo (PA); ☎091 6573466; fax 091 6572208. Courses run throughout the year.

CESA Languages Abroad: Western House, Malpas, Truro TR1 1SQ; ☎01872-225300; fax 01872-225400; www.cesalanguages.com. Organises language courses in Florence Venice, Rome and Siena.

Istituto Europeo: Piazza dell Pallottole 1 (Duomo), 50122 Firenze; ☎055-2381071; fax 055 289145; info@istitutoeuropeo.it. Language courses; also cultural, professional and music courses.

Istituto Italiano: Centro di Lingua e Cultura, Via Machiavelli 33, 00185 Rome; ☎06 704 52138, fax 0670085122; www.istitutoitaliano.com.

It Schools is an online directory of Italian language schools in Italy and around the world: www.it-schools.com.

Italiaidea: Piazza delle Cancelleria, 85, 00186 Rome; ☎06 68307620; fax 06 6892997; www.italiaidea.com

Italian for You (Online Course): www.italianforyou.it.

Scuola Leonardo da Vinci: Schools in Rome, Florence and Siena; ☎055 290 305; www.scualoaleonardo.com.

Susan Howard Rees: Via Matteotti 45, Arese, Milan; ☎02-93 80 256; fax 02-93 58 13 00. Made-to-measure language courses especially for commerce.

Italian Societies

It is essential to delve into Italian culture before leaving for Italy if you want to avoid feeling culturally stranded on arrival in Italy. Various societies exist in the UK, USA and other countries that organise social events and discussion groups of an endlessly diverse nature which will serve to soften the culture shock. The Italian Cultural Institute (see above) is the main Italian government agency whose function it is to promote cultural relations between the two countries. The Institute organises lectures, exhibitions and promotes concerts and has a library facility of approximately 21,000 books including subjects such as Italian literature, art, history, criticisms and essays. The library is open to the general public although only members are eligible to take the books out on loan. Anyone looking for a scholarship to study in Italy should contact the Italian Institute as all scholarships for study and research in Italy are awarded by the Italian Ministry of Foreign Affairs and other Italian institutions through them. Membership of the Institute is on an annual basis and entitles members to receive information on all of the cultural events that it arranges and gives free access to its facilities. There is a reduced annual membership for under 18's, full-time students, senior citizens and anyone with an address outside London.

Slightly different is the *Federazione Italiana Lavoratori Emigranti e Famiglie (FILEF)* based in London (96/98 Central Street, London EC1V 8AJ; ☎020-7608 0125; fax 020-7490 0938) the main aim of which is to keep Italians in Britain in touch with the cultural developments in their country and introduce Britons to Italian culture. FILEF provides advice, support and information to its members. They also publish a newsletter and provide an interpreting and translating service and can be a great place for making contacts.

SCHOOLS AND EDUCATION

ITALIAN CHILDREN ARE ONLY LEGALLY required to attend school until the age of fourteen, consequently, many children in the south leave school at fourteen to try to find a job which will contribute to the family's often inadequate income. However, they frequently only succeed in joining the swelling ranks of the Mezzogiorno's unemployed.

Regarding the quality of Italian schools, however, over the last ten or fifteen years, massive improvements have been implemented within the Italian state education system and Italy can now boast a system of education which equals most others in Europe. The system of education is administered centrally through the government, with the exception of elementary schools that are usually run by the local commune. Unfortunately, as in many countries there a wide disparity in the quality of education available between the rich and poor sections of the country. In Italy this is a further wedge between the north and the south of the country – the standard of schools in the large northern cities like Turin, Genoa, Rome and Milan are much higher than those found in Molise, Calabria or Campania. Although state education is free in Italy, parents are responsible for buying their children's textbooks and stationery.

Private schools also exist, of which nearly all are Roman Catholic (although pupils are not required to be) and most are day schools only. Although private schools do not carry the same kind of status with which they are often associated in Britain and America, they do form an attractive option to those who can afford them, especially where the local state school is not of the best. Like many large cities of the world, some of the large cities of the Mezzogiorno, particularly in Naples, some state schools are facing serious and growing drug problems.

The decision as to whether to educate children within the Italian, British, American or International system of education (see the section, *International Schools* below) is one which must include such considerations as the age of the child, the length of time you are planning to live in Italy, how much you want your child to be bilingual and your financial situation. Remember also that the watershed age for learning a language with relative ease appears to be around eleven to twelve and after this it becomes more and more difficult to pick up the language quickly. There is also the problem that important exams are much closer and there is therefore less time for the child to catch up on the work they missed whilst learning the language.

The Structure of the Italian Education System

Scuola materna or **asilo nido**: Optional pre-school education is available privately or through commune-run kindergartens, from the age of three. Italian women do, however, complain that the availability of pre-school care from a young age is limited. To a certain extent it seems that in Italy women have to choose between a career and parenthood.

Scuola elementare: Primary school, known as elementary or grade school in north America, begins at age six and continues until children enter the next level at age eleven. Lessons usually last for only four hours each day and this short time does not allow room for sports, music, drama, etc, which are largely regarded as not only extracurricular activities but outside school activities. The *scuola elementare* is the easiest stage at which to integrate foreign children into the school system; the younger the better as far as becoming fluent in Italian is concerned. After passing some fairly straightforward exams, children pass on to the next stage, the *scuola media*.

Scuola Media: Secondary school, known as Middle School in north America, covers the ages of eleven or twelve to fourteen or fifteen. To successfully complete the *scuola media*, exams must be passed and an average of not less than sixty percent maintained throughout each school year. The *diploma di licenza media* is awarded to all those who get this far. At this point, the less academic tend to go on to one of the vocational *istituti tecnici* to study anything from accountancy to farming (if they do stay in the system), while the academically better students stay at school for a further two years, taking either the *liceo classico* or *liceo scientifico*. This involves a certain amount of specialisation, although not to the same extent as the UK A level system. At 18 or 19, the *liceo* students take the *maturità* (the equivalent of the French baccalaureat), while the *tecnici* students take a diploma which bestows the equivalent qualification of a British City and Guilds.

University: Since the reforms of 1977, everyone who has obtained either the *maturità* or a *tecnici* diploma is entitled to go on to an Italian university. Consequently, universities are now flooded with students and Italy has one of the highest percentages in Europe of the relevant age group attending university. Italy, however, has far fewer non-university higher education courses than France and Germany, which probably accounts for much of this high percentage. Though a high percentage of young people attend university many of them do not graduate; in fact, only about one third of students enrolled for a university degree ever finish their course.

Italian universities are the victim of under-investment and a lack of courses and venues. Inevitably, there is an unofficial league table of the universities with graduates of some institutions being in a better position to get good jobs than graduates of others. Indeed, a survey found that some graduates were only marginally better off in the job stakes than holders of a high-school diploma. One of the much-needed reforms is to forge closer links between business and universities, thus ensuring that academic products are competitive and relevant to the job market.

The picture is not, however, entirely bleak. Some of Italy's universities have a very good reputation and are becoming internationally renowned. For example, the private Bocconi University in Milan is excellent, particularly in the faculties of business studies and economics, with fierce competition for the few available places each year. Rome's *Libera Università degli Studi Sociali* (LUISS) has a similarly high reputation. Both of these universities are private and their tuition fees run into several thousand pounds each year, with only a few scholarships and other awards available.

The state universities vary in quality but among the most prestigious are:

Politecnico in Milan (famous for its engineering faculty).

Bologna University, which is the oldest in Europe and has a very high reputation in most subjects.

Pavia University, which excels particularly in medicine.

Orientale in Naples boasts the oldest oriental language school in Italy.

The method of university teaching in Italy is similar to that in the UK, i.e. it requires students to do much of their work independently and without a lot of supervision from faculty members; if anything it is even more remote and reliant on each individual's often faltering, self motivation. Lectures are frequently over-crowded, sometimes to the point that it is practically impossible to squeeze into the lecture halls. One peculiarity is that exams can be postponed indefinitely until the student chooses to take them, while no degree can be completed in less than four years. If exams are failed then they can simply be retaken the next time round; consequently most students graduate one or two years late. A large proportion of all courses rely on oral examinations. Italian universities are not residential and do not even organise accommodation for their students, so many students live at home and go to a local university. One of the added problems of education in Italy is that every male should, in theory, do military service and attending university is an acceptable way to postpone it.

International Schools

International schools tend to be regarded as the best option for the children of expatriates who do not expect to remain in Italy in the long-term, or who want their children to have the option of attending university in their home country. Different schools within the category of International School offer UK, German, French, Japanese, Swedish, Spanish, and US curricula. Though international schools can be seen to isolate children from the communities in which they live, most International Schools admit students from many nationalities, including that of the host country, and students are given the chance to study the local language in a way suitable for non-native speakers. There are numerous schools in Italy that are possible options for expatriates, the majority of which are of high quality and offer a continuous style of education for transient expatriate children. They also offer easier access to UK and North American higher education and ensure that the level of English (or German, French or other language) of the expatriate child remains at native level.

The main English medium international schools are listed below, along with their address and phone number and the age range they cover. Schools whose classes are taught in other languages, as mentioned above, can be contacted via the appropriate embassies. The European Council of International Schools (21B Lavant Street, Petersfield, Hants GU32 3EL; ☎0730-68244; www.ecis.org), International Schools Services – ISS (15 Roszel Road, PO Box 5910, Princeton, New Jersey, USA; ☎609 452 0990; www.iss.edu) and the International Baccalaureate Organisation (www.ibo.org) maintain lists of English medium schools on their websites. A comprehensive explanation of the schooling options for expatriate children, including local school, British, US, International Baccalaureate and boarding schools, can be found in *Live and Work Abroad: A Guide for Modern Nomads*, also published by Vacation Work Publications.

English medium schools in Milan:

The American School of Milan, Via Marx 14, 20090 Noverasco di Opera, Milano; ☎ 02 530 0001; fax 02 5760 6274; www.asmilan.org. Ages three 18.

International School of Milan: Via Caccialepori 22, 20148, Milan, Italy; ☎ 02 487 08076; fax 02 487 03644; www.ism-ac.it. Ages three to 19.

Sir James Henderson British School of Milan: Via Pisano Dossi 16, 20134, Milan; ☎ 02 264 13332/13310; fax 02 264 13515). Ages three to 18.

Rome:

Ambrit School: Via Filippo Tajani 50, 00149 Rome; ☎ 06 559 5301/5; fax 06 559 5309; www.ambrit-rome.com. Ages three to 14.

American Overseas School of Rome: Vica Cassia 811, 00189, Rome, Italy; ☎ 06 3326 4841; fax 06 3326 2608; www.aosr.org. Ages three to 18.

Castelli International School: 13 Via Degli Scozzesi, 00046 Grottaferrata, Rome; tel/fax 06 943 15779. Ages five to 14 years.

Greenwood Garden School: Via Vito Sinisi 5, Rome 00189 (tel/fax 6 3326-6703).

International Academy of Rome: Via di Grottarossa 295, 00189 Rome (☎ 06 3326 6071). Ages three to 14.

Kendale Primary International School: Via Gradoli 86, Tombe di Nerone, 00189 Rome (tel/fax 06 366 7608). Ages 3 to 10.

Marymount International School: Via di Villa

Lauchli 180, 00191 Rome (☎ 06 3630 1742; fax 06 3630 1738. Roman Catholic school. Ages three to 19.

New School: Via della Camiluccia 669, 00135 Rome; ☎ 06 329 4269; fax 06 329 7546). Ages: three to 18 years.

Notre Dame International School: Via Aurelia 796, 00165 Rome (☎ 06 680 8801; fax 680 6051). Ages 10-18.

Rome International School: Viale Romania 32, Parioli (off Piazza Ungheria, Rome; ☎ 06 844 82650; fax 06 844 82651. Ages three to 18 years.

Southlands English School: Via Teleclide 20, Casal Palocco, 00124 Rome; ☎ 06 505 3922; fax 06 509 17192). Ages three to 14 years.

St Francis International School: Via Massimi 164 (Balduina) Rome; ☎ 06 353 41328; fax 06 353 48719. Ages three to 14. American system.

St George's English School: Via Cassia KM 16, 00123 Rome; ☎ 06 3790141/23; fax 06 3792490). Ages three to 18.

St Stephen's School: Via Aventina 3, 00153 Rome; ☎ 06 575 0605; fax 06 574 1941. Ages: 13 to 19.

Other Cities:

American International School of Florence: Via del Carota 23/35, 50012 Bagno a Ripoli, Florence; ☎ 055 640033; fax 55 644226. Ages 2½ to 19.

American International School in Genoa: Via Quarto 13/C 16148 Genoa; ☎ 010

386528; fax 010 398700). Ages three to 14.

Anglo-Italian School Montessori Division: Viale Della Liberazione, Comando NATO, 90125, Bagnoli, Naples; ☎ 081 721 2266; fax 081 570 6587.

European School: Via Montello 118, 21100 Varese; ☎ 0332 806111; fax 332 806202. Ages four to 18. Waiting list of 2 years and the school generally only takes children of EU employees.

International School of Naples: Viale della Liberazione, 1 H.Q. AFSouth Post, Bldg 'A', 80125 Bagnoli, Napoli; ☎ 081-721 20 37; fax 081-762 84 29. Ages three to 18.

International School of Trieste: Via Conconello 16, Opicina, 34100 Trieste; ☎ 040 211452). Ages three to 18.

International School of Turin (American Cultural Association School of Turin): Vicolo Tiziano 10, 10024 Moncalieri; ☎ 011 645967; fax 011 643298). Ages three to eighteen.

International School of Modena: Via Silvio Pellico 9, Fiorano, 41042, Modena, Italy; ☎ 0536 832904; fax 0536 911189.

United World College of the Adriatic: Via Trieste 29, 34013 Duino (Trieste); ☎ 040-3739111; fax 040-3739225. Takes boarding students aged 16 to study for the pre-university IB diploma. Entry is exclusively by scholarship.

MEDIA & COMMUNICATIONS

Newspapers

IN COMMON WITH THE SPANIARDS, the Italians are not avid newspaper readers compared with the British and only 60% of Italian families buy a daily newspaper. There is no real equivalent of the well established British tabloids and US supermarket newspapers and only the downmarket papers, e.g. *Il Messaggero* carry horoscopes, cartoons or fun features.

TABLE 5	ITALIAN PAPERS	
Newspaper	**City**	**Political leaning**
La Nazione	Florence	Socialist
Il Mattino	Naples	Christian Democrat
Il Messagero	Rome	Communist
Il Resto del Carlino	Bologna.	
L'Ora	Palermo; at the forefront of anti-Mafia movement in the media environs of Sicily.	
Il Tempo	(Rome)	
La Gazzetta del Mezzogiorno	(Bari)	
La Nuova Sardegna	(Cagliari)	
Paese Sera	(Rome)	
Il Piccolo	(Trieste)	
La Nuova	*Venezia* (Venice)	

The most popular Italian dailies are *Il Corriere della Sera* (Milan) and *La Repubblica* (Rome) – both of which boast a daily circulation of between five and six hundred thousand. *La Stampa* (Turin) follows with a dramatically lower circulation of just over four hundred thousand. *Il Giornale and Il Messaggero* trail in with less than two hundred thousand.

Il Corriere della Sera and *La Repubblica*, in particular, are constantly vying for circulation supremacy, mostly using free supplements on computers, health, money matters etc. and inserts including a women's magazine and TV guide. However, *La Repubblica*, an unusually liberal publication, tends to create the most controversy and excitement, with its talent for political insight and cultural reporting. By contrast, the conservative *La Stampa* tends to back whichever government is in power at the time – which has historically been some variation of the Christian Democrats. In the five most widely read newspapers above, articles on social issues are comparatively rare.

The two main financial dailies – *Il Sole/24 Ore* and *Italia Oggi*, – are reasonably extensive in their coverage, but not quite of the standard of *The Financial Times* or the *Wall Street Journal*. The three sports dailies are *Corriere dello Sport*, *Gazzetta dello Sport* and *Tuttosport*. The regional newspapers, which focus on national news but include several pages of local news and comment, are particularly popular and widely read in Italy. The most popular among these are listed in Table 5.

There are no separate Sunday papers as such in Italy; instead all of the national dailies print on Sunday and then have a day off on Monday.

The English-language newspaper, *The International Herald Tribune* (6 bis rue des Graviers, 92521 Neuilly, Cedex Paris; ☎+33-1 41 43 92 61; fax +33-1 41 43 92 10; subs@iht.com; www.iht.com), is published in Paris in conjunction with the *New York Times* and *Washington Post*. It is available in Italy at newsagents or by subscription in Italy from 800-780 040, in the UK from 0800-4 448 7827 and in America from 800-8822884. Those on the job hunt in Rome should try to get hold of a copy of the English-language newspapers, *Daily American* and *When in Rome*, both of which carry substantial job advertising.

Magazines

The Italian magazine market is swamped with publications that churn out the same themes, features and cover-spreads week after week. The main three publishing houses, Mondadori, Rizzoli and Rusconi are in constant competition to control a saturated market. The better-quality magazines include *Gente* and *Oggi*, both of which contain a good deal of serious and well-written news and arts coverage. At the other end of the spectrum, *Novella 2000*, *Eva Express* and the incredibly lurid *Stop* are pure gossip and scandal reading.

Italy also boasts some of the classiest women and men's fashion and home furnishing magazines in the world. The most popular of which are *Moda*, *Marie Claire*, *King* and *Vogue Italia*.

English Language Publications The English-language magazine, *Italy, Italy* (via M. Mercati 51, 00197 Rome; ☎ 06 322 1441, fax 06 322 3869) is full of useful articles on culture, politics, entertainment and general interest and is available by subscription from the above address. Another possibility is the expatriate website *The Informer* (www.informer.it), formerly published monthly but now totally online that contains a variety of both useful and interesting articles ranging from tax and money matters to general interest. *The Informer* also has electronic newsletters and extensive archives of information available online to its subscribers. *The Informer* is a gold mine of information and highly recommended for expatriates in Italy. Those interested in taking out a subscription should sign up online at www.informer.it. Also full of useful tips about how to survive daily life in Milan and northern Italy as a foreigner is *The Survival Guide to Milan*, available from the *The Informer*. There are two other fortnightly English-language papers published in Rome: *Wanted in Rome (www.wantedinrome.com)* sold on news-stands and in some bookshops, and the *Metropolitan*. There is also the *International Spectator*, a quarterly publication, and the *Rome Elite*.

The English Yellow Pages (via Belisario 4/B, 00187 Rome;   ☎06-4740861; fax 06-4744516; www.intoitaly.it) updated annually, will be invaluable to any new arrival in Italy. The directory contains listings for English-speaking professionals, businesses, organisations and services in Rome, Florence, Bologna, Naples, Genoa and Milan and is available at international bookstores and from news-stands. The online version also has listings for Palermo and Catania. For a free listing, contact the above address. Free classified ads can also be posted on the website. Also from the same publisher is the English White Pages, an alphabetical directory of English-speakers living in Italy.

Books

The Italian publishing market tends to cater for the extreme ends of the reading public; at one extreme the intellectual highbrow of contemporary literature; at the other downmarket, gossip and romance, Barbara Cartland-imitation junkies. The Italian best-seller list reflects the refined intellectual tastes of the literary minority. Surprisingly, foreign authors such as Milan Kundera and Gabriel Garcià Marquez often sell better than Italy's home-grown talents such as Primo Levi,

Leonardo Sciascia and Umberto Eco.

English-language bookshops:
Anglo American Bookshop: Via della Vite 102, Rome; ☎06 6795222; www.aab.it.
The Corner Bookshop: Via del Moro 48, Rome; ☎06 5836942.
Economy Book & Video Centre: Via Torino 136, Rome 00184; ☎06 4746877; fax
06 483661; www.booksitaly.com. New and used paperbacks, videos for sale and
rent, mail order, special order, seminars and other events, greeting cards and
gifts, discount cards, buys used paperbacks for cash/credit.
Lion Bookshop: Via dei Greci 36, 00187 Rome; 06 32654007; fax 06 32651382.
Paperback Exchange Bookshop: Via Fiesolana 3lr, 50122 Florence; ☎055 2478154;
fax 055 2478856. All fields, hardbacks and paperbacks, new and secondhand,
academic/library supplies, bibliographic service, special order and mail order.

Online bookshops and video suppliers:
www.amazon.com
www.amazon.co.uk (cheaper postage than Amazon.com for books sent to Italy)
www.bn.com
www.choicesdirect.co.uk (supplies UK PAL video by mail order).

Television

The Italians are telly-addicts and 99% of Italian homes own their own television.
With literally hundreds of channels of programmes to choose from, they have
ample fuel with which to feed their craving. This saturation of television space
was the unsurprising response to the deregulation of the television board in 1976;
before this time, there had only ever been one, black and white, state-run channel,
heavily influenced and censored by church authorities. The great majority of these
relatively new channels are crammed with rubbishy quiz shows and low quality
sitcoms and soaps, while the three state-run channels, RAI 1, 2 and 3 manage
to provide a higher quality programming and command higher viewing levels.
However, the standard is evidently not high enough and viewing figures are
falling for the state-run channels. The state channels (RAI 1, RAI 2, RAI 3) are
now no longer as subject to political patronage as they once were. RAI3 tends to
show more cultural programmes than the others.
    The important independent television channels are Italia 1, Canale 5 and Rete
4 that collectively account for about 45% of Italian viewing. Although Rete 4
is thought to be more highbrow than the other two, none of them offer really
serious news coverage although Canale 5 has been attempting to give greater
emhasis to documentaries and news.
    In recent years there has been something of a public crusade in Italy against the
probable dangers of certain types of television on the psychophysical development
of children and younger viewers. The result was a watershed of 10.30pm for
X-rated movies and other violent/sexually explicit programming. Italy was also a
pioneer of the so-called 'violence chip' a piece of technology designed to filter out
violent programmes on television when children are watching.
    When shipping personal belongings to Italy it is worth remembering that

Italian TV and videos operate on the PAL-BG system. The UK operates PAL-I, the USA and Canada operates NTSC and France operates MESECAM. TVs of one system do not correctly work with another (you can get black and white instead of colour, or have no sound). However, multi-system TVs and videos that play all system types are freely available in Italy – in fact, many TVs and videos now sold in Europe are multi-system.

Expatriates can find watching local television channels not as relaxing as what they are used to due to the concentration required to follow a foreign language. Thanks to satellite and cable technology it is now possible to receive a huge variety of international channels via satellite, including BBC World (free to air), BBC Prime (subscription only), CCNI (free to air), CNBC, The Disney Channel and other good quality English language channels throughout Europe. There are also many other channels available in the numerous European languages, plus the languages of the immigrant population – Arabic, Urdu, Hindi, etc. Local satellite suppliers can offer the best solution as not all areas are connected to cable networks and satellite dishes are not allowed in certain protected areas.

Video and DVD

For those unable to find enough substantial fare, at the right time of day, on Italian television and the available satellite and cable channels, there is always recourse to videos or DVDs.

Apart from *Amazon.com, Amazon.co.uk* and *Barnes and Noble* online, there are www.choicesdirect.co.uk and www.bbcshop.com who supply UK standard videos in English. Expats are well recommended to buy a multi-system video player so they can watch videos they collect around the world during their travels (see Television above for explanation). DVD players, however, offer the advantage that each DVD disc gives the viewer the chance to choose the language they hear – i.e. original language or a number of dubbed languages. With this capability, expats no longer have to search out the obscure shops that sell imported videos in their original language, or order them from outside the country and can instead buy DVDs in their local shops.

DVDs, like videos, come in different formats. There are, however, only two – American and European. They will, of course, not work on a player intended solely for the other format – so you have to buy a dual format player to ensure you can play American DVDs brought over to Italy. Blockbuster Video now operates rental stores in the larger cities and offers some videos in their original language. As most DVDs come with original soundtrack available, buying a DVD player can give you a much wider choice of films to rent.

Radio

The Italian radio network was deregulated in 1976, the same year as television, with the result that the airwaves are crammed with a diverse range of obscure stations; over two and a half thousand of them. However, the three main radio channels are Radio 1, 2, and 3. The first two feature light music and entertainment while Radio 3 is similar to the UK equivalent, broadcasting serious discussion programmes and classical music. Finally there are Radio 1 and 2 rock stations which, although technically part of RAI, are on separate wavelengths. The accumulated audience for rock stations is immense (12½ million listeners). The total audience for radio nation-wide is estimated at 35 million. However, there are so many stations that this audience is hopelessly fragmented and some local stations are estimated to have no more than a few dozen listeners.

As with television, the main radio channels are all under the wing of a powerful sponsor who consequently has a substantial influence over the station's output.

BBC World Service A monthly publication *BBC On Air* which gives details of schedules, and advice and information about BBC World Service radio and BBC Prime and BBC World Television, is available on subscription (£20 annually) from BBC On Air, Room 310NW, Bush House, London WC2B 4PH (☎020-7557 22875 (answer phone); fax 020-7240 4899); www.bbconair.co.uk.

Voice of America For details of Voice of America programmes, contact VOA, Washington, D.C. 20547; ☎1-202 619 2358. Details of programmes and frequencies are also online at www.voa.org.

The Post Office

The Italian postal system, the *Poste, Telegrafi e Telefoni* (PTT), has had the dubious reputation as one of the slowest and least efficient in Europe – hardly surprising considering the service had not been reorganised since the 19th century. However, the system is now being revamped and services are improving, though they still have some way to go to fully escape their old image. Mail deliveries are getting quicker, though overnight delivery can not be relied upon – nor is the system reliable enough to negate the need for courier services for important letters and packages. The overseas service is also slow and mail can take a week or more to arrive at a European or North American destination.

Stamps can be bought from post offices (*ufficio postale*) and also tobacconists (*tabaccherie*). Post offices are open Monday to Friday 8.15am to 6pm and until lunchtime on Saturdays.

There are various postal services available in Italy, including letter post, parcel post and registered post. Domestic letters can be sent either priority (*prioritaria* – almost guaranteed next day delivery), or ordinary (*ordinaria* – probable delivery within three or four days). With registered post insurance can also be purchased as can a request for proof of delivery. Parcel post can only be insured. International mail can be sent by airmail or surface mail – surface mail from any country can take many weeks and Italy is no exception to this rule.

For those who have no fixed address, the post restante (*fermoposta*) service is useful; just write the addressee's name, then *fermoposta* and the place name on the envelope; the addressee can then pick up his or her mail from the post office after providing a passport as identification. In large cities it is always better to address poste restante mail to the main post office. Lonely Planet guidebooks are helpful in suggesting the best ones to use.

The state-run ITALCABLE operates a telegraph service abroad by cable or radio; both internal and overseas messages can be sent over the phone.

In addition to the regular postal services, large post offices in major cities are now offering financial services, as do post offices in other parts of Europe. Services offered include banking services, savings schemes, money wire transfers and bill payment services for most bills you are likely to receive (gas, electricity, telephone, rent, etc.).

Telephones

The Italian telephone giant Telecom Italia was privatised in 1997, thus bringing Italy towards liberalisation of her telecommunications market in line with EU directives. Since the early 1990s the phone Italian phone system has been almost totally modernised and fibre optic cables installed throughout the country – except the usual remote rural districts that always seem to be left somewhere in the past. Public telephones take either coins or the phone cards that are available from tobacconists, news-stands, machines at telephone offices, stations and airports. The coin operated phones are being phased out in favour of the card phones. Note that the sign seen over public telephones, *guasto*, is Italian for 'out of order'.

American users will find having to pay as you go for local calls different to the system prevalent in many US locations. Local and long distance calls do not vary much in price, though the time of day affects the cost of a call – out of business hours is cheaper than during them. International calls within Europe are cheaper after 10pm, though the peak rate for North America finishes earlier in the day. As peak rates and off-peak rates and their applicability vary it is worth checking with Telecom Italia to find the best time to make your calls.

The cheap rate for evening calls in Italy doesn't come into effect until 10pm, which means it is quite usual to make long distance calls late into the night. However, there is a price structure known as *Numero Blu* that provides discounts on the numbers you call most often, including your Internet connection number.

Phone users need to dial the complete number of the person they wish to contact, including the area code, even for local calls. This system is common in Europe and possibly heralds the introduction of a seamless European phone system sometime in the future. When dialling Italy from abroad (except to mobile phones) it is necessary to dial the Italian country code (39) and then the complete phone number, including the zero of the area code.

Expatriates (*extracommunitari*) who use international phones more than most for keeping in touch with friends around the world have long used call-back services and other alternative phone services. These are advertised in international newspapers and magazines (*International Herald Tribune, Time, Newsweek*) and can be a great cost saver.

The latest innovation in reducing telephone costs is the utilisation of the internet for international phone calls. Services such as www.Net2Phone.com allow internet users whose computer is equipped with a microphone and sound card (most computer produced within the last two years allow a microphone/ headphone set to be plugged into their soundcard) to log on to their local Internet Service Provider (ISP) and call a standard phone, via the internet, in most

TABLE 6 — LOCAL TELEPHONE CODES

Alassio	0182	Naples	081
Aosta	0165	Palermo	091
Bologna	051	Pesaro	0731
Bolzano	0471	Pisa	050
Cagliari	070	Riccione	054
Cattolica	0541	Rimini	0541
Como	031	Rome	06
Cortina d'Ampezzo	0436	San Remo	0184
Diano Marina	0183	Sorrento	081
Florence	055	Taormina	0942
Genoa	010	Trento	0461
Grado	0431	Trieste	040
La Spezia	0187	Turin	011
Lido di Jesolo	0421	Venice	041
Lignano	0431	Verona	05
Milan	02	Viareggio	0584

Emergency & Useful Numbers

Ambulance	118
Breakdown Services	116
Carabinieri	112 or 113
International Directory Enquiries	170
Enquiries for Europe & the Mediterranean	176
Telephone faults/engineers	182

countries around the world. The cost of the call is then limited to the cost of being online.

Some phone users even avoid *Telecom Italia* completely by making long distance calls through France Telecom, or Deutsche Telecom or Sprint etc. To do this you need a hardware gadget than allows you to connect direct with the provider. You need to contact a private telecommunications broker to do this (see below) or look in the telephone yellow pages of your city under *telefonia e telecommunicazioni*. The attraction of this is lessening with the increase in quality of internet-to-telephone services.

Mobiles: The mobile phone (*telefonino*) has become the vital accessory without which no self-respecting Italian would dare to be seen. In common with other European countries, Italy has auctioned off mobile phone licences and there are now six operators available. TIM, WIND, BLU and OMNITEL who between them offer a bewildering range of price structures and payment options depending on the type of service required, the amount of time you spend on the phone per month, what time of day you phone and how often you want to phone abroad. The area of coverage also varies between providers.

When choosing a mobile phone it is important to check that the provider covers the areas where you live, work and visit. TIM is the mobile telephone subsidiary of *Telecom Italia* and has the widest coverage for those who travel extensively.

Roaming agreements, where you can use the phone outside of Italy, are another useful option for frequent travellers. In addition to the coverage, the level of usage needs to be considered. High monthly charges can counteract low call rates for some, while the reverse is the case for other users. If your Italian is not up to it, take someone along to translate for you – or risk facing a large bill.

International Calls to and from Italy: To telephone the UK from Italy dial 00, wait for the continuous tone and then dial 44 and continue immediately with the UK number, omitting the first number of the UK code. For example, to ring Vacation Work Publications from Italy you would dial: 00-44-1865 241978.

To telephone the US from Italy the country code is 1 followed by the ten digit number, including the area code, e.g. 00-1 123 456 7890.

To telephone Italy from the UK dial 00 39 and then the Italian number. The first zero of the provincial code must be included. For example to ring a Rome number of 06-123456 you would actually dial 00-3906-123456. From the US it is necessary to dial the international access code of your service provider, followed by 39-06-123456. Table 6 contains a list of some of the most important provincial codes:

The Internet

Italy was one of the slowest European countries to jump on the internet bandwagon, though it is now catching up – some Italian municipalities (e.g. Rome) even have websites where they provide information in English for expatriates.

The internet is a great resource for expatriates and email is an easy, cheap and reliable way to keep in touch with friends and relatives around the world. There are a number of free access (you pay for the phone call) ISPs in Italy, www.jumpy.it and www.kataweb.it are two, who give away CDs in store to attract new clients. Once you have a CD, insert it in your modem-equipped computer and follow the instructions. Within a few minutes you should have internet access – assuming *Telecom Italia* have installed your telephone line. As in other countries, heavy users may find it more cost-effective to pay for a subscription service as there are special deals available.

Expatriates should be aware that different phone systems around the world are wired differently. Modem sockets have four connectors, different Modems are wired to use either the inside pair or the outside pair. If your modem worked before you arrived in Italy but not after arrival, try changing the connector cable to one that is wired differently. Remember to keep the cable for when you go home again.

For expats who move frequently it can be worth having an email address that you can take with you each time. Hotmail (www.hotmail.com), Yahoo! (www.yahoo.com), iMail (www.imail.com) and Altavista (www.altavista.com), to name the most popular, offer free email service that you can access online, or have forwarded to your current local email address that comes free from your ISP. When you move you can access your email from an Internet café until you are set up at home, or just change the forwarding address of the email to your new ISP email and not have to tell everyone you have ever given your email address to that the address has changed.

CARS & MOTORING

Buying a Car

EXPATS HAVE THE CHOICE of importing their own cars to Italy (see Importing a Car, in the section: *Setting Up Home*), or buying a new one after arrival in Italy. All of the main European makes, and their spare parts, are available in Italy. American cars have not been so popular in Europe as, for many years, US manufacturers did not apply for European certification of their cars, which is expensive, to enable them to be sold through dealerships. Imported American cars are also more expensive to maintain and run as they frequently have large engines that consume quantities of expensive European petrol. If need be, the local ACI office can direct you to the nearest car dealer of whatever make of car you are interested in, though dealerships should be relatively easy to find through the personal recommendations of colleagues. To buy a car with an Italian registration plate, you must be an Italian resident. If you do buy a car in Italy then you will be liable to pay ownership transfer fees (*passaggio di proprietà*), which cost about €440,000 (£300, US$480). When considering buying a car, it is worth bearing in mind that hiring a car in Italy is very expensive compared to UK and North American rates. It currently costs around £200 (US$320) a week to rent a medium-sized car with unlimited mileage. However, there are an increasing number of budget rental agencies that are offering more competitive rates, especially for long-term rentals.

Italy does not have an abundance of second-hand car dealers and once you have had a brush with the bureaucracy and expense involved it becomes clear why this is not a booming market. First, you have to pay ownership fees (*passagio di proprietà*), you then have to wait up six months for the arrival of the car log-book (*libretto di circolazione*). As it is an offence to drive without having the log-book (commonly called the *libretto*) to hand, you must obtain interim documents (*foglio sostitutivo*), which have to be renewed every three months. Additional irritations are likely to include reminders to pay fines incurred by the previous owner – the inevitable consequence of the inefficient Italian bureaucracy.

There is also the problem of persuading dealers to give expatriates hire purchase agreements. One US expatriate couple had the following experience when trying to buy a car.

The dealer seemed reluctant to sell us a car at first, even though my husband's colleague, who also speaks English, was friends with the owner and accompanied us. They told us that there is more paperwork for them to fill out because we are foreigners. They were also concerned with the fact that we are here on a temporary basis. My husband's employer had to call the dealer to put in a good word for us. We were only able to finance the car for 18 months, I think because we told them we were going to be here for 2-3 years. The whole process took several weeks, but we did manage to buy the car we wanted in the end. We were advised to buy either German or Italian made cars because they are the easiest to resell, diesels are also popular.

When selling a car, the popular motor magazine, *Porta Portese* is invaluable. Alternatively, simply stick a 'for sale' sign (*vendesi*) in the car window. Alternatively, you may prefer to sell your car to a garage in part-exchange for a new one. A general proxy (*procura*) must first be obtained through a notary, empowering the garage to sell the car on your behalf. The buyer then pays ownership transfer fees (see above). At least in this version of second-hand car dealing, the legwork generally has to be done by the garage.

Car Tax A tax stamp (*bollo*) must be purchased for your car and is obtainable from the ACI and renewable at the post office. The tax is dependent on the power rating of the engine and whether it is diesel or petrol driven.

Driving Licences

EU drivers licences are a standard pink and holders of these may drive their home registered car in Italy with no alteration to their licence at all. However, holders of the old UK green coloured driving licences must first obtain a translation, available free of charge from the Italian State Tourist Office (1 Princes Street, London W1R 8AY;   ☎020-7408 1254), or update them for the new style. Owners of Italian-registered cars should theoretically have an Italian-registered licence, this involves converting your EU driving licence for an Italian one. To do this a certificate confirming that you have never been convicted for a driving offence in the country of issue is required – such certificates are available from the nearest Embassy or Consulate. In practice, however, many expatriates avoid doing this and carry an international driving licence instead.

Non-EU drivers licence holders are in a slightly different situation and the usefulness of their drivers licence depends on where it was issued. Some countries have reciprocal agreements with Italy to recognise each other's driving licences, other do not. Further information can be obtained from your embassy. If your country does have a reciprocal agreement with Italy (America does not) you can apply to exchange your current licence for an Italian one. The Italian licence replaces your previous one – it is not in addition to it.

If your country does not have a reciprocal agreement with Italy you will need to take a two-part driving test, in Italian. The first part is a written test and the second part (after passing the written test) is the road test. Exams must be taken at a driving school, who will also apply for the licence for you after you have passed the tests.

It is possible to drive in Italy on an International driver's licence, though you must always carry your national licence to show at the same time. International licences can be obtained from your national drivers association (e.g. the AA in the UK, or your state organisation in the US). However, international licences can also be obtained via the internet from sites such as: IDL International (www.idl-international.com) who can supply five year licences.

All Nationalities will find that though it is not essential it is definitely advisable to carry an international green card for your car and remember that it is a legal requirement to carry your driving licence (*patente),* all of your car documents (*libretto*) and passport with you while you are driving. You may be required to present any or all of the papers if you are stopped by the police and can be fined for failing to do so.

An EU-approved driving test has recently been introduced to Italy, replacing the slightly ridiculous and typically Italian test which involved a mass of paperwork about mechanics and road safety, but very little actual driving. Driving schools (*scuola guida*) are widely available, and listed in the *Yellow Pages*.

Insurance

Italian car insurance covers the car, not the driver, and is nearly always third party. Full, comprehensive cover (*kasko*) is available, at a price, upon consultation with the insurance company. Note that insurance is rather more expensive than in other EU countries. Unfortunately, Italian insurance companies are both notoriously slow and mean in honouring claims and be prepared for a hard battle and an even longer wait before a cheque is actually signed, delivered, and in your bank account. This is partly why so many minor road accidents in Italy go unreported.

An insurance broker used to handling the expatriate community's requirements is John Thorpe S.r.l., Insurance Brokers, Lloyd's Correspondents, (Via Dogana 3, 20123 Milan; ☎02-867141; fax 02-809250) who provide most insurance needs for expats, though they can only insure Italian registered cars in Italy. Royal International Insurance (Royal & Sun Alliance, Via F.lli Gracchi, 30/32, 20092 Cinisello Balsamo – (Mi); ☎02-660791; fax 02-66011760; www.royal.it.), also sell motor insurance through direct marketing in Italy. Copeland Insurance (230 Portland Road, London SE25 4SL; ☎020-8656 8435; fax 020-8655 1271; www.andrewcopeland.co.uk) can also provide insurance in Italy in certain circumstances.

Roads

Driving in Italy can be a costly business. The tolls (*pedaggi*) on Italian motorways (*autostrade*) are expensive at about €0.50-€0.60 per ten kilometres. As you drive on to an *autostrada* you will pick up a toll ticket which you pay on exit. *Strade Statali* (SS) are the equivalent of British A roads. Both *autostrade* and *strade statali* are numbered, while smaller roads *strade provinciali* and *secondarie* are not. For drivers new to roads outside the UK and North America, it is as well to realise as soon as possible that the law of the jungle applies to the Italian roads. It takes courage and an ability to learn to drive like an Italian to survive on Italian roads and only the fittest and most adept will survive without at least a couple of minor prangs as proof of having negotiated the Italian road system. Information in English about the *autostrade* network, including tolls, service stations and rescue services can be found at www.autostrade.it/pagine-1/english/e-homep.html.

In Europe it is customary to give way to cars entering traffic from the right – even if it is a small side road they are coming from. Not all drivers approaching you from the right will slow down to make sure you will give way. Unless the road joining the one you are on has a solid white line across it where the two roads meet, you do not have right of way. As road rules become harmonised across Europe, drivers are confused by the new rules as much as foreigners getting used to the alternative way of doing things. One of the biggest changes in Europe has been who has right of way at roundabouts. Though it is supposedly the person on the roundabout, this was not the case until recently in Italy and some other European countries. Therefore, it is important to take great care whilst driving in Italy as everyone gets used to the new traffic rules.

Italian petrol (*Benzina*) is cheaper than that in the UK, but more expensive than US residents are used to. Unleaded petrol comes in two octane ratings, 95 and 98, and cars are set-up to take only one of these. *Gasolio* (diesel) is popular in Europe because it is much cheaper than unleaded petrol and is as widely available as unleaded petrol. Leaded petrol is to be phased out through the whole of Europe, though lead replacement petrol is available in some places for older cars that do not have catalytic converters. LPG (Liquified Petroleum Gas), known as GPL in Italy, is becoming increasingly popular because of its lower price and environmental cleanliness. Only those petrol stations displaying the GPL symbol sell GPL. Petrol stations along the *autostrade* are open 24 hours while those on secondary roads usually open between 7am and 12.30pm and then from 3.30 to 6.30pm and close on Sundays.

24 hour self-service petrol stations are becoming more common. In most cases standard garages will have one or more pumps, alongside traditional pumps, that are entirely self-service. The self service stations require you to insert a credit or debit card into a slot on the pump, then enter your PIN number, as in a cash point machine (ATM), before petrol can be pumped. The machine authorises the transaction and charges your card for amount of petrol received.

Accidents

Italy has one of the highest road accident rates in the whole of the EU. This is a result of lax enforcement by the Italian traffic police (*Vigili Urbani*), inadequate road laws (see below) and the frenetic style of driving which the Italians favour in the built-up areas of Italy. However, although the accident rate is astronomical (approximately 250,000 injured each year), the death rate is mercifully lower (estimated at 7,000 deaths each year) – probably because the streets are so crowded nobody can go very fast anyway.

Part of the insurance documentation that is required to be carried in every car is an insurance claim form that has space for the parties involved to sketch the accident scene as well as other questions that need to be answered. If the two parties have differing views on what happened, ensure that you sketch your version on your form. Also call the police to review the scene and if you are correct they should support you in their official report. As with all accidents, never admit liability or your insurance company has good grounds not to pay up, which leaves you financially liable. Both parties are required to sign the accident claim forms.

If you have an accident it is mandatory to stop. If you see an accident happen, even though you are not involved, you are required to stop and help. After an accident you are expected to take the names and addresses of witnesses and their car details if applicable. Always inform your insurance company of any accident you have whether or not you file a claim – the small print of most European

TABLE 7	ROAD SIGNS
Accendere i fari in galleria	Switch on headlights in tunnel
Attenzione	caution
Caduta massi	fallen rocks
Casello a ....metri	toll in ....metres
Curve	bends
Dare precedenza	give way
Deviazione	detour
Divieto di accesso	no entry
Divieto di sorpasso	no overtaking
Divieto di sosta	no stopping
Divieto di transito	no right of way
Lavori in corso	roadworks
Passaggio a livello	level crossing
Pedoni	pedestrians
Rallentare	slow
Senso unico	one way
Sosta autorizzata	parking permitted
Strada ghiacciata	icy road
Tenere la destra	keep to the right
Transito Interrotto	no through road
Uscita camion	truck exit
Veicoli al passo	dead slow

insurance policies requires you to do so (unless the accident is a fender bender) and failure to do so can invalidate your insurance.

The red triangle that it is 'recommended' you carry in your car becomes mandatory to have after an accident, as you are required to place the triangle 50 metres (approximately 60 yards) behind the accident to warn approaching drivers.

Breakdowns

The Italian Automobile Club, *Automobile Club d'Italia*, is the Italian equivalent of the RAC and the AA. The head office of the ACI is at Via Marsala 8, 00185 Rome (☎06-49981; fax 06-4457748 – General Secretariat; 06-49982426 – Presidency; 06-49982469 – Tourism Department; www.acit.it).

The emergency 24-hour phone number is Rome 06-4477 with multilingual staff providing round the clock assistance.

If your car comes to an unprompted and definitive halt, then dial 116 (ACI breakdown Service) from anywhere in Italy, from either a telephone box or a mobile phone.

On motorways, you can also use SOS phones that are placed every 2km along the road and connected with the motorways radio centres – road assistance can be provided either by the ACI 116 or by a local operator. The service is permanently available on all roads throughout Italy. In all emergencies (personal injury and all kinds of accidents or mishaps) dial 113 (police), 112 (Carabinieri) or 115 (Fire Brigade).

Breakdown service comprises transportation of the car from the place of breakdown to the nearest ACI garage or, in major cities, the roadside repair of the vehicle if possible. Road Assistance provided by the ACI is free of charge only for tourists with an AIT or FIA Assistance booklet, otherwise the service for all motor vehicles up to 2.5 tons is chargeable. An annual subscription can be purchased from the ACI that covers breakdown service either within Italy only, or throughout Europe, depending on the fee paid.

Driving Regulations

In theory, the Italian speed limits are as follows: 130 kph (80 mph) on the *autostrada*, 90 kph (55 mph) on highroads *(le strade statali)* and 50 kph (30 mph) in all built-up areas. Although the police have become a lot more enthusiastic over the last few years, they are notoriously slack at enforcing driving regulations. Nonetheless, be warned that if you are caught then hefty fines are often made on the spot.

It has only been compulsory for motorbike riders to wear helmets since 1986 (it is still legal to ride a moped without a helmet if you are over 18). Wearing seatbelts became law in 1986 and only as a result of EU directives and Italy planning to introduce drink drive legislation. Italian drink drive regulations are not quite as strict as in the UK, though the police can perform random testing without having to have due cause.

Italian road signs are standardised by European norms, which helps UK expatriates – though North Americans should have no trouble working out what most of them mean either. Note that circular signs are used to announce restrictions (or the end of them), rectangular green ones are used on the *autostradas* and rectangular blue ones on the secondary roads. Table 7 gives translations of the more common road signs.

TRANSPORT

Railways

THE ITALIAN RAILWAY SYSTEM, *Ferrovie dello Stato* (FS) runs one of the cheapest railway services in Western Europe. This is more remarkable than you might think, considering the substantial reforms that were made to services during the last two decades which resulted in a greater network of inter-city lines and a generally modern, fast and reasonably reliable service. Unlike the UK and North America, branch lines reach the most remote areas, with connecting buses that will get you to the most obscure spots. Despite the heavy subsidies handed out to the rail network, the railways still run up a huge deficit; part of the solution to reduce this will be the introduction of higher ticket prices.

Tickets. There are usually formidable queues for tickets at main stations. You can

TABLE 8	STATION SIGNS AND PHRASES
Al Binari/Ai Treni	to the platforms/trains
Arrivi/Partenze	arrivals/departures
Biglietteria	ticket office
Deposito Bagagli	left luggage
Entrata/Uscita	entrance/exit
Orario	timetable
Sala d'Attesa	waiting room
Vietato l'Ingresso	no entry
Andata/Andata e ritorno Firenze	single/return to Florence
Il primo/l'ultimo/il prossimo treno	the first/last/next train
A che binario?	Which platform?
C'è un posto?	Is there a seat?
È questo posto libero?	Is this seat taken?
Dove siamo?	Where are we?

find automatic ticket machines, but these are usually a problem for newcomers, though you can ask someone to help you (*Può aiutarmi per favore? Voglio un billete por ....*). Also, it is compulsory to validate all tickets by inserting them in the yellow machines on the platforms, which clip and stamp them. Failure to punch your ticket can make you liable for an on the spot fine. Self-punching of railway tickets is a common practice on European railways, though the machines are not always yellow.

There is a complete national pocket timetable (*Il Pozzorario*), which can be bought at stations and newspaper kiosks. It has useful maps, and tables to work out costings. Travelling by train in Italy is by far preferable to the localised and sluggish bus system. The FS website (www.fs-on-line.com) has service information and Thomas Cook produces a European railway timetable (in English) that includes many Italian services – available from www.Amazon.co.uk in the UK, or www.railpass.com/eurail/cooks.htm in North America.

The *rapido* and *IC* (Inter-city) trains are invariably the fastest and most expensive, stopping only at the major cities. For these a supplement (*supplemento rapido*) is required according to mileage. Remember that the best prices are for tickets bought in advance, as tickets bought on the train are subject to a surcharge. Reductions of around 50% are available to children under 12 and people over 65.

The Milan to Rome *rapido* train takes under four hours, with an onward link to Naples. There is also a *Super Rapido* or TEE (Trans-Europe-Express), which has first class only and compulsory reservation. Using the Channel Tunnel from the UK the trip to Paris takes three hours; from there you get a Paris to Milan connection.

The *espresso* and *diretto* trains are the next fastest, and more reasonably priced, stopping at most large towns. Lastly, and to be avoided wherever possible (unless you are hoping to enjoy the leisurely pace of Italian rural life) are the painfully slow *locale* trains which seem to stop at every small village and country backwater imaginable.

Railchoice are the UK agents for Italian Railways (☎ 020-8659 7300; fax 020-8659 7466; www.railchoice.com); visits can be made by appointment only to their office address at 15 Colman House, Paris Square, High Street, London SE20 7EX. In Canada contact CIT Montreal 666 Sherbrooke Street West, Suite 901, Montreal, Quebec H3A 1E7;   ☎514 845 9101; 514 845 9137; www.cit-tours.com and in North America tickets can be ordered from European Vacations (☎1.888.TOUR.404, www.europeanvacation.com).

Buses

Italian cities are dotted with bright orange town buses weaving chaotically through the traffic as Italian motorists resolutely refuse to acknowledge the function of bus lanes. Italy has more buses than any other European country but no national bus company. Bus tickets are fairly inexpensive (though more expensive than train tickets) and are obtainable from tobacconists (*tabaccherie*) which have the black 'T' sign displayed, from ticket offices at the bus termini (*capoline*) and from some news-stands, tickets should be cancelled at the ticket machine once you are on the bus.

There are a number of ticket types, including single tickets (*corso semplice*), morning or afternoon tickets also known as half-day tickets (*biglietti orari*) and season tickets *(abbonamenti)* of varying length. A season ticket can include use of bus, tram and subway routes (*intera rete*) if necessary.

Buses in the provincial areas of Italy can be a nightmare and bus services are often severely reduced at the weekends. Provincial bus journeys are long and slow and timetables erratic. Tickets can be bought on the bus and most of them will stop for you if you flag them down along the road and look desperate, though tickets can be bought in advance and used as necessary. Although travelling by train is preferable, especially between large cities, the buses and coaches are a reasonable alternative for shorter trips and are a useful alternative during a train strike.

The Metro

Both Rome and Milan have metros. The Rome metro (*Metropolitina*) consists of two lines which exist principally to ferry commuters in and out of the centre to the suburbs. However, the metro is less crowded and less hot than the buses, so it can be worth catching the metro if you're travelling around the city; there are stations at the Colosseum, the Spanish Steps and the Piazza Barberini. A transport map (available from the *Piazza dei Cinquecento* information booth) is invaluable when attempting to negotiate your way through the metro system. Books of five or ten tickets can be bought in advance from *edicole* (news-stands) and *tabaccherie* (tobacconists).

In Milan, stations are marked MM and tickets can be bought from places where the black and yellow sign *Biglietti ATM* is displayed. Tickets are also available from stations. A single ticket gives integrated access to other city transport above ground, but only allows one metro trip.

Taxis

Italian taxis are a cheerful canary yellow in colour (like the New York cabs) and more expensive than London cabs. This is partly due to the list of hefty surcharges that are imposed for countless sins including extra luggage, night trips and rides to the airport. Often the meter is 'forgotten', in which case it is worth negotiating a price for the journey in advance rather than recklessly jumping in the cab and finding the price outlandish later.

Air

The Italians indulge in internal flights far more than the British, though not as much as North Americans. This is partly due to the distances which separate Italy's most important cities, principally Milan and Rome (flight time about 50 minutes). Alitalia and its sister companies, Alisarda and ATI, fly to eleven major cities throughout mainland Italy and the islands and Air One does flights between Rome and Milan. However, internal flights do tend to be pretty expensive, so bear in mind that passengers of ages 12 to 25 qualify for a 35% discount over normal fares, as do students. There are also reductions of 50% for group family travel, 30% for night travel and children up to two years of age only have to pay 10% of the adult fare while children aged two to twelve pay half fare.

Italy has its share of little airlines, which sprang up following the opening up of the skies to the free market. Air Dolomiti is the best known, though the current state of flux in the airline industry is likely to mean consolidation and change in the airline industry in Italy as elsewhere.

Milan has two airports, Malpensa and Linate, which are 46km and 8km respectively from the city centre. Airport buses run between Linate and the Garibaldi Central Station, a journey of about 30/40 minutes. The Italian government only allowed international airlines to land at Malpensa, while Alitalia used Linate. Not surprisingly the airlines objected and complained to the European Commission. The situation is likely to change and so it is always worth checking which airport your plane is scheduled to land at.

Rome also has two airports: Leonardo da Vinci/Fiumicino, 32 km west of the city for scheduled flights, and Ciampino airport for charter flights. Buses run every quarter of an hour between Fiumicino and the Termini Station of Via Giolitti; a journey of about an hour. There are also trains, which take about half an hour to reach Ostiense station.

It is possible to arrange personal transport to and from the airport, which is well worth the cost when arriving in a new country for the first time. Allegro Italiano offer a private car service, with English speaking driver, and bookings can be made online at: www.allegroitaliano.com/bus.htm. Other service providers can be found through Yahoo! using the search string: +Italy +limousine +service.

Ferries

There are regular ferry connections between the mainland of Italy and the islands. Large car ferries run from the ports of Genova, Civitavecchia and Naples to Sardinia and Sicily. There are also ferry connections from the mainland to the smaller Tremiti, Bay of Naples and Pontine islands. The ferries also make international trips from the mainland to Malta, Corsica, Spain, Greece, Turkey, Tunisia, Egypt and Israel. Fares are reasonable although you may have to book well in advance, especially over the holiday season in the summer months. In the winter the number of crossings is greatly reduced. In Italy the tourism office and travel agents can provide information, which can also be found on the website: www.traghettionline.net or the websites of the ferry operators, some of whom are listed below.

Minoan Lines: www.minoan.gr
Agoudimos Lines: www.agoudimos-lines.com
Strintzis Line: www.strintzis.gr

BANKS AND FINANCE

The Banking System

BEFORE BECOMING INVOLVED in the Italian banking system it is advisable to become acquainted with its peculiarities. It is ironic that from the tenth to the fourteenth centuries parts of Italy, mainly Venice and Lombardy, were responsible for some of the most innovative banking practices in Europe. The Italians virtually brought banking to England (hence Lombard Street in London) and then the rest of the world. Since then, alas, Italian banking services have slipped into a morass of bureaucracy. Italy is generally recognised to have one of the least efficient banking services in Europe.

In recent years there have been a number of mergers and acquisitions among Italian banks thus reducing the number of smaller banks. There are hundreds of banks operating in Italy (well over 900), including a number of foreign banks who operate local branches (*filiali di banche estere* or *FBEs*). In the past the phenomenon of the single-outlet bank meant that customers found it virtually impossible to obtain cash outside the town where their account was held as other banks were certain to refuse to cash the cheques of other banks. The consolidation of the banking system is alleviating this problem, as is the Bancomat network of automatic cash dispensers, which dispense cash to clients of other banks. Expatriates can also use the ATMs to withdraw cash from their accounts outside of Italy, as long as both the machine and their card carry a matching pair of symbols such as Cirrus, Maestro, Visa, MasterCard or Plus. depending on the account accessed and the issuing bank, the charges levied on the transaction can vary significantly and it is worth checking with your bank before utilising this service.

Italian bank staff are often no more co-operative than their technology. Owing to the fact that around 80% of the banking system is state owned, banks are grossly overstaffed and employees have jobs for life, which has produced a similar mentality to that found in the state bureaucracy – inefficiency, slowness and masses of paperwork. History has frequently shown that state industries are inclined to put the welfare of their employees first and that of their clients second – Italian banks are a good example.

The frustration of dealing with Italian banks runs a close second to that experienced in close encounters with the state bureaucracy. Bank facades are often impressive, but once inside, the image crumbles. The most simple transaction can take a preposterous amount of time and queuing is a random affair in Italy, necessitating an opportunistic approach to any window that may become vacant. If you are fortunate enough to attract the teller's attention, the chances are that the bank computer will be down – they nearly always are, or if not, the employee is incapable of working it (technical training is abysmal).

Until recently it was extremely difficult to get a personal loan from an Italian bank and, as in other European countries, issuing a cheque for which there are insufficient funds, is illegal. Italian banking practices are still a far cry from the credit largesse characteristic of banks in the UK and North America. Months of negotiation with an Italian bank and copious paperwork are required for any reasonable overdraft to be granted. Even if the loan is approved, the interest charges will be exorbitant (25% or higher), as are all charges connected with Italian banking. Small wonder then, that Italians are amongst Europe's least keen holders of current bank accounts; about 25% of Italians have such an account, whereas in the UK there are 1.9 accounts per head of the population.

The governing body of Italian banks is the Banca d'Italia (Via Nazionale 91, 00184 Rome). The biggest bank is the Banca Nazionale di Lavoro which is state owned and comes fifteenth in the league table of European banks. Other larger national banks include: Credito Italiano, Banco di Roma, Banco di Napoli, Banco di Sicilia and Banca Commerciale Italiana.

Expatriates may find that the foreign banks are more helpful: National Westminster and HSBC both have branches in Italy. Barclays Bank only provides banking services to larger multinational clients and not to individual clients, instead Barclays refers existing clients looking for personal banking services to *Banca Commerciale Italiana*.

Opening an Account

Anyone who is considering living and working in Italy on a long-term basis will need an Italian bank account. Accounts are available for foreigners with non-resident and resident status, though anyone working in Italy will need to wait for their *residenza* (residence permit) before being able to open their residents account. The only option if you are not yet in possession of this invaluable document is to enlist the assistance of an influential Italian who may be able to persuade a bank manager to let you have an account. Alternatively, if the institution you currently bank with has a branch in Italy near where you will be living or working, you can ask for a letter of introduction that may smooth and quicken the process of opening an account. HSBC banks are particularly popular with expatriates because of the number of countries where HSBC operate and the process of referrals that they operate between their various branches. If you can not open an Italian bank account before receiving your *residenza* you will have to manage with Eurocheques, cash and credit cards until you receive the piece of paper in question – see above for advice on obtaining cash from your accounts outside Italy.

Once an Italian bank account has been set up the customer receives a *libretto di assegni* (cheque book) and he or she will be able to cash cheques (*incassare un assegno*) at their branch. When paying for goods and services by cheque a *carta di garanzia* (cheque guarantee card) is obligatory. For larger purchases a bank draft (*assegno circolare*) is normally required.

Using an Italian Bank Account

The majority of expatriates do not normally choose to transfer all their assets into their Italian bank account. There are sound reasons for this as not only are bank charges very high in Italy, but one is liable to attract the grasping hands of the Italian tax authorities. The consensus seems to be that one should maintain an account outside of the country (either 'at home' or 'offshore somewhere') and transfer the minimum funds needed as cash to Italy. Credit and/or debit cards linked to accounts outside the country can be used to make purchases in Italy and also have the advantage that it can take weeks for the charge to reach the account in question. If UK citizens do maintain accounts in the UK it is essential to inform the British tax authorities and the bank that they are resident abroad in order to prevent double taxation.

When calculating the amount of funds needed in your Italian account you should err on the generous side as there are various ways you can be caught out. For example there are charges levied per cheque written and the gas and electricity companies may automatically adjust your standing orders after the bi-annual meter readings (see Chapter Three, *Setting Up Home*, Utilities). Banks do pay a small amount of interest, usually two or three per cent, on current accounts in credit, but this is minimal when compared to the horrendous bank charges. If one is unfortunate enough to issue a bouncing cheque (*un assegno a vuoto*), albeit by accident, it can lead to legal problems, being disbarred from holding any bank account and even to having your name gazetted in the local press so doing this should be avoided at all costs. On the other hand pre-arranged overdrafts may be possible, if you can afford the interest and have the patience to arrange one.

Transferring Funds from Abroad into Italy

For retirees and expatriates paid in their home country, transferring funds to Italy is necessary on a regular basis. It the old days, bearing in mind the dinosaur qualities of the Italian banking system, transferring money could be a protracted process; three weeks was about the minimum, though for those living in Tuscany and Umbria months could elapse before the transfer arrived. By using the same bank at each end of the transfer the process could be speeded up, which was a good reason for using a larger bank. However, nowadays the system has been greatly improved and Swift transfers that go directly to your local branch rather than via the head office of the bank in Milan, Rome, etc. are one of the best ways to transfer money. Online banking services from banks such as Citibank and HSBC allow customers to submit transfer instructions such as this 24 hours a day through their computer and can be very convenient for expatriates with internet access. Other banks have telephone banking service which can be just as convenient, though the cost of international phone calls to deal with them, especially when the lines are busy and you get put on hold, can be much higher.

Lastly, if the bank cards issued by your bank outside Italy carry the Maestro symbol and your Italian bank accepts Maestro payments, you can draw out money into your Italian bank account whilst sitting in the managers office. Both the issuing bank and Italian bank can limit the amount of cash you can draw down at any one time. The issuing bank will place a limit on how much you can charge to your card in a specified time period and the Italian bank can have what is known as a floor limit, which limits how much they are allowed to accept via a single Maestro payment.

With these options in mind, it behoves the prospective foreign resident to base the selection of an Italian bank account and bank on what services are available, not just the charges levied and the nearness of the branch to your place of work or residence.

Choosing a Bank

Despite the problems within the Italian banking system in general, some banks do enjoy a better reputation than others in their dealings with foreigners. These include: *Istituto Bancario San Paolo* based in Turin, with 500 branches nationwide, and *Creditwest*, which is the product of a joint venture between the Italian bank *Credito Italiano* and the UK bank National Westminster. *Creditwest* has about 30 branches in the Milan, Rome and Naples areas many of which employ staff familiar with the banking needs of expatriates. Some of the smaller, privately-owned banks may also be worthy of closer acquaintance: in particular, *Credito Emiliano* (Milan, Rome and central Italy), has a policy of encouraging clients from the foreign community.

Useful Addresses

Abbey National Bank: Via Nizza 48, 00198 Rome;　☎06 841 3890; fax 06 841 3896. Via G. Fara 27, 20124 Milan; ☎02 66 7291; 02 66 981755.

ABN Ambro Bank N.V.: Via Principessa Clotilde 7, 00196 Rome;　☎06 321 9600; fax 06 320 4851. Via Mengoni 4, 20121 Milan;　☎02 722671.

American Express Bank:, Piazza San Babila 3, 20122 Milan;　☎02 77901; fax 02 76002308.

Banque Nationale de Paris: Via Lazio 6, 00187 Rome;　☎06 4817041; 06 4818508. Via Meraavigli 4, 20123 Milan;　☎02 721241; fax 02 865 948.

Chase Manhattan Bank: Via M. Mercati 39, 00197 Rome;　☎06 844 361; fax 06 844 36220. Piazza Meda 1, 20121 Milan;　☎02 88951; 02 88952229.

Citibank: Via Bruxelles 61, 00198 Rome; ☎06 854 561. Foro Bonaparte 16, 20121 Milan;　☎02 85421.

Credito Emiliano: Via Emilia San Pietro 4, 42100 Reggio Emilia;　☎0555 5821; fax 0522 *Creditwest:* Via Santa Margarita 7, Milan;　☎02-8813.

Istituto Bancario San Paolo di Torino: Via della Stamperia 64, 00187 Rome; ☎06 85751; 06 857 52400. Piazza San Carlo 156, Turin;　☎011-5551. 433969; www.credem.it.

National Westminster Bank: Via Turati 18 20121 Milan;　☎02 6251; fax 02 6572869.

More banks are listed in the *Regional Employment Guide* section in the chapter on *Employment* later in the book.

Offshore Banking

One of the financial advantages of being an expatriate is that you can invest money offshore in tax havens such as the Isle of Man, the Channel Islands and Gibraltar, thus accruing tax-free interest on your savings. Many such facilities are as flexible as UK high street banking and range from current accounts to long-term, high interest earning deposits. Mortgage facilities are also available. Many of the banks that provide offshore facilities have reassuringly familiar names and include a number of building societies that have moved into this field since demutualising.

Useful Addresses

Abbey National: PO BOX 824, 237 Main Street, Gibraltar; ☎ 010 350 76090; www.abbeynationaloffshore.com.

Alliance & Leicester International Ltd.: P.O.B. 226, 10-12 Prospect Hill, Douglas, Isle of Man IM99 1RY; ☎01624 663566; fax 01624 617286.

Barclays International Personal Banking: PO Box 784, Victoria Road, Georgetown, Jersey JE4 8ZS, Channel Islands; ☎ 01534 880 550; fax 01534 505 077; www.internationalbanking.barclays.com.

Brewin Dolphin Bell Lawrie Ltd. Stockbrokers: 5 Giltspur Street, London EC1A 9BD; ☎020-7246 1028; fax 020-7246 1093.

Bristol & West International: P.O.B. 611, High Street, St Peter Port, Guernsey, Channel Islands GY1 4NY; ☎01481-720609; fax 01481-711658; www.bristol-west.co.uk/bwi/.

FT Expat: Subscriptions, Oakfield House, 35 Perrymount Road, Hay-wards Heath, West Sussex RH16 3DH; England; ☎01444 445520; fax 01444 445599; www.ftexpat.com

Halifax International (Jersey Ltd): P.O.B. 664, Halifax House, 31-33 New Street, St. Helier, Jersey; ☎01534 59840; fax 01534 59280.

HSBC Bank International: P.O. Box 615, 28/34 Hill Street, St. Helier, Jersey JE4 5YD, Channel Islands; ☎01534 616111; fax 01534 616222; www1.offshore.hsbc.co.je.

Lloyds TSB Offshore Centre: P.O. Box 12, Douglas, Isle of Man, IM99 1SS; ☎01624 638104; fax 01624 638181; www.lloydstsb-offshore.com.

Nationwide Overseas Ltd: 45-51, Athol Street, Douglas, Isle of Man; ☎01624 663494.

Woolwich Guernsey Limited: P.O. Box 341, La Tonnelle House, Les Banques, St. Peter Port, Guernsey GY1 3UW; ☎01481 715735; fax 01481 715722.

ITALIAN TAXES

THERE ARE NUMEROUS TAXES in Italy and so only the main ones that expatriates will be most likely to come across will be covered below. As the tax regulations change frequently it is worth checking frequently what the current situation is. Information is available on the internet to help employees understand what taxes their employer is deducting, though self-employed expatriates are well advised to employ an accountant with experience of working with expatriates of their nationality. *The Informer,* an English language website (www.informer.it) for expatriates in Italy is a goldmine of advice on tax issues and goes into much more detail than is possible here. The main taxes expatriates will encounter are:

Imposta sul redetti delle persone fisiche(IRPEF). This is levied in a format most people are used to, i.e. it is a progressive tax that increases with the amount you earn. US citizens in particular are likely to consider the rates very high. However, Italians get a lot in return for their taxes in the form of pensions, health care and other social security benefits and the rates are not the highest in the EU. Tax rates begin at 18% and go up to 44.5% for high earners. Employees have the taxes deducted at source every month by their employer based on an estimate of the year's tax – any necessary adjustment will be made early in the following year. Self-employed workers operate under a complicated system whereby some taxes are paid at source and some in arrears – expert advice from an accountant is recommended.

Imposta regionale sulle attivita produttive (IRAP). This is a corporate tax that is charged to every business no matter how small. The rate is decided by the region in which the business is located. IRAP also includes health contributions. It is a tax on services and goods produced, on the difference between the value realised after specified production costs (except labour costs) have been deducted. The basic rate of IRAP is around 4.25%, but as with ILOR there is a reduced agricultural rate (3%). The rate for banks, insurance companies and other financial services is approximately 5%. In 1998 and 1999 IRAP was levied directly into the National Treasury; after that it began to be a regionally payable tax, so local rates can vary.

Imposta sul reditti delle persone giuridiche (IRPEG). This is a corporate tax levied on S.r.l. and S.p.A. type companies; not generally applicable to self-employed workers.

Imposta sul valore aggiunta (IVA). This is known as VAT (value added tax) in the UK and is levied on all sales, whether retail or wholesale, and even by consultants and other businesses who do not sell an actual product. There are three rates of 4%, 10% and 20%, the standard rate being 20%. Most foodstuffs are taxed at 10%. For other goods including most clothing, shoes, records, cassettes and certain alcoholic goods the rate is 20%.

Social security contributions. Whilst these are not really a tax, they amount to approximately 10% of income – information on the benefits obtained in exchange for the contributions is included in the *Social Security and Unemployment* section of this chapter.

When trying to estimate your tax bill it should be borne in mind that a number

TABLE 9	INCOME TAX RATES (IRPEF) FOR 2002	
Income in Euros	**Tax rate**	**Tax payable**
up to 10,239	18%	1,843 (max)
10,330 to 15,494	22%	1,187 (max)
15,495 to 30,987	32%	4,957 (max)
30,988 to 69,722	38.5%	14,912 (max)
69,723	44.5%	22,899 + 44.5% on amount above 69722Euro
Regional IRPEF charged at 0.9% and municipal IRPEF up to 0.4%.		

of allowances are available that can be deducted from the taxable income and therefore reduce the amount of tax payable. Therefore, a married employee with a dependant spouse and two children in full-time education will pay much less tax than a single, childless employee. Housing allowances, education allowances, overseas living allowances and many of the other benefits that expatriates may enjoy are all counted as part of the income and their value will be taxed and added to the tax liability.

Personal allowances as listed below are allowed to reduce tax liability:

O Basic deduction between €52 and €904, depending on income (Higher income, lower deduction).

O Allowance for a dependant spouse of €422 toEuro546 depending on household income.

O An allowance for each child of €285.

O Other allowances, up to a maximum of 19%, including medical expenses, life assurance, mortgage interest on property in Italy and limited university tuition fees can also be claimed in certain circumstances.

Apart from the main taxes listed above there are a multitude of other taxes payable by residents, including expatriates: these include:

O Rubbish disposal (*nettezza urbana*),

O Water rates (*acquedotto comunale*.

O *Imposta Comunale sull'incremento di valore degli immobili (INVIM)*. This is the equivalent of Capital Gains Tax paid on profit from the sale of property. This tax is subject to wide abuse but rarely completely evaded. For further details see Chapter Three, *Setting Up Home*.

O *Imposta sulle Successioni e Donazioni* (Inheritance and Gift Tax). In common with some other European countries, Italian inheritance tax levels vary according to the nearness of the deceased's relatives: direct relatives, e.g. spouse and children, pay the least, cousins more, and non-relatives the most. For further information see Chapter Five, *Retirement*.

- Car (or other motorised vehicle) tax.
- TV licence fee.
- Property tax.

(Note that the first two listed above are based on the floor area of the property. House owners with their own independent water supply such as a well or spring are exempt from water rates).

Tax evasion in Italy is a popular topic of conversation and supposedly occurs on a massive scale. Though Italians reputedly do it all the time, expatriates should consider the implications of doing it themselves and getting caught – being put in an Italian prison, deportation, the financial burden of playing catch-up with the tax authorities. It has been estimated by the tax inspectors' organization, *Il Servizio Centrale degli Ispettori Tributari*, that 83% of the self-employed category declare an annual income of less than £4,000. The reason such modesty does not attract the attention of the *Guardia di Finanza*, a.k.a. *i Finanzieri*, the tax police) is that they are often in on the fraud at the highest levels. It is probably a mark of their schizophrenia that from time to time, *i Finanzieri* feel obliged to indulge in advertising campaigns to remind the public and themselves that they are there to root out the culprits, and not to co-operate with them. However, despite the enormity of the problem facing them, the Finance Ministry has been making some attempt to catch tax evaders, especially as far as high income earners are concerned. The *i Finanzieri* have proved more effective than might have been expected in pursuit of offenders. Foreigners become taxable as residents if they are working in Italy for 183 days or longer and technically all their worldwide income is taxable.

Deciding to pay one's taxes gives rise to its own set of problems, particularly if one is in business or self-employed, as the system is constantly being amended. Unfortunately, new taxes are often brought in without the old ones being cancelled. This induces a permanent state of chaos in the tax system so that it is extremely difficult to ascertain which taxes one is actually liable for. However, it is undoubtedly better to pay some taxes rather than none at all. It is probably unwise to proceed without the services of an accountant (*commercialista*) preferably obtained through personal recommendation.

To combat tax evasion that the authorities decide to investigate, but that they can not actually prove, they have devised a cunning, if arbitrary, scheme for assessment based on perceivable assets. For instance, yachts, expensive cars, estates and household staff are all deemed to represent, according to their size and quantity, a specific amount of income. Since Italians are born showoffs, there is little chance that they will resort to driving around in battered Lancia's in order to conceal their assets and lower the likelihood of being hit with a perceived wealth tax bill

There are other peculiarities regarding the Italian tax system: unlike Britain where the tax office will chase you to fill in a tax form, in Italy it is up to the individual to present him or herself at the *Intendenza di Finanza* (local tax office) to fill in a standard tax form (known as a '740') and be given a *codice fiscale* (tax number). A *codice fiscale* is needed in order to work, and for various transactions such as property and car purchase, rentals and bill payments.

Owing to the fact that Italian personal taxation rates can be very high at the higher levels it is advisable not to have all one's assets in Italy if one can avoid it. The alternatives, as already mentioned, are to maintain offshore accounts or investments in such places as Luxembourg. Owing to the complexity of taxation it is strongly recommended that you take independent, expert financial advice before moving to Italy as well as after arrival. A list of such advisors in the UK can be obtained from the Financial Services Authority (25 The North Colonnade, Canary Wharf, London E14 5HS;   ☎020-7676 1000; www.fsa.gov.uk).

You will almost certainly need to consult a *commercialista* to work out how the new tax regulations apply to your particular circumstances.

In addition to IRAP there is an additional regional tax to allow for the portion of IRAP, which the regions need to replace the taxes such as ICIAP which have been abolished. The regions themselves decide the amount of additional local tax that needs to be levied as a subsection of IRAP.

The estimated amount of both income and business taxes are payable in two tranches in May and November. There are big fines for non-payment and under estimation of the amount due. Late payment is also penalised with fines.

Further information and advice can be obtained from:

British Chamber of Commerce in Italy: www.britchamitaly.com.

American Chamber of Commerce in Italy: www.amcham.it.

Penta Consulting, Business & Fiscal Advisor Firm; tax-law-firm@geocities.com; www.geocities.com/WallStreet/4019/.

Invest in Italy, Investor Advisor; http://investinitaly.com.

Studio di Consulenza Aziendale, Accountant, Largo Augusto, 3 – 20122 Milano, Italy; ☎02 796141; fax 02 796142; info@cosver.com; www.scaonline.it.

EXPATS AND HOME COUNTRY TAX

UK *Citizens and Residents*

UK CITIZENS AND EXPAT RESIDENTS who leave part way through the tax year (the UK tax year runs from April 5 to April 4) may be able to reclaim part of the tax already paid. For salaried employees UK taxes are deducted at source and the estimated amount of tax payable on a full year's income is deducted in equal amounts from each salary payment throughout the year. Departure part way through the year means that a larger percentage of the earned income is deductible and therefore less tax is due. Application forms for a tax refund are available from tax offices and should be returned to the office responsible for your tax file. Declaring non-residency status can also reduce, or eliminate, tax liability on rental income from property and interest on savings in the UK.

Specialist expat tax advice firms can provide individual advice, particularly useful high-income expatriates and those with property and savings in the UK. These include the Fry Group, Crescent House, Crescent Road, Worthing, West Sussex BN11 1RN (☎01903-231545; fax 01903-200868; www.wtfry.co.uk. They also have offices in Hong Kong and Singapore.

US Expatriates

US citizens must file a tax return no matter where they live if they have any income whatsoever. US expatriates are liable for tax on income over US$80,000, though taxes paid in the country where they are resident can, in part, be offset against what Uncle Sam wants. There are penalties for not filing tax returns and late filing, just as there are for US residents. US embassies can provide tax forms for their citizens, though many expatriates utilise the services of specialist expatriate tax consultants, especially if they are high earners resident in countries that levy low tax rates (which does not include Italy). Yahoo! has a limited directory of expatriate accountancy firms athttp://dir.yahoo.com/Business_and_Economy/Shopping_and_Services/Financial_Services/Taxes/Expatriate/. Expatriate magazines and websites aimed at US expatriates also carry adverts for firms offering such services.

Canadian Expatriates

Canadians moving overseas for an extended period of time need to inform their tax authority that they will be non-resident. This means Canadians can avoid having to pay tax on income earned outside of Canada during their time abroad, among other benefits. Expert advice should be taken on how non-resident status affects investment regulations and other aspects of financial planning. Information and advice should be sought from specialists in expatriate financial advice, two such firms are listed below:

The Expatriate Group Inc., Suite 280, 926 5th Ane SW, Calgary, Alberta, Canada T2P ON7; ☎ 403 232 8561; fax 403 294 1222; expatriate@expat.ca; www.expat.ca.

Canadian Relocation and Expatriate Taxation and Resource Center, Braemar Place, Suite 330, 1201 – 5th Street S.W., Calgary, Alberta, Canada T2R 0Y6, ☎403 531 2200; fax (403) 263 1826; www.expatax.com; peter@expatax.com.

The Yahoo! directory listed in the section for US expatriates above has a subsection for Canadian firms. Some US firms in the directory also offer services for Canadian expatriates through Canadian affiliate offices.

HEALTH CARE, INSURANCE AND HOSPITALS

IT WOULD PERHAPS BE A SALUTORY lesson for those who are accustomed to bash the British National Health Service to be sent for treatment in an Italian state hospital. They would be guaranteed never to complain again. In common with other systems under state control in Italy, the state medical system costs the government (i.e. the taxpayer) a fortune and is a disaster area to be avoided if at all possible.

Italy has a glut of doctors and produces more medics than any other European country. Some of these, however, are theoretical graduates who may never have seen a surgical procedure or even a corpse! Practical experience is usually gained by becoming the acolyte of a consultant (*primario*) and following the great man or woman on their ward rounds. Despite the erratic standard of Italian medical training, there are many excellent doctors, especially in private clinics. Italy has a clutch of world-renowned specialists including a Nobel prize winner (Daniel Bovet) and a singing heart surgeon with a string of hit records as well as medical successes under his gown (Enzo Jannacci). Simultaneously with some of the best doctors in Europe Italy possesses some of the most appalling hospitals, where treatment is irregular, care haphazard and facilities inadequate. Unsurprisingly, many Italian residents, both nationals and expatriates, take out private health insurance (see below) to cover themselves in case they need basic care, let alone long-term, expensive hospitalisation. Note that a list of local national health centres and hospitals is available from your local health authority (*Unita Sanitarie Locali*) in Italy; also most local embassies or consulates should be able to provide a list of English-speaking (private) doctors in your region.

When purchasing private healthcare it is essential to read the small print to ensure that the coverage is as complete as possible and covers all your possible future requirements – exclusions can be extensive. Paul Wolf of Innovative Benefits Solutions (www.ibencon.com) says, 'There are no bargains out there, you get what you pay for'.

The E111

It is essential that anyone resident or domiciled in the UK who intends to move permanently to Italy register their change of address with International Services, Inland Revenue National Insurance Contributions Office (Newcastle upon Tyne NE98 1ZZ: ☎0845-915 4811 from the UK or +44-191 225 4811 from overseas; fax 0845-915 7800 inside the UK or +44-191 225 7800 from overseas) before leaving the country. They will then be sent the paperwork required to obtain an E111 (allow one month for processing), which entitles all EU nationals whether they are tourists or working abroad to medical treatment by the national health service in any EU/EEA member country. Details are available on the Inland Revenue Website www.inlandrevenue.gov.uk/nic/intserv/osc.htm. The E111 is valid for twelve months, and is renewable on the proviso that the applicant still makes their UK National Insurance contributions.

Although the E111 covers emergency hospital treatment while abroad it does not include the cost for prescribed medicines, specialist examinations, X-rays, laboratory tests and physiotherapy or dental treatment. Consequently, private insurance should still be taken out for the required period, as this will provide financial protection against medical treatment costs which are not regarded as emergencies and which are not covered by the E111.

Leaflet SA29 which gives details of social security, health care and pension rights within the EU is also available from the International Services (see above) and is useful reading for anyone intending to live and work in Italy. Students studying abroad should, however, be aware that they need an E128, not an E111, to cover them. An E128 can be obtained in the same way as an E111.

For those who are not moving to Italy full-time, an E111 can be obtained from the Post Office. E111 forms issued by European countries other than the UK expire after one year and this can lead to problems having an UK E111 accepted around Europe if it has been issued more than 12 months previously. To avoid this potential problem replacements can be issued by the International Services office listed above.

UK National Insurance Contributions

If you start paying into the Italian social security system you become eligible for their benefits. However, if you are planning to return the UK it is advisable to keep up your UK contributions in if you want to retain your entitlement to a UK state pension and other benefits. Class 1 contributions are for those in full-time employment with a British-based employer, but there are alternatives if your employer is not paying: class 2 (self-employed) and class 3 (voluntary) contributions. Many UK tax advisors advise that you should pay UK NICs if you possibly can for future benefits available. Further details from your local DSS office, though the DSS website (www.dss.gov.uk) also contains useful information and contact details for those looking for official advice and information. Financial consultants such as KPMG (020-7311 1000; 8 Salisbury Square, London EC4; www.kpmg.co.uk) can advise expatriate employees.

Using the Health Service

Anyone who makes social security payments in the EU, who receives an EU state pension, is unemployed, or under the age of 18 is entitled to the dubious benefits of medical treatment on the Italian state health service free of charge. These include free hospital accommodation and medical treatment and up to 90% of the cost of prescription medicines; a contribution (*il ticket*) of 10% is required from the patient. Social security payments, which account for approximately 8% of a worker's gross income, are deducted from the employee's gross salary by the employer.

Foreigners working for foreign firms will almost certainly be insured for treatment under a private medical scheme and thus will be spared the trauma of public health care in an Italian hospital (*ospedale*). If you are not insured by your employer the cost of purchasing your own private coverage can be well worth it if you ever need hospital treatment. The numerous private hospitals in Italy are often run by the church and being both hygienic and efficient prove a pleasant contrast to the state-run hospitals.

Any foreigner who has become a resident and who wishes to receive treatment under the Italian state system is obliged to register with and obtain a national health number from the local *Unita Sanitaria Locale* (USL). You will need to produce your *permesso di soggiorno* and a letter from your employer which states that you are working for him or her. Self-employed or freelance workers should first register with the INPS in Piazza Augusto Imperatore 32, Rome, where they will be given the necessary documentation to take to the local USL office together with their *permesso di soggiorno*. USL addresses can be found in the *Tuttocittà*, a supplement that comes with Italian telephone directories, or alternatively in the local newspaper. Once you are registered with the *Unita Sanitaria Locale*, the next step is to register with *un medico mutualistico* (general practitioner). The system of free treatment is known as *il mutuo*. Outpatients are normally treated at a *studio medico* or *ambulatorio* (surgery). A private clinic is *una clinica private*.

If you are unlucky enough to find yourself in an Italian state hospital it is essential that your relatives know where you are and that someone visits you regularly to provide you with a regular intake of food. Italian hospitals are notorious for providing inedible food, or none at all. In the latter case the cause is almost certain to be because the kitchen staff have sold off the ingredients or are on strike. However, the food is the least of the patient's worries: only 25% of urgent cases get a hospital bed within a month of diagnosis and 700,000 patients contract further infections in hospital owing to the appalling standards of hygiene.

Some of the better hospitals are in Rome: the *Salvator Mundi,* the *Fatebenefratelli* (Via Cassia 600) and the Roman American Hospital. In Milan there is the *Ospedale Maggiore di Milano Policlinico* (via Francesco Sforza 32). Local advice should always be taken from other expats as certain doctors and hospitals will be better set up to meet the needs of expatriates.

Emergencies

If you are involved in or at the site of a serious accident then get to the nearest phone box and dial 113, which will put you through to the emergency services; ask for an *ambulanza* (ambulance). Less serious injuries should be treated at the casualty (*Pronto Soccorso*) ward at the nearest hospital. Alternatively, most major railway stations and airports have first-aid stations with qualified doctors on hand – many of these first aid stations are reputed to be more effective than the hospitals.

In the event of minor ailments, aches and pains it may well be worth avoiding the chaos of the state hospitals and applying directly to your local chemist (*farmacia*). Chemists are generally extremely well qualified in Italy, and will probably be able to prescribe something for you. The *farmacia* are usually open all night in larger towns and cities and if the one you end up at is closed, there should be a list displayed on the door that lists which chemists in the area are open that night.

Sickness and Invalidity Benefit

Any EU citizen who is moving to Italy permanently and who claims sickness or invalidity benefit in their home country is entitled to continue claiming this benefit once in Italy. Strictly speaking, to claim either benefit, you must be physically incapable of all work, however, the interpretation of the words 'physically incapable' is frequently stretched just a little beyond literal truth. If the claimant has been paying National Insurance contributions in the UK for two tax years (this may be less depending on his or her level of income) then he or she is eligible to claim weekly sickness benefit. After receiving sickness benefit for 28 weeks, you are entitled to invalidity benefit.

Anyone currently receiving either form of benefit should inform their local branch of the DSS that they are moving to Italy. They will then send your forms to the Overseas Branch of the DSS who will ensure that a monthly sterling cheque is sent either to your new address or direct to your bank account. The only conditions involved are that all claimants submit themselves to a medical examination, either in Italy or the UK, on request.

Italian sickness benefit for workers (*operai*) and salaried staff (*impiegati*) in commerce and industry is paid partly by the employer and partly by the state national sickness fund (INPS). Salaried staff get 100 per cent of their salary (at the employer's cost) for up to six months. For manual workers the amount is dependent on their labour contract and the length of service

Private Medical Insurance

In contrast with the lack of organisation in the public sector, the private sector of the health service is amazingly well organised. However, it is also expensive; charges at private hospitals and clinics are a minimum of £150 (US$210) per day for a room, so private health insurance is a must. If you currently hold a private health insurance policy for the country in which you are currently resident, you may find that the company will switch this for European cover once you are in Italy. However, with the increase in insurance companies offering this type of cover, it is worth shopping around to find the best cover for you and your family. If you have not organised insurance cover before leaving home you can organise it from Italy just as easily. Of course, if you are employed in Italy, you and your family may be able to join (or be provided with) a health insurance scheme (*il mutuo*) through your employer, which tops up the state health service.

Private health insurance can be arranged through organisations such as BUPA, PPP or Expacare, all of which offer international health insurance schemes. The cost, coverage and conditions of private health schemes vary enormously and the small print should be checked carefully. The annual premiums on the policies will vary according to age group of the insured and some will include dependent children at reduced rates, or even for free (though their premiums may be higher to start with).

ExpaCare – high-quality health insurance cover, for individuals or families living abroad. To find out more...

The policies can offer a full refund for medical treatment undertaken in hospital up to pre-set limit. Some also provide cover for out-patient treatment, and visits to a general practitioner and the dentist, also with pre-set limits. The premiums can be paid monthly, quarterly or annually by direct debit, credit card or cheque – though it should always be borne in mind than failure to make a stage payment invalidates the coverage. Optional extras that can significantly add to the cost of coverage, include:

- Nursing at home
- Pregnancy and childbirth (natural and caesarian).

- Stress counselling.
- Disability compensation
- Cover during travel outside of the country where you live.
- Emergency evacuation and repatriation.

Self-employed expatriates are liable to INPS contributions as a percentage of their annual taxable income. However, if you wish to join the Italian National Health scheme, you are required to pay 7½% of your taxable income, quite apart from what it may cost to keep your non-Italian pension rights going. It is very doubtful if the benefits achieved by such a contribution in Italy outweigh the disadvantages of possible unnecessary involvement in the Italian tax system and the answer is almost certainly recourse to a private health insurance policy, some of which will even pay GP and dental charges.

The Italian for first aid is *pronto soccorso*.

Useful Addresses

BUPA *(British United Provident Association)*: 15 Bloomsbury Way, London WC1A 2BA; ☎020-7656 2000; fax 020-7656 2728. Aimed mostly at UK nationals.

BUPA *International:* www.bupa-international.com for non-UK Europeans and north Americans living and working around the world.

Expacare: email info@expacare.net or visit www.expacare.net. Specialists in expatriate healthcare offering high quality health insurance cover for individuals and their families, including group cover for five or more employees. Cover is available for expatriates of all nationalities worldwide

Innovative Benefits Consultants Ltd.: 40 Homer Street, London W1H 1HL, UK; tel/fax 0870-737 9000 ext 6129 (Paul Wolf). In New York (212 328 3030 ext 5854; info@ibencon.com; www.ibencon.com.

Private Patients Plan:: PPP Healthcare Group plc, Vale Road, Tunbridge Wells Kent TN1 2PL; ☎01892-512345).

United Healthcare: BUPA partner providing services for North Americans.

Worldwide Travel Insurance: ASA Inc. USA; ☎1-602 968 0440.

SOCIAL SECURITY AND UNEMPLOYMENT

Social Security

T HE ITALIAN STATE SOCIAL SECURITY SYSTEM, (*lo stato assistenziale*), is generally regarded as being disastrously inadequate and wasteful. There were massive cutbacks in the system in order to meet the strict rules for being part as the Euro. However, as in many European countries there are serious reservations among the Italian populace about cutting back too much of the social welfare system – one of the more popular of the Berlusconi election pledges was his promise to increase the minimum level of pension payments. The

Italian system provides an array of old age and disability pensions, sickness and unemployment benefits and health and medical services. However, these services are lacking in facilities, finances, are sometimes corrupt, always ridden with bureaucracy and mostly inefficient.

If you have a regular job with an Italian firm you will be paying INPS contributions, the equivalent of National Insurance in the UK. The rate of contribution is on average about 50%, of which around 9% is paid by the worker.

For UK citizens it is possible to keep up National Insurance contributions (the equivalent of Italian social security) in the UK on a voluntary basis after moving to Italy. This can be quite a canny move for anyone who is not working, but who hasn't yet reached retirement age, as you will be eligible to claim a UK pension from the age of 60 (for women) or 65 (for men) throughout your time in Italy. However, continuing UK National Insurance contributions will be unnecessary for those who intend to work in Italy as EU regulations ensure that social security contributions made in one member state are counted as a contribution period in the contributor's own country's social security system for the purpose of determining their future benefits from that system.

Unemployment Benefit

Considering Italy's inclusion in the group of the world's seven most industrialised nations, the country has a high unemployment rate. The unemployment figures peaked at 14.2% in 1985 and now stand at around 9%. Unsurprisingly, unemployment is worst in the poor *Mezzogiorno* which, although only comprising a total of 36% of the Italian population, accounts for 52% of the total number of unemployed. On the other hand, unemployment is less than half the national average in the prosperous north. However, Italy's thriving black economy (which contributes, by some estimates, up to 25% of GNP) provides thousands of jobs for those officially out of work and undermines the representational value of these statistics. Moreover, many of Italy's unemployed refuse to do certain jobs, such as street sweeping, washing dishes, making pizzas; leaving such menial chores to the millions of illegal immigrants who scrape a living off the country's black economy. Others indulge in the notorious Italian practice of taking second or third jobs (*il secondo/terzo laboro*), which is a frequently-used means of topping up the often low incomes (as compared to other European countries), which exist in Italy. The second and third jobs will often be cash in hand and therefore not taxed.

Any worker who registers as being unemployed within 45 days of losing their job is entitled to unemployment benefit (*sussidio di disoccupazione*), administered by the provincial unemployment office, the *Ufficio di Collocamento*. Family allowances (*assegni familiari*) also exist which cover offspring up to the age of 26 who are still in full-time education.

For any EU national who is unemployed and contemplating a tentative work-finding trip to Italy, unemployment benefit can be transferred to Italy for thirteen weeks while you look for employment there. Benefits can be claimed at the UK rate throughout this period. This arrangement only exists in the European Economic Area that is made up of the EU plus Iceland, Liechtenstein and Norway.

If you are British and thinking of going to Italy to look for work, it is worth knowing that you can continue to receive UK unemployment benefit at UK rates for three months in Italy. This is only applicable if you have already been unemployed for a month in the UK. It is essential to apply as soon as you can, as entitlement to transfer benefit expires within three months of becoming unemployed. You will need to have paid full Class 1 contributions during the two tax years previous to the one you are claiming in. You should contact your usual benefit office who will in turn contact the International Services branch of the Inland Revenue (see under *The E111* above for address). They will issue a form E303, the document which is needed to claim benefit in another EU country. In order to receive the medical care you are entitled to under Italian regulations for unemployed people you should also ask for the form E119 at the same time. For general information about benefits and social security in EU countries, ask for forms SA29 and JSAL22, either from your Jobcentre or from the Pensions and Overseas Benefits Directorate, Department for Work and Pensions, Tyneview Park, Whitley Rd., Benton, Newcastle-upon-Tyne NE98 1BA.

LOCAL GOVERNMENT

RUNNING PARALLEL TO CENTRAL GOVERNMENT in Italy are three tiers of local government listed in order of ascending importance: *il comune* (the town council), *la provincia* (province) and the twenty *regioni* (regions); the latter comprising the country's largest administrative units. Of the twenty regions, only five have evolved any kind of semi-autonomous powers; Sicily, Sardinia, Trentino-Alto Adige, Friuli-Venezia-Giulia and Valle d'Aosta. The devolution of power in these regions was necessitated by both geographical and ethnic history.

For example, Trentino-Alto Adige was only annexed to Italy after World War I and has a strong German-speaking contingent with pro-Austrian sympathies. It remains an uncomfortable Italian annexe with a strong move towards political and administrative independence, mirroring to some extent the long-lived dissension between Northern Ireland and the UK. The five regions are known as *regioni a statuo speciale* and they differ from the other fifteen regions in that their assemblies resemble mini-parliaments which enjoy varying economic and administrative powers – simmilar to the Scottish Parliament and Welsh Assembly in the UK and Federal Parliaments in Germany and Switzerland.

Sicily is the only region of the five that has total control over its own education system, although legislation passed in 1970 provides, theoretically, for limited powers of autonomy in the assemblies of the remaining fifteen regions. In practice, however, central government remains very much the dominant force in these areas. Additionally, legislation as recent as 1989 created boroughs in the five main cities of Italy, Milan, Naples, Tome, Genoa and Turin that have a great deal of power over local spending and which are entitled to levy their own taxes.

Each of Italy's 94 provinces has a two-letter sign which forms part of the post-code and is also evident on official documents like driving licences and identity cards. The bureaucratic function of the provinces is obscure, since the other two tiers of local government duplicate almost everything they do. A good deal of their budget goes into sponsoring often costly cultural and other prestige projects, which are thought to further their reputation and tourist potential. Finally, the *communes*, elected once every five years (as are all other tiers of government), deal with all matters of local administration – local taxes, administration of social security services, housing, roads and transport etc. The *communes* are headed by the *sindaco* (mayor) who is assisted by *gli assessori* (the councillors).

CRIME AND THE POLICE

Crime

MOST EUROPEAN COUNTRIES have experienced a high increase in crime over the last two decades, and Italy is no exception. However, whereas in Britain the increase has been in theft and malicious offences against property, particularly cars, in Italy nearly three-quarters of all crime is drug-related. The three areas with the highest crime rates are *Latium,* the *Marche* and *Campania*. The last two in particular have shown a spectacularly rising crime rate based on the statistics for reported crimes of theft and robbery in recent years.

Organised violent crime in Italy is infamous and needs little elaboration here. There are Mafia black spots where murder is a regular occurrence and vicious kidnappings where the perpetrators have the charming custom of sending the odd ear or finger of the victim to the family as an *aide-mémoire* to pay the ransom are not uncommon, but most expatriates will never knowingly come face to face with Mafia crimes. In fact, although kidnapping regularly occurs, predominantly in Calabria or Sardina, instances have fallen to a handful a year (in the 60s and 70s, it was up to sixty a year). A law forbids victims' families to mediate privately with kidnappers and allows magistrates to freeze the family's assets in order, it is argued, to discourage kidnapping. However, the state is allowed to intervene and has discretion to pay the ransom, which seems rather to negate the law's deterrent value – other than saving the finances of the victim's family.

Apart from Mafia violence, which is on the increase in well-recognised areas, there is less violent crime, i.e. muggings and street violence in general, than in many other Western countries. This may be connected to the fact that drunkenness, which proves a spur to much crime in the UK, is very rare in Italy. Indeed the Italians look with consternation upon the hooliganism of drink-inflamed British football supporters. Also little-known in Italy are the type of crazed gunmen found in North America, who blast away a few dozen complete strangers in an orgy of gunfire. Private arsenals, except for hunting rifles, are a rarity (except of course amongst the Mafia). Until recently, serial killings and crimes against children were a rarity in Italy, but sadly these types of crime are on the increase – or they are being reported more frequently as in other countries.

A new crime wave that has erupted in the last few years is connected with the influx of refugees and immigrants from Albania – the Albanian Mafia are reputed to be more ruthless than the indigenous groups. Milan has the dubious reputation of being the capital of the Albanian Mafia. According to local police chiefs the Albanian criminal element is much more aggressive and ruthless than other foreign criminals and they are simply murdering the Italian, African and Arab competition out of the way.

The Police

It is unfortunately the case in Italy that the police have a dismal record in beating crime – around three-quarters of all crimes committed in Italy go unsolved. This is mainly because the bulk of crime occurs in the far south and Sicily – in other words Mafia territory. Italy has four main, separate police forces, for historical reasons. Liaison between the forces is extremely bad with the result that when representatives of two different ones are called out to the same incident, unseemly scuffles are liable to break out amongst the policemen from the different forces! Owing to the singular ineffectiveness of the police in combating organised crime in cities such as Naples and Reggio Calabria, the provision of private security forces has become a booming industry. Often bizarrely uniformed, the private security men are nevertheless a more effective deterrent against underworld-inspired violence than the regular police are. The official police forces are:

I Carabinieri: The military-associated *carabinieri* are the largest force, numbering nearly 86,000. They have been striving in recent years to shake off their thick image, and they are generally more personable and helpful than the other forces. *Carabinieri* are recognisable by their dark blue uniforms (designed by Giorgio Armani) with red stripe and matching peaked cap. Accessories include white belts with matching cartridge holder and holster. They may also carry machine guns (e.g. when looking for kidnappers in the Calabrian Mountains). *Carabinieri* squad cars are also dark blue, but with a white stripe. Their dress uniform features an ostrich-feather decorated bicorn hat, white gloves, sword and cloak. *Caribinieri* police stations are known as *la Caserna* or *il Comando*. The *Carabinieri* are responsible for stopping motorists in contravention of traffic regulations and administering on-the-spot fines.

La Polizia: There are around three thousand fewer *Polizia* than *Carabinieri*, and around 5% of the force is comprised of women. Their uniforms are lighter blue than the *Carabinieri* and have a deep pink stripe. The riot squad section *La Celere* who wear green uniforms are not as high profile as they were during the seventies, and are often found guarding important buildings. *La Polizia* have a reputation for uncouthness and being rather trigger happy. Their plain-clothes section is often mistaken for armed robbers. A *Polizia* station is *la Questura* and *Polizia* chiefs are *questori*.

La Guardia di Finanza/I Finanzieri: These are the customs police who can trace their origins back to the eighteenth century. Their force level is half that of the *Carabinieri*. They wear light grey uniforms and dark green berets with a yellow badge. Their poor reputation reached its trough when their former head, Generale Raffaele Giudice, was jailed for corruption on a multi-billion dollar scale, but has marginally improved since. When leaving an Italian bar or restaurant it is obligatory to carry your till receipts for 100 metres after leaving the premises in case *i Finanzeri* wish to inspect it, as a check on whether restaurant owners are fiddling their VAT.

I Vigili Urbani: These are the local police forces. They are normally dressed in navy blue, with white jackets and a matching helmet. Of all Italian police they are the least professional. Like the *Carabinieri*, they can stop and fine motorists. They are responsible for checking residence permits, investigating planning infringements and other local matters. In Rome their on-going feud with the *Polizia* provides regular street entertainment for local citizens.

It is generally agreed that the *Carabinieri* are the preferred force if one needs to call out the police. Their emergency number is 113. Theft being one of the most common crimes in Italy, the chances are that sooner or later you will require the police to make out a stolen goods report (*la denuncia*). It is equally likely that they will be unwilling to do this, which can be very frustrating if you need a *denuncia* for insurance purposes. It is best to go to a *Comando dei Carabinieri,* or *Questura*, in person to exercise your powers of persuasion.

If you are unfortunate enough to be accosted by any type of police, be warned that they expect you to be awe-struck. If you show any signs of unwillingness to co-operate, they may arrest you on a charge of insulting a state official. Under Italian law the police have powers to detain you for twenty-four hours without informing a magistrate. You may also be interrogated without a lawyer being present. Owing to the congestion and inefficiency of the Italian judicial system it is legally possible to be held in police custody for up to three years before being brought to trial.

RELIGION

A S THE HOME OF THE HISTORIC administrative centre (the Vatican), as well as the focal point of world Catholicism, Italy has a unique religious heritage that has permeated almost every aspect of Italian culture. Although the Vatican ceased to be a political power in the eighteenth century, its spiritual influence, backed up by the Papal road show, is still capable of producing profound awe amongst the Catholic populations of underdeveloped countries worldwide. The Vatican is also a member of the United Nations which belies its claim to have no interest in politics. In Italy itself, however, there exist extreme attitudes of both devotion and profanity to *Cattolicesimo* (Catholicism). The traditional areas of fervour are the poor regions of the south and the area around Venice, while from Emilia Romagna to Umbria has a reputation for sacerdotal antipathy; there is even a pasta named *strangolapreti* (priest-stranglers).

The Vatican has often caused controversy in Italy by not limiting itself to religious pronouncements, which has not done its reputation much good. For instance it had a long-running feud with the Italian government on the basis that it regarded parliament as ideologically unsound and all its members were therefore ineligible for Communion. This state of affairs was finally remedied by the Lateran pact of 1929 that secularised the Italian state. The Vatican showed equal implacability towards members of the former Italian Communist Party and anyone of that persuasion was excommunicated, despite the fact that many of them were fervent Catholics. During the liberal seventies, the Catholic church came in for some sacrilegious lampooning, the most notorious example of which is probably the scene in Frederico Fellini's film *Roma*, in which flashing fairy lights are incorporated in the sacred vestments during a glitzy clerical fashion parade.

In contemporary times, the present Pope, one of the few non-Italian popes, has caused concern for his conservative views on current issues of concern and many people believe this conservatism will have devastating effects on some countries. For instance, the Papal commendation of large families while on visits to the faithful in Africa shows his blinkered disregard for what is probably the main problem facing that continent, namely an ecological crisis exacerbated by poverty often caused by overpopulation. Meanwhile, back on home ground, Italian Catholics have reacted to papal dictums with common sense. Despite a religious ban on 'non-natural' birth control and abortion on demand, Italy has one of the lowest birth-rates in the world, whilst also having one of the most prosperous condom industries.

Away from the developed areas of Italy, religion moves in mysterious ways. Although generally more devout than their metropolitan countrymen, the country people mingle Catholicism with older beliefs inherited from pagan times.

English Speaking Churches and Services

Aviano: US Air Force Base Chapel; ☎04 1520 0571.

Bologna: ☎081 411 842.

St Mark's Church: Via Maggio 18, 50125 Florence; ☎055-294764. Reverend Richard Major. Founded in 1877 and considered a minor masterpiece of the Pre-Raphaelite movement. Located on the ground floor of the 15th century Palazzo Machiavelli at the above address on the south bank of the Arno. Sunday mornings 9 am Said Eucharist (also Thurs. 6pm & Fri 8pm). Sunday 10.30am Sung Eucharist followed by drinks in the ballroom of the Palazzo Machiavelli is a good way to meet people and if necessary network for jobs. The notice-board in the church foyer is 'full of job and house offers for anglophones'.

Città della Pieve (near Perugia): Anglican worship is offered in the Palazzo Crinelli in Città della Pieve, in the Umbrian hills every Sunday: for details contact Peter Hurd (0578) 29 92 60.

American Church of the Anglican Communion in Florence; fax 055-294417.

Church of the Holy Ghost: Piazza Marsala, 16122 Genoa; ☎010-3291383.

All Saints' Church, Via Solferino 17, 20121 Milan; ☎02-655 2258.

Methodist Church (Evangelica Metodista): Via Porro Lambertenghi 38, Milan; ☎02-6072631. Pastor Paul Perry, English-speaking service.

Christ Church: Via S. Pasquala a Chaiai 15b, 80121 Naples; ☎081-411842. Also serves Bari, Capri and Sorrento.

Church of the Holy Cross: Via Mariano Stabile, 90139 Palermo; ☎091-585220.

At University Church: Perugia; ☎055 294 764.

Anglican Church of All Saints: Via del Babuino 153, 00187 Rome; ☎06-36001881. Reverend Peter Marchant.

St Andrews Church of Scotland: Via XX Settembre 7, 00187 Rome; ☎06-4827627. Reverend John Ross.
Roman Catholic Church: San Silvestro in Capite, Piazza San Silvestro, 00187 Rome; ☎06-6785609. Father Larry Gould.
Methodist Church: Via Banco di San Spirito 3, 00186 Rome; ☎06-6868314.
St Peter's Siena: Anglican. Small Victo

SOCIAL LIFE

BUSINESS AND SOCIAL LIFE are so intertwined in Italy that anyone who is considering living and working there will almost certainly have to socialise with Italians. The first indispensable step in finding a social life that encompasses expatriates and host nationals is to acquire a knowledge of the Italian language (see Chapter Four, *Daily Life*, The Italian Language). Without a good grasp of Italian an expatriate will miss much of the exciting and pleasurable aspects of living in foreign country and almost certainly not be as happy as they could be.

Every country's population has its idiosyncracies and expatriates in Italy will undoubtedly find the Italian social mores annoying, entertaining, frustrating, enjoyable and entirely incomprehensible by turns. Italians will also find your idiosyncracies equally perplexing. Learning the language will go a long way towards helping an expatriate through the maze of Italian social etiquette and also allow them to apologise for their latest faux pas.

The Italians

Stereotyping a nationality always leads to problems, as few countries are homogenous enough for any general statements to apply to more than a limited number of its citizens. In the case of Italians, who are an incredibly varied group of people that lack even a well defined sense of their own nationality, few general statements can even be contemplated. There are, however, some traits that are recognisably Italian, for instance the importance of the family. Where the Italian family differs though is their closeness, which means that every Italian has a highly developed support system from birth. Not only will *mamma e papa* indulge their children's every whim and support them financially *ad infinitum* if possible, but a network of relatives will aid and abet their progress in life. This type of string pulling was practically invented, in Europe, by the Italians whose word for nephew is *nipote*, hence nepotism. The closeness of the relationship between mothers and sons, *mammisimo*, is generally recognised as another typically Italian trait, whereby mothers do everything for their sons. More than half of all Italian men live at home with one or more parents until their mid-thirties. For foreigners, particularly women, becoming romantically involved with Italians usually means taking on an exhausting number of responsibilities across the family network; far more than one would expect from a similar relationship in the UK or North America.

Another manifestation of the Italian group-oriented social life is the urge to cluster, which is particularly noticeable amongst teenagers, *ragazzi*. This phenomenon is known as *stare insieme* (hanging out) and youngsters usually congregate on streets in groups with no discernible objective other than to operate as a mutual admiration society – rather than cause trouble as they seem to do in other countries.

Italians will often show warmth towards a new acquaintance, much like outgoing North Americans, but unlike northern Europeans with their traditional Anglo-Saxon reserve who wait until they know someone better before getting really enthusiastic towards them. This willingness to communicate on the part of Italians is a great help in breaking the ice on social occasions, particularly if you are feeling inhibited about speaking Italian. Being born gesticulators, Italians are very receptive to sign language, which is a gift to foreigners wishing to enhance their shaky Italian with hand gestures.

Other fairly uniform Italian traits are an obsession with personal appearance (*la bella figura*), which often leads them to dress beyond their means. Italians also pride themselves on their *xenofilia*, an approval of foreigners – though this is wearing thin with the recent influx of legal and illegal immigrants from Albania.

Manners and Customs

The Italian concept of individualism can appear to be incredibly selfish and anti-social to some non-Italians. Loyalty and consideration are reserved for the family or those of one's immediate, intimate circle. This contrasts with the northern European idea of having a responsibility to society at large. Thus litter-dropping in Italy is considerably less frowned upon than in the UK, Switzerland and Scandinavia, since to Italians it is always someone else's (usually the hated state's) problem. In matters of friendship, it is customary for Italians to go out in a group; one-to-one friendships along UK lines are not common.

Shaking hands is considered paramount at meetings and social occasions. Social kissing is also reasonably prevalent as in most Mediterranean countries, though the practicalities do vary from country to country. In Italy men and women kiss both their own, and the opposite sex on social occasions; two kisses, one on each cheek, not three as in Russia or France. If you do not feel comfortable with kissing then just shake hands – though holding back from a kiss can make you appear stand-offish and arrogant. On social occasions it is considered good manners to take presents. Generous to a fault themselves, Italians resent meanness in others, so expensive presents are called for, such as quality whisky or champagne, generous bouquets, handmade chocolates or other sweet delicacies.

In Britain it is common to go drinking with your friends, sometimes to the point of excess, as a way of letting off steam. North American attitudes towards alcohol are almost to the opposite extreme, lunchtime drinking and hard liquor often being frowned upon. Italians, however, enjoy social drinking but they regard drunkenness as totally unacceptable behaviour. Whilst you may see heroin addicts by the dozen shooting up in public in certain areas of the larger Italian cities, you almost never see a drunkard. Italians release pressure by shouting and gesticulating, which is probably healthier than bottling it up British fashion before indulging in a fit of temper or road rage and cheaper than going to therapy US-style.

Making Friends

Undoubtedly, one of the most rewarding aspects of living and working in a foreign country is meeting host country nationals, making local friends and forming long-lasting friendships. Making friends in a foreign country can be slower than at home, because cultural differences and the language problem can constitute formidable impediments – as can the attitude of foreigners to the locals. In Italy, as in most countries, taking the time to make host national friends can be well worthwhile, as, once their hearts are won, Italians can be loyal and generous friends. However, despite Italian enthusiasm on first acquaintance, it can take a long time before the Italian mask of formality drops and you are considered part of the family. As already mentioned in Chapter Four, there is a formal and an informal version of address, *lei* and *tu*. It should be noted that *lei* is considered even more formal than the French *vous,* and thus slipping into *tu* without being invited to can cause offence. Likewise *ciao* (hello/goodbye) should never be used with *lei,* use *buon giorno/buona sera* (good morning/afternoon) and *arrivederci/arrivederla* for goodbyes.

Despite the joys of having host national friends, most expatriates find it necessary to have friends of their own nationality. Being able to pass sarcastic comments, make jokes and generally let off steam without the fear of being misunderstood and causing offence is an important aspect of life abroad. A selective list of expatriate social clubs is included later in this chapter.

Homosexuality While the narcissistic habits of the Italian male may suggest otherwise, homosexuality in Italy keeps mainly in the closet. It is frowned upon, largely due to the oppression of the Catholic Church and the tradition of machismo in Italian society. The national left-wing gay and lesbian organisation, *Arcigay* (information on www.gay.it), based in Bologna, campaigns against hypocrisy (the Vatican staff includes several homosexual noblemen) and the persecution which is inflicted on Italian gays. In the south of Italy you risk being murdered by your own family or the Mafia if you are not heterosexual. Rome has one or two clubs where gays can meet. The only pink magazine is *Babilonia*. Information on gay life in Italy can be found on websites such as www.gay.it and www.gay.com.

Entertainment and Culture

As already mentioned, entertainment in Italy is always pursued as a group activity. The idea of eating out or going to a film alone would be strange to Italians, with their predominant group mentality. Single expatriates should therefore get into the habit of collecting telephone numbers so that when they fancy a night out they can ring round everyone on their list, however slight the acquaintance, to see who might be interested in going out. The alternative, if one goes out alone, is to be regarded as eccentric, or even an object of compassion.

Tourist offices are a possible source of information on entertainment and cultural events, as are the national newspapers *La Repubblica* and *Corriere della Sera,* both of which publish listings in their weekly magazines.

Italy has a *patrimonio culturale* (cultural heritage) second to none and many outsiders believe the Italian government could do more to conserve it. Like Greece and Turkey Italy has so much heritage lying around and there are so many unscrupulous collectors willing to buy it, it is almost impossible to protect it comprehensively. However, there is no doubting Italian pride in their Classical and Renaissance art and architecture. Italy does not lack exponents in the performing arts either, perhaps most notably in the field of opera, which had a heyday in the nineteenth century, thanks to amongst others, Verdi, Donizetti and Puccini. Likewise, the Italian cinematic tradition, together with the French, is universally accepted as one of the greatest – among modern Italian films worth seeking out are *Il Postino* and *Cinema Paradisio*.

In common with many other European countries, increasingly so the further south you go, culture in Italy has a general appeal. This contrasts with the elitist reputation of the arts for which Britain in particular is notorious. This may come as a pleasant surprise to foreign residents who can fall back on the arts, especially cinema, as a topic of conversation with Italians of all backgrounds.

Nightlife: Italian city nightlife may not compare with the bright lights of New York, Barcelona or London in terms of quantity, but the *ragazzi* can do their heads in at the huge discos, especially in Emilia, Turin and Milan, which are also some of the venues for rave parties. Elsewhere, as already mentioned the *ragazzi* make do with 'hanging out' in groups which is less effort than making the logistical arrangements necessary for any positive action. Italian teenagers are however, avid consumers of *il fast food*, which hit Italy in the form of American hamburger joints in the late eighties and early nineties, and which continues to blossom there at its usual rate. For other Italians, bars with outdoor tables are the main form of nightlife, not that the Italians are great drinkers (see above), but they enjoy the company and the gossip. For those who like music with their whisky, retro jazz and other live music clubs exist in most cities. Also popular are video bars showing non-stop rock videos.

Opera and Classical Music: Surprisingly, for a country so closely linked to opera, the season is short – running only from December to May. There are around a dozen important opera houses the best known of which are: *La Scala* (Milan), *Teatro dell'Opera* (Rome), *Teatro Communale* (Florence) and *San Carlo* (Naples). Venice's *La Fenice* was destroyed by fire in the eighties, and has yet to be restored. In addition, most provincial towns have an opera season showing productions of a varying standard from reasonable to good.

Despite a venerable musical tradition, there are few Italian musicians of international renown – apart from Pavarotti and the best symphony orchestras are usually attached to opera houses. Compared with other European countries including Britain and with the big orchestras in North America, the standards of other Italian orchestras are not high. However, Italy has produced three outstanding conductors in recent years: Riccardo Muti, Claudio Abbado and Carlo Maria Giulini.

Cinema: Italian cinema provides rich ground for the enthusiast. Over the years Italian audiences have become very discriminating and Italian films have a

THE ITALIAN NATIONAL ANTHEM

Most Italians consider the national anthem *Fratelli d'Italia*, (Brothers of Italy) archaic and uninspiring. It was written by the youthful patriot Goffredo Mameli who died while defending the Roman Republic in 1849 and its sentiments are somewhat romantic and high flown for these days. Although meant as an interim anthem it was never replaced. A recent contender as a replacement anthem is reported to be the'Chorus of the Hebrew Slaves' (*Va, pensiero, sull'ali dorate*) from Verdi's Nabucco.

reputation for being stylish and sophisticated. Unfortunately for the foreign resident whose Italian is not up to following dialogue, films from the English-speaking world are customarily dubbed into Italian. Cinema listings are given in every newspaper and cinema categories are *Prima Visione (*new release and smart cinema), *Seconda Visione* (older cinema and re-run films) and *Cinema d'Essai* (classical world cinema with original soundtrack). Some cities have *Cinema all'aperto* (open air movies) during the summer. The *Pasqunio* cinema (Vicolo del Piede 19, 00153 Rome) in Rome may be worth a visit for expats weary of long Italian-speaking days as it shows a good selection of films in English. Dedicated film freaks might like to take advantage of AIACE (Italian Cinema-goers' Association) membership, which entitles patrons to half-price tickets on weekdays (not Fridays). Details can be obtained from local cinemas.

Main Art and Arts Festivals. *Venice Film Festival:* The Venice Film Festival is held annually, during the first two weeks of September and is one of the big three, the others being Cannes and Berlin. It is however smaller, and therefore less commercially influential, than the other two. The Festival programme is available from the tourist office a few weeks in advance. Festival premieres are held in the *Palazzo del Cinema* and the *Astra* cinemas, and the public can queue for tickets on the day of the performance.
Venice Biennale: The Venice Biennale is a prestigious international exhibition of contemporary art first held in 1895. Now held in even-numbered years from June to September, it has a permanent site is the *Giardini Pubblici*, where exhibits from over forty countries are housed in separate pavilions.
Spoleto Festival dei Duo Mondi: The Spoleto Festival of the Two Worlds is Italy's main international festival of the performing arts including classical music and ballet, held in and around the walled mediaeval town of Spoleto (Umbria), during two months in summer. Further details from the Italian Tourist Office.
Panatenee Pompeiane: The Pompeii music festival is held in the dramatic surroundings of those famous ruins during the last week of August.
Verona Music Festival: One of the oldest Italian annual music and opera festivals, held in the spectacular surroundings of the Roman Arena di Verona from June to August. Further information from the Verona tourist offices: APT, Via Dietro Anfiteatro 6, and Piazza delle Erbe 42.

Sport

The concept of sports like squash and golf as fashionable recreation activity has yet to seize Italy with quite the same force as it has northern Europe and North America. This objection to after-work exertion is generally held to hearken back to Italy's peasant culture when backbreaking work left no spare energy for active pursuits. The exception to this is probably cycling, of Tour de France type, which is a popular recreation, especially in the north.

Football, which is played by virtually every man and boy, is almost as important as the Church and it is not uncommon for there to be lighting strikes when one of the big clubs or the national team is playing an important game during working hours. The introduction of football to Italy occurred at the turn of the last century, courtesy of British industrialists who imported factory sports clubs as part of their workers' welfare ethos. Sports generally were slow to evolve until Mussolini built many large stadia in the twenties and thirties, thus promoting a body cult whose inspiration came not so much from Classical Rome as from Nazi Germany. In 1960 Rome played host to the Olympic Games which led to the building of Nervi's Palazzo and Palazzeto dello Sport di Roma. However, as in the UK, Italy's would be champions are seriously hampered by a lack of adequate facilities and funding. Additionally, unlike Britain and North America, sports are not part of the school curriculum in Italy. Children who want to participate in sports will do so outside of the school system.

Though sports are not popular, the health and fitness boom of the 1980's has left its mark it Italy and tennis clubs and gymnasia have mushroomed. However, there is always the sneaking suspicion that the attraction of such places for Italians is that they provide a place to hang out and show off their designer sports gear and their toned bodies.

Cycling: The Italians, especially in the north, have taken to *il ciclismo* (cycling) in much the same way as the French. The Italian version of the *Tour de France* is the *Giro d'Italia*. The majority of the recreational *ciclisti* can be spotted at weekends, crouched over Bianchi or Campagnolo racing bikes in the Po Valley.

Football: To the foreigner Italian football *il calcio* is perhaps best known for its 1982 World Cup win and ability to buy the hottest foreign players for mind-boggling sums and then find they have feet of clay. Maradona livened up Napoli for a while before his cocaine habit led to his being sent back to Argentina, while Lazio (Rome) are probably regretting the day they ever signed up the auto-destructive talents of 'Gazza'. Most of the top league teams (known as *Serie A*) are in the north where big cities have two teams each: Turin has Juventus and Torino, Milan has Internazionale and AC Milan and Rome has Roma and Lazio. The fans (*i tifosi*) are noisy and boisterous but need only Latin blood not an alcohol transfusion to galvanise them.

Until 1996 Italian football clubs were non-profit organisations. Now that the Italian government has allowed them to raise profits which they desperately need to improve facilities, some have been doing so on the financial markets and others are doing so via the stock exchange. With huge profits to be made from football products and with

Italians keener than most to buy them, any club that believes it can make a profit (which many have not done previously) by converting to a business and then listing on the stock exchange is likely to do so at the earliest opportunity. A stipulation of the stock exchange, however, is that any company has to show three consecutive years of profit in order to qualify for stock market flotation.

Tickets for matches can be obtained from local stadia or team headquarters, well before the game and are standing (*in tribuna*), *non numerato* or *numerato*.

Motor Racing: After football, motor racing is Italy's second national sport – speed and Italians go together. Throughout motoring history the Italians have produced some of the world's most thoroughbred sports cars: Bugatti, Ferrari and Alfa Romea to name a few. Originally, only Italian aristocrats could afford such cars and the sport of motor racing. However, out of these illustrious beginnings such classic races as the *Mille Miglia* and the *Targa Florio*, which takes place in Sicily, were born. The best known Italian racing circuit is probably Monza, just outside Milan. San Marino is also host to a Grand Prix circuit too.

English-Language Clubs

At any age, socialising in a foreign country requires a certain amount of innovative thinking to locate people with similar interests who you can communicate with. Expats on a short term posting will find many clubs and societies aimed at them, whose members will be in a similar position to them – i.e. suffering from culture shock, struggling to learn Italian and trying to explore as much of Italy as is humanly possible in the few short years they will be living there. Such clubs can be great sources of information, friends and cultural sanctuary, where expats can meet and put into perspective the stresses and strains of expatriate life.

For retired people and other non-working expatriates, who are at liberty to follow their own interests, in their own time, whenever they like, few countries compare to Italy for the range of outdoor, historical and artistic related pursuits available. Despite there being plenty of options for activities and hobbies, the expatriate clubs as mentioned above and the associations of permanent foreign residents have grown up from a need among the foreigners to mix and socialise with people of their own nationality. The dream of rustic Italian life can be filled with olive groves, vineyards and beautiful Tuscan scenery populated by welcoming and friendly locals, but the reality can, on occasions, be frustrating, isolated and lonely. Those considering a permanent move to, or a retirement in Italy should seriously and realistically contemplate where and how they will socialise with both locals and other foreigners.

Whether you decide to revive a long-neglected passion for Scottish dancing, cultivate a dormant theatrical talent, learn to play bridge, or even if you simply wish to share some of your time and experiences with other expatriates over an espresso or a stronger beverage, then the list provided below should be a good starting point in your search for an English medium social life. Other social reference points include International Schools, Churches and Chambers of Commerce. These have been listed elsewhere in this book, or they are easily found through telephone directories and expatriate websites (www.expatexchange.com, www.expatnetwork.com, etc.). The Federation of American Women's Clubs Overseas has nine branches in Italy (see below for details). The British, Canadian, Australia and American embassies and consulates should be able to provide the address of the various expatriate clubs for their nationals in the area they cover. The organization *American Citizens Abroad*, (www.aca.ch; e-mail acage@aca.ch) has local affiliates in Rome, Sorrento, Palermo and Saramo.

Bari: *The International Women's Club of Bari*, Via Petrarca 2, I-70010 Adelfia; ☎08 04592672.Florence, Genoa, Milan, Palermo, Rome, Turin and Vercelli.

Bologna: *The International Women's Forum* for international women who speak English: www.iwfbologna.org.

Cagliari: *Associazione Italia Inghilterra:* Via Machiavelli 97, 09100 Cagliari, Sardinia; ☎070-402835; fax 070-402966.

Florence: *British Institute Library and Cultural Centre*, Palazzo Lanfredini, Lungarno Guicciardini 9, I-50125 Florence; 055 2677 8270; www.britishinstitute.it.

English Language Library of Florence, voiale redi 49, 50155 Florence; 055 8998089; www.ellf.it.

American International League of Florence, Casella Postale No 33, Via Fratelli Orsi, 50012 Bagno a Riploi; ailo@ailoflorence.org; www.ailoflorence.org.

Genoa: *New-comers' Club:* meets at the Hotel Astor ☎Via delle Palme 16, Nervi, Genoa).

American International Women's Club of Genoa, Via Ribloi 6/7, 16145 Genoa; ☎010 316 179; info@aiwcgenoa.fawco.org.

Italo-Britannica Centre for Cambridge Language Courses and Examinations. Also houses the British Library (13,000 books in English). Same address as the British Consulate (Piazza della Vittoria 15; (☎010-564833). The cultural centre also has other activities.

The Anglican Church: (Piazza Marsala, Genoa).

Milan: *Benvenuto Club for English-speaking ladies of any nationality:* Meet every second Tuesday of the month 10am-3pm at the Circolo A. Volta, Via Giusti 16, 20154 Milan; ☎025468719; benvenutopresident@yahoo.co.uk.

Naples: *American Women's Club of Naples,* ☎081 575 0040.

Palermo: *Americans Abroad Palermo*, Via Vaccarini 1, 90146 Palermo; ☎0348 510 4196.

Rome: *The American Women's Association*, c/o Savoy Hotel, via Ludivisi 15, I-00187 Rome; ☎06 4825268; fax 06 482 5268; www.awar.org.

The Commonwealth Club.: ☎06-58330919.

The Luncheon Club of Rome: ☎06-50913274.

Professional Women's Association: ☎06 20404613; www.pwa-milan.org.

Rome Labour Party: tel 06-6384227.

United Nations Women's Guild: ☎06-57056503.

Turin: *Esprit Club.* Contact Peter Allen (☎011-8111623).

American International Women's Club, refer to www.fawco.org for information.

Umbria: *English Speakers Club,* Harry and Margaret Urquhart, San Lorenzo di Rabatta 1M, 06070 Cenerate; ☎075 690693.

Varese: *Bienvenuto Club of Varese:,* ☎0332-949815.

Food & Drink

Many myths surround the Italians, and their eating habits are no less liable to exaggeration or misconception than other aspects of their lives. Admittedly, whether the pasta is cooked *al dente* (just right) *or una colla* (sticky and overcooked) is a subject treated with an almost religious reverence. However, despite the world-famous ice creams, pizzas and pasta dishes, the Italians boast one of the lowest incidences of heart disease in Europe (and consume less ice cream than most of their European neighbours). The basis of Italian eating tends towards quality, not quantity, and as with all matters of Italian life, is subject to the rigorous demands of *la bella figura* (cutting a fine figure). Just as the majority of Italians looks upon drunkenness as a disgusting and unnecessary foreign fetish, obesity is similarly unacceptable, unless accompanied by a corresponding amount of Pavarotti-like charisma.

Although every Italian region proclaims the excellence of its own cooking, the region of Emilia-Romagna is thought by some to boast the finest and richest of Italian cuisine. However, Tuscany is renowned for its high-quality meat and Genoa for its herb-based dishes while the food of the south is the most spicy. The three main meals of the Italian day are treated with varying degrees of importance. Breakfast, *(colazione)* is usually a frugal offering of croissant *(cornetto)* or biscuits *(biscotti)*; although cereals are gaining popularity in the Italian market. Lunch *(pranzo)* is treated as the main meal of the day in the southern regions although home-cooked food is increasingly being superseded by convenience food. Finally, dinner *(cena)*, as in the majority of Mediterranean countries, is eaten late in the evening, usually between 8pm and 10pm, especially during the summer months.

Traditional Italian restaurants are signalled by the *ristorante trattoria* or *pizzeria* signs. Sparse or unpretentious decor is common and does not reflect on the quality of the food or service. When eating out with Italians you should offer to split the bill *alla romana* – dividing it by the number of those present. However, if you have been invited out to dinner, your host or hostess will probably insist on paying the entire bill. As far as giving tips is concerned, service was traditionally added at the customer's discretion, usually at around 10%-15%. These days though, a 10% charge is generally included in the total bill, as is a cover charge per person. The easiest way to tell if service is included is by looking at the bill *(il conto)*, it will have *servizio* and *coperto* for service and cover charges respectively.

As mentioned above, the Italians are not great drinkers and being drunk *(ubriaco)* carries a special disapproval amongst the majority of Italians, which would be thought curious amongst the beer-swilling section of the British pub population. Though drinking wine from a young age is an accepted part of the culture, unlike in the USA. Alcohol sales have flagged in Italy, as mineral water *(acqua minerale)* sales escalate nationwide. Italy is now second only to France in annual consumption of mineral water and is ahead of Germany and Belgium. Another beverage that has taken off in Italy is beer. According to the Italian Statistics Institute, ISTAT, the majority of men and a significant percentage of women now choose beer above wine. This may be a result (or a cause) of the mushrooming of English-style pubs in the larger cites (there are scores in Rome alone). The new pubs appeal mainly to the twenty-something party crowd of cosmopolitan Europeans that can be found in most major commercial cities of Europe. In contrast to the increase in beer sales, the annual consumption of wine is dropping to such a level that the wine marketing board is now advertising it in order to encourage sales. If you prefer wine-bars then look for the signs *vineria* or *enoteca* above the door.

Thus, far from fulfilling the image of a nation of pasta-stuffing, wine-guzzling Pavarotti prototypes, the reality of the Italians' eating habits is far more discerning and infinitely more healthy. The Italians are now spending 10% less of their incomes each year on food than they did a decade ago, and while still providing a role model for every aspiring *buongustaio* (food and drink connoisseur), the national gastronomic motto seems to be, enjoy, but not to excess.

Wine. Most of Italy is wine country and there is no time to do justice to the many varieties here. Suffice it to say that some areas have gone in for professional production and export while others have kept their traditions and best wines a secret from the outside world. The northwest (Piemonte) is famous for its vermouths and spumantes and purplish wines and barolo and barbera grapes. The north-east, particularly the part under Austrian influence, has gone in for mass production. Probably the best known wines abroad are those from central Italy, especially the Chianti wines from the Tuscan hills between Florence and Siena. Southern Italy has the Neapolitan wines of Ischia, Capri and red and white wines from the area around Mount Vesuvius. Sicily's best-known wine is probably the sweet and treacly Marsala.

TABLE 10   WINE LABEL GLOSSARY

DOCG – *Denominazione di Origine Controllata Guarantita*: the highest quality, similar to France's *appellation contrôleé*.
DOC – *Denominazione di Origine Controllata*: the second highest quality.
DS – *Denominazione Semplice* – the equivalent of the French vin de table.
Messo in bottiglia del produttore all'origine/nel'origine: estate-bottled.
Classico: from the central, i.e. best area of the region.
Imbottigliato nello stabilimento della ditta: bottled on the premises of the firm.
Riserva: wine that has been aged for a statutory period.
Wine Colours: Bianco (white), Rosso (red), Rosato (pink), Chiaretto (very light red), *Nero* (very dark red).
Secco: dry.
Amaro: bitter or very dry.
Amabile/Abboccato: medium sweet.
dolce: very sweet.
Spumante: bubbly.
Frizzante: slightly fizzy.
Vin/Vino santo: sweet dessert wine made from dried grapes.
Stravecchio: very old, mellow.
Vino liquoroso: fortified wine.

SHOPPING

Non-food Shopping

NEXT TO TAX EVASION, the other favourite Italian pastime is shopping. Consumption, especially in luxury goods including *firmato* (designer) clothes, is more conspicuous in Italy than in most other European countries. As the old class distinctions have all but disappeared in Italian society (though they have been replaced by the new system based on wealth), everyone aspires to the same high standards. While some are certainly less able to afford designer goods than others, everyone has them. To fund their passion for expensive shopping, some Italians are prepared to go without decent housing and the best food, in order to dress the same as the *nuovi ricchi*. It is therefore difficult on a night out in Italy, to distinguish a car mechanic from a high-flying executive, as they are both likely to be wearing a Giorgio Armani suit and Gucci loafers. Italians have become addicted to a hedonistic lifestyle that leaves most other Europeans standing – apart from the Spanish who also like to party all night in best clothes they can afford. To sustain this exhausting pursuit of pleasure and *bella figura* (looking your best at all times) Italians take the line that nothing but the best will do and are constantly seeking out the newest fads and fashions.

Italy's preoccupation with fashion, not unexpectedly, means that much of their shopping revolves around clothes and accessories. Partly because of the natural flair of Italian designers and partly to meet the high expectations of the domestic Italian market, Italian suits, knitwear leather goods, jewellery, sunglasses, etc. are often considered the best in the world. The Italian brand names of Louis Vuitton, Bulgari and Rayban, among many others, now have an international reputation and cachet.

The Italian love affair with designer labels has rubbed off on other nations and helped to inspire a well-publicised boom in the production of counterfeit brand-name goods. Much of the pirate production goes on in the Far East, however, in Italy itself there are hundreds of Mafia-run sweatshops where illegal immigrants churn out fake goods. For instance, in December 1997 the *Guardia di Finanza* impounded a complete shoe factory at, Caserta in Campania, that was about to begin production of fake Timberland shoes. The foreign resident should therefore beware of improbable bargains – though if the quality is as good as the original the temptation to buy can be irresistible.

One way to have your cake and eat it, in this case have designer clothes but not pay the outrageous prices, is to buy from factory outlets. Expat groups and websites are good places to find out about the best places to shop, as is the website, www.made-in-italy.com, which is a good source of information about shopping in general as well as factory outlets.

Food Shopping

Unfortunately, the cost of living in Italy is one of the highest in Europe. Food prices especially can come as a nasty shock to foreign residents, since many of the items which enjoy an international reputation such as Parma ham and

TABLE 11	SHOPPING GLOSSARY
abbligliamenti	clothes
agenzia di viaggi	travel agency
calzoleria/calzatura	shoeshop/footwear
calzolaio	cobbler/shoe repairer
cartoleria	stationery/bookshop
confezione	clothes
drogheria	grocer
ferramenta	hardware
fioraio	florist
fornaio	baker
fotocopisteria/typografia	photocopying/printing
frutta e verdura/fruttivendolo/	fruit and vegetables/greengrocer
giocattoli	toys
gioielleria	jeweller
ipermercato	hypermarket
latteria	dairy
lavaggio a secco	dry cleaning
libreria	bookshop
macelleria	butcher
merceria	haberdashery
oreficeria	jeweller (lit. goldsmith)
orologiaio/orologeria	watchmaker/repairer
ottico	optician
panificio/panetteria/panettiere	breadshop/bakery/baker
pasticceria	cake/pastry shop
pastificio	fresh pasta
pelleteria	leather goods
pescheria/pescivendolo	fishmonger
rosticceria	shop selling cooked food to take away
salumeria	delicatessen
sarto/sarta	tailor/dress-maker
surgelati	frozen food
tintoria	dry cleaners

various cheeses are more expensive to buy in Italy than in Britain and the US. Supermarkets, although not ubiquitous as in the UK and North America, are on the increase. In Ferrara there are two large shopping centres outside of the city with grocery stores (*supermercato*) that have the best selection and prices for food items, they also carry household items like electrical appliances and clothes. Hypermarkets are even more scarce and represent only a small percentage of the Italian food market, compared with the vast majority of the market in the UK. Those living in the countryside of Tuscany and Umbria will have to plan their shopping trips to the nearest city carefully, as relying on the village shop for forgotten items can become very expensive.

Each city has one morning or afternoon a week when the shops close – in Ferrara for example, the shops close on Thursday afternoons. Many shops, though, are opening on Sunday afternoons and some do not close for lunch.

Small, family run businesses will also close for funerals and vacations and they will leave a note on their door to notify their customers about the length of the closure. Most businesses close for at least a couple of weeks summer vacation in August (in France a month in more common). All *Tabacchi* shops, which sell various items like stamps and prepaid phone cards in addition to cigarettes, remain open for lunch. There are fruit and vegetable shops in most neighbourhoods in the city where the shopkeeper will pick out the produce for you, so it is best to find one you like, and frequent it, as they give the best selection to regular customers.

Pasta is the universal diet of all Italians. However, in the north *polenta* (a porridge made from maize meal) and rice are as common as pasta as a basic constituent of main daily meals. Italian meat is patchy in quality as it often is in countries that suffer from a lack of rain and green grass. Pork and famous pork products, like *prosciutto crudo* from the north, are excellent but much of the veal (*vitello*) is imported. The best beef (*vitellone*) is considered to come from Tuscany. In the mountainous regions of the south, prime lamb (*agnello*) is produced. Italians also eat farmed rabbits and fowl, and a variety of small birds (including skylarks *allodole,* blackbirds *merli,* sparrows *passeri* and thrushes *tordi*) that will have little attraction for British and North American diners. These small songbirds are usually trapped with nets and sold skewered, in similar fashion the how the Chinese eat small birds. It makes one wonder whether Marco Polo took the dish with him to China, or brought it back to Italy. After grilling, each bird constitutes a small and bony mouthful. Meat is purchased from a *macelleria* and poultry from a *polleria*.

One of the other main dietary constituents, cheese, comes in many delicious specialities, a number of which (e.g. Parmesan, Gorgonzola and Mozzarella) will already be familiar to most expatriates. Parmesan increases in price with age, the most expensive being *stravecchione* (very old) and no self-respecting Italian would dream of buying it ready grated. Sheep's milk cheeses (*pecorino*) are specialities of Sardinia and the Genovese region. If you are in doubt about what cheese to buy a good cheese monger (*formaggiaio*) will always let you taste before buying. See below for further details on Italian eating habits.

If there are some consumables that you have grown up with and for which there is no Italian substitute (Marmite, digestive biscuits, Bird's custard, Maple Syrup, etc.), or the substitute is just not the same then there are a few specialist shops that stock these and other familiar items. Another good reason to join an expatriate club is to find the best place to buy your favourite imported food items. The availability of these items can be variable and when you see a rare item it is often a good idea to buy it on the spot, because it probably will not be there next week.

The online shop, www.expatshopping.co.uk, will deliver many of the delicacies that expatriate desire, though they do have a minimum quantity, so a joint order with friends can share the burden of postage.

METRICATION

ITALY USES THE METRIC SYSTEM in all respects: the standards of measurement are recognisable to English speakers. Temperature is always measured in celsius.

In the long run it is much easier to learn and think in metric rather than to always try to convert from metric to imperial. To facilitate this process a metric conversion table (including clothes and shoe size conversions is) given: see table 12.

In all cases measurements are quoted as a decimal and not a fraction; for example, on road signs, 'Napoli 12.7 km'.

TABLE 12   CONVERSION CHART

LENGTH (NB 12inches 1 foot, 10 mm 1 cm, 100 cm 1 metre)

inches	1	2	3	4	5	6	9	12	
cm	2.5	5	7.5	10	12.5	15.2	23	30	

cm	1	2	3	5	10	20	25	50	75	100
inches	0.4	0.8	1.2	2	4	8	10	20	30	39

WEIGHT (NB 14lb = 1 stone, 2240 lb = 1 ton, 1,000 kg = 1 metric tonne)

lb	1	2	3	5	10	14	44	100	2246
kg	0.45	0.9	1.4	2.3	4.5	6.4	20	45	1016

kg	1	2	3	5	10	25	50	100	1000
lb	2.2	4.4	6.6	11	22	55	110	220	2204

DISTANCE

mile	1	5	10	20	30	40	50	75	100	150
km	1.6	8	16	32	48	64	80	120	161	241

km	1	5	10	20	30	40	50	100	150	200
mile	0.6	3.1	6.2	12	19	25	31	62	93	124

VOLUME

1 litre =	0.2 UK gallons		1 UK gallon = 4.5 litres
1 litre =	0.26 US gallons		1 US gallon = 3.8 litres

CLOTHES

UK		8	10	12	14	16	18	20
Europe		36	38	40	42	44	46	48
USA		6	8	10	12	14	18	

SHOES

UK	3	4	5	6	7	8	9	10	11
Europe	36	37	38	39	40	41/42	43	44	45
USA	2.5	3.3	4.5	5.5	6.5	7.5	8.5	9.5	10.5

TIME

THE 24-HOUR CLOCK SYSTEM is used for all times in Italy. For example, shop opening hours are given as 09.00 à 17.30 (9am to 5.30pm) or train times as 20.20 (8.20pm) or 00.15 (12.15am).

Italy follows Continental European Time (CET) as do most EU countries with the exception of Greece, the UK and Eire. Summer time lasts from the last Sunday in March at 2am to the last Sunday in September at 3am, when clocks are advanced one hour. Consequently Italy is one hour ahead of the UK for most of the year, whether the UK is operating to Greenwich Mean Time (GMT) or British Summer Time (BST). However, clocks in the UK are changed later in the autumn than in Italy so for a time, in September and October, the two countries are actually sychronised: there are currently proposals to synchronise the times throughout the EU.

PUBLIC HOLIDAYS

NOTE THAT ON ITALIAN NATIONAL HOLIDAYS (*feste*) offices, shops, banks, post offices and schools are all closed. Whether museums, parks, etc, are closed will vary from region to region:

PUBLIC HOLIDAYS

1 January (New Year's Day; *Capodanno*)
6 January (Epiphany; *La Befana)*
Easter Monday *(Pasquetta*)
25 April (Liberation Day; *Anniversario della Liberazione*)
1 May (Labour Day; *primo maggio*)
15 August (Assumption; *Ferragosto*)
1 November (All Saints'; *Ognissanti*)
8 December (Immaculate Conception; *L'Immacolata Concezione)*
25 December (Christmas Day; *Natale*)
26 December (Boxing Day; *Santo Stefano*)
The festival days listed below are held to honour each specific city's own patron saint. Shops and offices usually remain open on these days although it is as well to check with the local tourist board for specific information.
25 April (Venice, St Mark)
24 June (Turin, Genoa and Florence; St John the Baptist)
29 June (Tome, St Peter)
23-25 July (Caltagirone in Sicily, St James)
26 July (island of Ischia in the Bay of Naples, St Anne)
19 September (Naples, St Gennaro)
4 October (Bologna, St Petronius)
6 December (Bari, St Nicholas)
7 December (Milan, St Ambrose)

RETIREMENT

CHAPTER SUMMARY

○ A modest pension that is just enough to survive on in the UK would probably not be enough to live on in Italy.

○ Italy offers those who can bear the higher costs of living abroad a higher quality of life in terms of climate, history, culture and pace of life.

○ Those considering retiring to Italy are advised to try !a six month stay first, a period that should ideally include both the cold of winter and the heat of summer.

○ To obtain the *permesso di soggiorno* (residence permit) you will need to be able to prove that you have sufficient funds to live on.

○ Those entitled to a British pension can arrange to collect it in Italy: it will be subject to Italian tax.

○ EU nationals resident in Italy are entitled to use the Italian state healthcare system, but this is not as comprehensive as the UK National Health Service.

ANYONE CONSIDERING ITALY as a place to retire to will do well to realise that Italy really is the land of frescos, ancient culture and the *bella figura* (personal aestheticism). It is definitely Italian, with little allowance for the needs of foreigners who want to have what they had at home, with a bit more sun. So, if you are after an abundant supply of fish and chips, English beer and imported foodstuffs, or lots of people who speak English, try Spain! Many retirees in Italy also retain homes in their country of origin, splitting their time between the two countries each year. The bulk of retired expatriates in Italy are Britons, who have planted themselves in the beautiful country spots of Tuscany and Umbria, where living and property costs continue their upward spiral. These areas are well away from the industrial centres of Milan and Turin and also the services associated with large centres of population. Despite being remote and rural, it is worth remembering that in the northern regions of Piedmont, Lombardy, Veneto, etc., the cost of living is considerably higher than that in the UK, other European countries and North America. Living abroad also brings additional costs, not just bigger versions of what you are used to – international telephone costs, medical insurance, travel to and from your home country, administration costs and internal travel to regularise your status. Survival, therefore, on a modest pension that just about allows you to live in your current country would be difficult in Italy, if not impossible. There is also a noticeable lack of welfare and after-care services for the elderly throughout Italy, which is especially noticeable in rural areas.

However, potential retirees will almost certainly find the excellent climate and the easy-going nature of the people, the progressive upgrading of the infrastructure and the lively expatriate community, combined with an ambition to make the most of Italian art and culture are all the excuses needed to justify retirement in Italy. Some of the very real benefits include a quality of life that is often higher than that offered in the UK and much of North America, in terms of climate, history, culture and pace of life. Additionally, away from Umbria and Tuscany, property bargains are still to be found in some of the less-discovered regions of La Marche, Puglia and Liguria.

THE DECISION TO RETIRE ABROAD

MOST IMPORTANTLY, anyone considering retiring to Italy must be able to afford the move financially. No less vital is being aware of the stresses involved in moving to another country and the ultimate effect lack of proximity to friends and family will have on you. You have to have the stamina to deal with the move not only practically but also emotionally. *Live and Work Abroad: A Guide for Modern Nomads* (also published by Vacation Work, ISBN 1-85458-256-9) covers the practicalities of living abroad in detail and the relevant parts of it should be read by anyone considering retiring abroad.

Also essential before moving to a new country under your own auspices is the willingness to upgrade language skills, in this case Italian (see *The Italian Language* in the *Daily Life* chapter). Trying to negotiate the Italian bureaucracy with little or no Italian is likely to ruin any stay in the country before it has really begun.

As many decisions to move abroad grow out of a love of the country discovered through past holidays of only a few weeks at a time it can be a good idea to have an extended stay in the country before making the final decision to complete a permanent move. A six month stay, perhaps through a home swap or a long-term rental (see *Setting up Home*) that should ideally include the winter period or the heat of summer, depending on what you have already experienced, can be a good way to help clarify the reality of retiring abroad. Ideally the stay should be in the area in which you are most interested, so that you can get to know it really well and do your research before buying property moving there. If you have yet to decide which region to move to, a succession of more long-term stays in various areas would also be possible.

If funds are not a problem, purchasing a second home in Italy and sharing time between it and your home country residence can ease the transition until you decide where you want to settle permanently, or allow you to have the best of both worlds if the decision is too hard to make.

Residence Requirements

Anyone intending to retire to Italy must first obtain a permit to stay (*permesso di soggiorno*) from the local police station (*Questura*) three months after arrival in Italy. The *permesso di soggiorno* will be renewed after a five year period and annually thereafter on condition that proof of funds are presented in the form a bank letter or statement to the sum of approximately £12,000 (US$17,000) each year. The basic regulations regarding permanent residence both before and after leaving your home country can be found in Chapter Two, *Residence and Entry Regulations*. Additional documents required from retirees by the *Questura* in Italy include proof of retirement or old age pension, indicating the amount received monthly and proof from a bank in Italy that you have opened an account with them.

CHOOSING AND BUYING A RETIREMENT HOME

THE MAIN and very obvious points to make regarding buying a retirement property in Italy is to choose something which is within your financial scope, which is both suitable for year-round living and for you to live in for many years to come. You will need to keep a firm grasp on reality when it comes to house prices, the lowest prices are often for derelict, isolated farmhouses in need of much renovation work. This may be perfect for someone with plenty of enthusiasm, energy and financial backing and with strong hermitic tendencies, but equally inappropriate for someone retiring to Italy to make new friends and enjoy their retirement in the peace and comfort of an Italian home. The other extreme is to be tempted by something beyond what you can really afford, which may then become a financial liability. Further information regarding property prices throughout Italy and a list of agents can be found in the Chapter, *Setting up Home*. However, property prices can change rapidly as can the ease of selling one bought in the heat of the moment but no longer wanted, manageable or affordable

Most people will have to budget carefully the expenses involved in moving abroad and will need to take into consideration the running and upkeep costs of the property in question. For instance, the *palazzi* (blocks of flats containing several different apartments) where maintenance and renovation costs are shared on a communal basis may work out more expensive than you think and you may not have a choice as to when renovation is done and needs to be paid for. Some of your budget should be allowed for these maintenance costs, which are always accrued when keeping a home in reasonable repair.

Proximity to health services and other facilities is also an important consideration for anyone reliant on public transport.

Once you have decided on where you want your new home you will need to follow all of the procedures regarding property purchase that are outlined in full in *Setting Up Home*.

Avoiding the Con-men

Time after time expatriates, especially retirees, show an inexplicable naivety by involving themselves financially in 'money-making' scams. Smooth-talking salesmen, peddling everything from 'precious stones' to dud shares make these proposals of quick returns. The temptation to increase a retirement nest egg through seemingly easy means, that involves no work, is evidently too much for the over-credulous retiree to resist. The usual procedure is for a salesman to telephone, introducing him or herself as being a representative from a company with a respectable-sounding name. The conversation somehow turns to shares and stock markets, with the unsurprising result that the caller has stock available in a small company that will shortly be on the receiving end of a juicy take-over bid from a large multinational company e.g. IBM, ICI. The caller promises the share price is sure to double and add that they would so hate to see you miss out on this once-in-a-lifetime opportunity that if you send in a cheque today, you will be able to share in the profits. Amazingly, people do just this and invariably the brief thrill of anticipation is replaced by a long period of regret. Often the money disappears totally and even if 'Mr Smith' the salesman is ever tracked down, the shares really existed and were actually bought in the right name, they can often only be sold at a fraction of the price for which they were originally bought. The moral is, if a salesman calls offering quick cash, hang up. Nobody but a fool sends a cheque to invest in a company he has never heard of, in response to a phone-call out of the blue from someone he has never met. If you do want to invest in shares, consider whether you want to be cautious or to indulge in a more risky scheme and then take truly professional advice. Commodity traders and stockbrokers are listed in the Directory of Major Employers in the *Employment* section of this book and many of the offshore banks that provide services to expatriates also offer reputable investment schemes.

HOBBIES

ONCE YOU HAVE SETTLED into your new home, waded through the lengths of red tape and obtained all the relevant permits and documents, thoughts will necessarily turn to socialising and the pursuit of hobbies and interests. Italy offers a host of possibilities in this area, which is one reason why so many people retire to the country.

Keen gardeners will find that Italy offers a variety of gardening climates and the Italians themselves are renowned as brilliant horticulturists but not, however, as particularly keen gardeners. You can derive hours of pleasure not only from growing exotic plants in different growing conditions, but also learning the Italian names for the common garden and wild plants: *giglio* (lily), *papavero* (poppy) and *violaciocca gialla* (wallflower) to name but three. Remember that although it is legal to take seeds into Italy, it is against the law to import plants and bulbs without a phyto-sanitary certificate issued DEFRA. An inspector will have to see the plants in question and an inspection can be arranged with a local office through DEFRA, Plant Health Division (Room 340 Foss Fouse, Kings Pool, 1-2 Peasholme Green, York YO1 7TX; ☎01904-455188; fax 01904-455199; www.defra.gov.uk). One potential problem for the keen gardener in Italy is the water shortage that affects most of the country. There are solutions for drought areas, such as recycling water used in the kitchen and for bathing to the garden and also using well water if your property has one.

For those with sporting inclinations, activities abound both strenuous and gentle. Cycling (*ciclismo*) is a particularly popular national sport but if this is too energetic and you would rather be a spectator, there are plenty of spectacles on offer from rugby and football to motor racing. For further details on sport see the *Daily Life* section.

Lovers of old properties, ancestral homes and formal gardens will find that the Italian equivalent of the National Trust in the UK and historical associations in the US, the FAI (Foundation for the Italian Environment) organises trips to the many places of interest which form Italy's almost inexhaustible architectural heritage. Although barely twenty years old and with a membership in the thousands (compared to the National Trust's two million), interest in the FAI is growing as the Italians become more aware of the need to protect their heritage if it is to survive into the future. The annual membership cost is minimal and entitles members to free entry to all FAI properties and a regular newsletter, as well as the outings mentioned above.

Studying is another way of enhancing retirement. The most obvious subjects are those connected with Italy itself, the language and culture. For something more ambitious you can enrol with the UK based Open University through their office in Milan (c/o The British Council, via Manzoni 38, 20121 Milan; ☎02-772221; fax 02 781119; www.britishcouncil.org; www.open.ac.uk). The Open University offers over 150 courses which can lead to a degree and many others that lead to diplomas and certificates. Studying for pleasure does not have to result in an academic qualification however and there are numerous organisations in Italy and around the world that offer courses, both in traditional classrooms, via correspondence or online through the internet.

Useful Addresses

Edupoint.com an online (www.edupoint.com) marketplace for continuing education providing centralised access to thousands of learning opportunities worldwide.

Gruppi Archaeologici d'Italia: Via Degli Scipioni 30/A, 00192 Rome; ☎06-39733786; fax 06-39734449. Season tickets and subscription to the magazine *Archaeologica*.

Lifelong Learning offers a searchable database online (www.lifelonglearning.com) of distance learning courses.

Entertainment

If you are one of those for whom life without television would be unthinkable, even if only to keep up with world outside your country retreat, BBC Prime, BBC World, CNN International and Sky TV are available in Italy and provide the best of British and American entertainment and news services. Choices Direct, Amazon.co.uk and Amazon.com can also supply English language videos and DVDs, by mail order, to Italy too – see the *Daily Life* section earlier in the book for further details.

Alternatively, there is BBC Radio and Voice of America. Most countries operate an Overseas Service for their own nationals too, but the BBC World Service, relayed by satellite and broadcast on FM in many parts of Italy, is in a class of its own. British newspapers are expensive abroad, tend to arrive late and are obtainable only in the large towns – though many are now available online and some also offer weekly editions for overseas readers that summarise the daily editions. Listening to the World Service is therefore the easiest and cheapest way to keep in touch with home. By day, reception is best on higher frequencies (15-21 mHz) but at night the lower frequencies (around 6-7 mHz) are preferable while early in the morning and evening, the middle bands of 9-11 MHZ provide the best quality reception. The BBC broadcasts continuously over a 24 hour period, 365 days a year. Programmes and frequency charts can be found in the monthly magazine *BBC On Air* and subscriptions are available from BBC On Air, Room 310NW, Bush House, London WC2B 4PH (☎020-7557 22875 (answer phone); fax 020-7240 4899); www.bbconair.co.uk. The magazine lists all overseas radio programmes as well as listings for BBC Prime and BBC World (see above and below) and much additional information such as a wavelength guide, useful tips on reception, suitable radios to buy and similar matters.

BBC World is a 24-hour international news and information free to air television channel which can be received in Italy. For further information contact Customer Services, Telepui (via Piranesi 46, 20137 Milan; ☎02-757677). A monthly programme guide is given in *BBC On Air* (see above).

English videos are available by mail order as mentioned above, but also through Atles Videa, whose outlet in Milan is located at Via Varese 8, 20121 Milan (☎02-29005474) or Economy Book and Video Centre in Rome (Via Torino 136, Rome 00184; ☎06-4746877; fax 06-483661).

For a list of some English-speaking clubs in individual cities, see *Social Life* in the *Daily Life* chapter.

FINANCIAL CONSIDERATIONS

Pensions

ITALY IS WELL-KNOWN for having one of the highest European rates of expenditure on social security in general, and pensions in particular. In 1998 the government, after many months of consultations introduced radical changes.

These included making pension requirements in the public sector the same as for the private sector i.e. employees in both sectors will have to pay contributions for the same number of years (40) in order to claim a full pension. The changes are being phased in gradually until parity is achieved in 2008. Italy will probably still come out well on top over the UK as regards pension entitlements. This parity of the public and private systems will end the extremely high number of state workers claiming substantial pensions after 'retiring early'. The old so-called super pensions (starting at 3.5 million lire a month) have been partially reduced in recent years. Silvio Berlusconi, however, has pledged that every pensioner will receive a minimum of 1 million lire a month, which will surely add to the social security bill, not reduce it.

One of the reasons that pensions (*pensione di vecchiaia*) were so high was because they were on a sliding scale, rises of 2% of each individual's earnings for every year in which contributions were made. For instance, someone who had worked for 30 years received an Italian pension of 60% of their earnings in the five years prior to retirement; after working in Italy for 15 years, a worker could earn 30% of his or her salary in pension. By contrast, British workers have only been eligible for a full UK pension after approximately 40-45 years of work and this represents only approximately 18% of average earnings. Moreover, the employee's contribution in Italy can be less than 2% of earnings, compared with 9% in the UK. The minimum contribution period to result in entitlement to any Italian pension varies but can be as little as three months. Once a worker has paid contributions for this minimum period, there is an absolute right to receive the pension wherever he or she lives in the EU. The pension is paid by the country in which it was earned at the appropriate pension age. If someone has not worked abroad for the minimum period to entitle them to any pension, then another rule comes into effect and calculates what is called a pro rata pension. This is the theoretical pension they would have earned if they had worked abroad for a longer period, which is then scaled down in proportion to the actual time spent working there.

UK Citizens.   UK citizens and those entitled to a UK pension who want to receive it in Italy should apply to DWP Pensions and Overseas Benefits Directorate, Newcastle-upon-Tyne NE98 1BA (☎0191-218 7777) who will send out a form which should then be taken to the nearest social security office (*Unità Sanitaria Locale*) in Italy. The *Unità Sanitaria Locale* will then make the necessary arrangements for your pension to be transferred to Italy. If you became entitled to a UK pension before leaving for Italy, this can either be paid to you in Italy or in the UK.

Alternatively, if you reach retirement age after taking up residence in Italy, again you need only apply to the Directorate and they will ensure that your pension is delivered to your Italian (or a UK) bank account each month. Anyone who moves to Italy before reaching retirement age should continue to pay National Insurance contributions in the UK in order to qualify for a British state pension. Depending on which country you have paid the majority of contributions in, you are eligible to draw the pension in either country. Note that pensions are not frozen at the level they reached on arrival in Italy and instead the pension will rise in accordance with any increases that take effect in the UK. Retired expatriates in most other non-EU countries (with the exception of Mauritius, the USA and Switzerland) are not so lucky as pensions in these cases are frozen at the level levied in the year the expatriate left the UK to retire abroad. Leaflet SA29 (available from the Directorate on receipt of an s.a.e.), provides details on EU pension and social security legislation.

It would be advisable to inform the Inland Revenue office with which you last dealt about your plans; they will supply leaflet IR138 *Living or Retiring Abroad? A guide to UK tax on your UK income and pension* or you can contact the Inland Revenue's two specialist offices for non-residents (Non-Resident Claims, Fitz Roy House, PO Box 46, Nottingham NG2 1BD; ☎0115-974 1919; fax 0115-974 1919; www.inlandrevenue.gov.uk; or Centre for Non-Residents (CNR), Residence Advice & Liabilities Unit 355, St. John's House, Bootle, Merseyside L69 9BB; ☎0151-472 6202; fax 0151-472 6003).

Italy itself also offers invalidity pensions (*pensione di invalidità*), which are widely abused in the south of the country where able-bodied workers are certified as being unable to work in order to decrease the unemployment statistics. There is also something called *la pensione di anianità* (a long-service pension) to which someone is entitled after thirty-five to forty years of work. As recently as 1998 the government brought in new regulations to abolish a scandalous variant on this system, awarding pensions to certain state employees, such as teachers, after only ten years' service (allowing 30 year olds to retire and get another job on the quiet). Political parties also found the generous pension system invaluable for bribing the electorate when it came to voting time.

The *Instituto Nazionale di Previdenza Sociale* (INPS) effectively dominates the Italian pensions system though there also exist several pension funds linked to certain state industries (water, gas, the railways, etc.). Private pension plans, of which there was a dismal shortage of choice only a few years ago, are likely to prove a booming sector for the newly wealthy Italians in the north, who will eventually start looking to invest their money rather than spend it.

If you are employed by a UK company but working in Italy you should check how long you are able to contribute to the UK company pensions scheme; normally, employees are able to remain with the UK scheme for at least three years, and with the approval of the Inland Revenue, for longer. However, UK citizens who leave the UK and cease to earn an income in the UK, are often not allowed to contribute to traditional UK-based pension schemes. To continue saving for the future they need to invest in US-style funds-information and advice should be sought from professional financial advisers, preferable ones who are registered in the UK and not ones who phone you up out of the blue.

Finally, if you are subject to tax in Italy it is worth checking whether your employer's pension contributions are taxable there. Previously, as a UK taxpayer you would not be taxed on your employer's contributions. Also take advice from an independent financial adviser as to whether it is best for you to continue with a personal pension scheme in the UK and for how long, and what other conditions and/or restrictions apply to the scheme once you are resident in Italy.

Other Pension Entitlements: The European Commission has recently put forward proposals for a pension directive. Current differences in pension provision between member states are seen as barriers to the total freedom of movement of employees within the European Community. The proposals now under discussion are intended to remove the obstacles and to encourage pension provision by employers. These are to include freedom to manage pension funds within the EU, freedom of cross-border investment and cross-border membership of pension fund schemes. The last clause is the one that is causing the most controversy, as it allows for the creation of pan-European funds, and the final outcome is still being awaited.

Note that it is always worth checking on your entitlements to a foreign state pension if you have worked abroad for any length of time. For instance, a British ex-expatriate discovered that she was entitled to a pension of approximately £50 a week and more than £20,000 in payments backdated to her 55th birthday as she had contributed to the Italian state pension scheme for about ten years while working in Rome.

Advice regarding, and administration of, offshore pension funds is available through Bacon and Woodrow Pension Trustees Ltd (Albert House, South Esplanade, St Peter Port, Guernsey, Channel Islands; ☎ 01481-728432; fax 01481-724082) as well as many of the Offshore Banks in Jersey, Guernsey and the Isle of Man. The UK tax authorities have tightened up the rules on offshore investments, especially trust funds that were popular with expatriates, and it is always worth seeking up to date professional advice before making decisions on investment activity.

Finance

Anyone considering retiring to Italy should take specialist financial advice regarding their own personal situation. Most people in a position to retire overseas have an amount of capital to invest, or will have once they sell their UK home and it is essential to take good advice on how and where this may best be done. Moreover, those who intend to maintain connections with both the UK and Italy will need advice on how their taxation affairs can be arranged to their own advantage. However, there is no reason why one should not continue with bank accounts or investments already established in the UK and in most cases interest will be paid on deposits paid without deduction of tax where one is non-resident, providing the correct paperwork is completed at the bank.

Taxation

Inheritance taxes in Italy have changed during the revision of this book. A new law was passed on October 25th 2001, and became effective immediately, under which gifts and legacies to relatives no longer attract inheritance tax, though some taxes relating to the transfer of ownership still apply. For non-relatives, large legacies (more than €175,000 approx) will attract some taxes such as Registration Tax. Transfers of all inheritances/gifts still remains complex and legal advice should be sought to avoid conflict between Italian and UK/US/Canadian law and ensure that the correct paperwork is filed punctually after the death, as late filing can attract large fines.

UK pensions paid to British expatriates are subject to Italian tax unless the pensioner is exempted by a double taxation agreement, or he or she is a former public service employee who worked abroad (in which case the pension is taxable in the UK, although sometimes not liable to any tax at all). The double taxation agreement only taxes pensions in Italy if you are resident there. If your pension is going to be liable for UK income tax or Italian tax, it may be better to elect to take a tax-free lump sum pension option, thereby reducing the level of pension liable to tax. A recent survey found that a UK couple who retire to Italy on a pension of £20,000 with no other income would take home significantly less than they would have in France, Germany and Switzerland, but more than they would have done in any Scandinavian country.

Non-EU retirees resident in Italy should take specialist tax advice to avoid paying tax in both the country where their income is generated and Italy.

Offshore Banking

Retired people with a lump sum of money to be invested, or put into a long-term deposit account, will find it well worth looking at the tax-free interest bearing accounts that financial institutions offer through offshore banking centres such as Gibraltar, the Isle of Man and the Channel Islands. The minimum amount of money required to open a deposit account ranges from £500 to £10,000. The deposit account interest rates work on the basis that the more inaccessible one's money, the higher the rate of interest paid. Interest can be paid monthly or annually, although the account holder will receive slightly less overall on the monthly payments because of the number of transaction charges involved. The monthly payments, however, offer a steady income flow and seem an invariably more popular option with retirees. A list of banks which offer offshore banking facilities is given in the *Banking* section of the *Daily Life* chapter.

SOCIAL SECURITY AND HEALTH

EU PENSIONERS who are resident in Italy on a permanent basis are entitled to free or subsidised healthcare under the Italian social security system (*lo stato assistenziale*). However, although free benefits include hospital and emergency treatment, routine visits to the GP or dentist are not included (see below). Those who are retired or who are otherwise eligible for UK social security should apply in Britain as far in advance of departure as possible to the Department of Work and Pensions Overseas Branch (address provided above) for form E121, and on arrival in Italy should register with their nearest government health centre.

The Italian social security system provides particularly poor outpatient and after-care treatment and facilities. Social security will only cover about 75% of a patient's treatment costs, thus the patient has to meet 25% of the costs him or herself or budget for payments for insurance to cover this instead. Those who have worked in Italy and paid into a private top-up scheme, as most people do, have the bulk of this contribution covered, but those who are retired and move to

Italy may not.

A list of English-speaking doctors is available from British and US Consulates and Embassies, though these lists will, however, often only list private doctors and medical facilities.

For details of private health care plan organisations, see *Private Medical Insurance* in the *Daily Life* chapter.

WILLS

THE EASIEST and most effective policy regarding the disposal of his or her estate for foreign citizens resident in Italy is to make a will that follows the law of their own country. If a will involves the dispersal of property both within and without Italy, it is advisable to consult a lawyer (*avvocato*) with experience of both your own country's and the Italian legal systems to avoid legal complications later on. In this case, you may find that it is simplest to make two wills, which deal with non-Italian and Italian assets separately, rather than trying to combine the two. If you wish, you can make an Italian-style will, but unless you have taken on Italian nationality during your time in Italy, this will be executed in accordance with the law of your home country. Non-Italian wills also avoid the Italian system of *Legittime*, common to most Western European countries, which gives those directly related to the deceased an absolute right to a share in the estate, regardless of the wishes of the deceased as expressed in the will. Remember that to validate an Italian will you will need to obtain a certificate of law from your consulate which will state that the will is being made under the terms of your own country's law and includes a provision for the free disposition of property. Any good lawyer will be able to organise this for you.

Death

Death is the unwanted eventuality that affects us all sooner or later. Dying abroad complicates matters slightly, in that one's near relations are often not on the spot to deal with the formalities surrounding burial or cremation. It is therefore advisable to make your wishes concerning the matter i.e. what form of burial is desired and where, known in advance and preferably also written down in a will. Note that burials in Italy must take place within 48 hours of death.

All deaths must be registered with the local *municipio* (town hall) within 24 hours. The attending doctor issues a death certificate, though you will need an international death certificate if the body is to be transported back home. Cremation, particularly in the north of Italy, is fairly common, although practically every Italian commune has its own cemetery in which all residents are entitled to be buried free of charge. There are also British cemeteries in large cities like the one at Staglieno in Genoa.

The British Embassy warns that sending a coffin back to the UK by air is an expensive business – to North America is of course even more expensive. Freight charges depend on weight but the minimum cost is about £2,000; prolonged storage will also add to your costs. The body will have to be picked up once it arrives home and some Italian funeral directors have contacts in other countries who will see to it that the body is safely delivered to its final destination. It is advisable to get a few quotations from Italian undertakers who offer such a service. An alternative is to have just your ashes returned home, which is much cheaper. Courier companies should be able to handle this if a friend or relative cannot do it.

Section 2

WORKING IN ITALY

EMPLOYMENT

BUSINESS AND INDUSTRY REPORT

REGIONAL EMPLOYMENT GUIDE

TEMPORARY WORK

STARTING A BUSINESS

EMPLOYMENT

CHAPTER SUMMARY

○ The official national unemployment rate is at 9.2% the lowest it has been for some years.

○ Unemployment remains lowest in the north and highest in the south.

○ The European Union has set up a system under which professional qualifications obtained in one member country are recognized in another.

○ Sources of information about jobs include the pan-European job information network EURES, professional organizations, online job resources and Chambers of Commerce in Italy.

○ Possibilities for temporary work in Italy include working on a farm or as an au pair, teaching English, and in the summer and winter tourist industries.

○ Each industry in Italy has its own national minimum wage. Overtime is paid at 130%-150% of the normal rate, but in some fields of work it has been banned by the unions.

○ All employees receive an extra month's wages in December.

○ **The economy.** Although there has been some privatisation in recent years there remains a large state interest in a variety of industries.

  ○ Small businesses have dominated Italian industry over the last decade.

○ **Industry.** The main industries offering prospects for permanent work include aerospace, agriculture, the automotive industry, chemicals, clothing and textiles, electrical household appliances, high technology, iron and steel, the IT sector, machine tools, mining and oil and gas.

  ○ The different industries are not evenly spread around the country so some research into what takes place where is necessary.

THE EMPLOYMENT SCENE

IF YOU ARE KEEN to live and work in Italy, as are an increasing number of Europeans and North Americans, but you are neither being sent to Italy by your current employer nor retiring then you will have to find employment yourself. The prospects for finding a job are better now than they have been as unemployment rates in Italy have normally been slightly higher than the rates in other countries of the European Union. But in recent years there has been a downward trend: since 1999 the Italian labour market has shown a slow but constant growth and the unemployment rate has dropped from 11.4% to 9.2% according to figures released by the National Statistics Bureau (www.istat.it) in July 2001, although some dispute the way the lower figure was calculated.

This growth in the economy is a consequence of the introduction of more flexible working arrangements (see *New Regulations* under *Aspects of Employment* below), and a directly linked dip in the unemployment rate. The progressive diffusion of atypical contracts (part-time, seasonal, work training, temporary, etc.) had an important effect on employment. The role of flexible work contracts is especially important in the tertiary sector starting from the services industry and professional services. Amongst these contracts you will find the following:

Train & Work Contracts (CFL)

These types of contracts are intended for paid work on a fixed term basis, with a non-renewable maximum of 24 months, with vocational training objectives. CFL's have been designed for unemployed people between 16 and 32 years of age. Special certificates or diplomas are not required for CFL contracts.

Apprenticeships

This is a special work contract where the employer is required to provide the young employee with sufficient training for the acquisition of skills comparable to a qualified worker's experience, while taking advantage of the apprenticeship. These types of contracts may last from 18 months up to 4 years. It is important to note that apprenticeship wages are less than those of a normal employment contract.

Work in the private sector

The government issued decree 469/97 that allowed individuals to act as mediators in the labour market (i.e. recruitment consultants) and no longer bans, within certain limits, intermediary activities in job placement. These measures are in accordance with the decision of the Court of Justice of the European Union.

This decree introduced temporary jobs (*lavoro interinale*) to the job market. Its goal was to make the working environment more dynamic, thus making the job supply truly meet the needs of the demand.

Current Trends

There is a special dynamic trend in the north-eastern areas. The manufacturing sector of Emilia Romagna, Abruzzo, and Molise show greater increases in employment, although it involves mainly the services sector, which is somewhat dynamic in the rest of the country as well. You can find great differences in the unemployment rates between the Northern, Central, and Southern areas. As of July 2001, the unemployment rate in Northern Italy was 3.9%, 7.6% in the Central regions, and 19.1% in the remaining areas. Nevertheless, there is a constant growth in overall employment in all the regions.

The Euro is expected to affect the Italian economy as a whole. New measures will be taken by the government to guarantee the further reduction of the inflation rate, currently above the European average levels. Unemployment rates are expected to drop, as shown by the recent trends discussed above. The creation of new jobs in the ICT sector, which has a deficit of at least 120,000 staff, and the constant growth of the services and manufacturing industries will certainly boost the economy, thus helping the labour market to grow further still.

Special contact. *CESOP Communication* (Via San Felice 13 - Galleria Buriani, 40122 Bologna BO, Italy; ☎051 272441; fax 051 272265; t.joel@recruitaly.it) operate www.recruitaly.it, a website providing comprehensive information on the working world in Italy, and a window for Italian companies interested in recruiting staff from abroad. The site allows a direct approach to recent graduates interested in working in Italy, helping companies that have difficulties in finding qualified personnel in Italy, especially in the ICT sector.

RECOGNITION OF DIPLOMAS, CERTIFICATES AND DEGREES

IT CAN BE DIFFICULT to have your diplomas, titles, certificates, and any other special qualification, fully recognised in Italy as there are significant differences between training courses and diplomas from country to country. Nevertheless, the European Union has set up systems for recognising diplomas and training which enable EU job seekers to make full use of his/her training and skills in another EU country: see *European Union Professional Qualifications Directives* below.

If you are an EU citizen qualified to exercise a profession in your home country, you are supposed to be qualified to do it in any other EU country. If you want to work in a profession that is regulated in the country of employment (teacher, lawyer, engineer, psychologist, etc.) you must apply for recognition of your qualifications in that country. The wait-and-see period is no longer than four months, so you should receive an answer in a relatively short time.

If you are a doctor, a general nurse, a dentist, a midwife, a veterinary surgeon, a pharmacist or an architect (professions for which qualifications have been co-ordinated at EU level), your national qualifications are, in principle, recognised automatically, allowing you to practice in any other EU country. If your profession is not regulated in the country in which you wish to work, no recognition of your qualifications is necessary. You are entitled to go and work in that country without any formalities linked to your training or qualifications.

These procedures vary for non-EU citizens. It is advisable that you check with the Italian embassy before starting the process of looking for a job. In order for non-EU nationals to get a work permit an employer must sponsor them and they will be required to prove they have special skills, not available in Italy at that moment. Graduates in the ICT sector are currently one such specialist in demand.

European Union Professional Qualifications Directives

The booklet *The Single Market, Europe Open for Professionals, EU Professional Qualifications Directive* is obtainable from the DTI (Kingsgate House, 66-67 Victoria Street, London SW1E 6SW; ☎020-7215 4648; www.dti.gov.uk) and gives further information of the first diploma directive dealing with professional qualifications awarded after more than three years study.

Further details of the qualifications covered by the second diploma directive (everything from hairdressing to insurance brokering) can be obtained from the same address. This booklet is also available from the Association of British Chambers of Commerce in Coventry.

Prospective job seekers are advised to consult the association relevant to their profession for the exact conditions for acceptance in Italy. This can be at one of the 40 European Documentation Centres (EDCs) in the UK. To find the address of your nearest one, contact the European Commission, Information Centre, 8 Storey's Gate, London SW1P 3AT; ☎020-7973 1992; fax 020-7973 1900/1910; www.cec.org.uk.

Although some professionals, such as doctors and dentists, have been able to practise in any EU state for a decade, it has not been the case for other professions who want to practise in the EU area but outside their home country. In Italy, foreign teachers are not taken on as permanent staff in state schools (though this has been challenged) as staff are civil servants and therefore should be Italian citizens. There may also be an *equipollenza* (equivalence) exam (see below) for some professions.

Certificates of Experience: Member states, other than the one in which qualifications referred to in the second directive were attained, may require evidence of one or more years of professional experience. In order to do this the home state can issue such a Certificate of Experience. In Britain, those wishing to practise their trade or profession in another EU state can contact the Certificates of Experience Department of The Department of Trade and Industry (Kingsgate House, 66-74 Victoria Street, London SW1E 6SW; ☎020-7215 4004; fax 020-7215 4489; www.dti.gov.uk.) requesting an application form for a

European Community Certificate of Experience. The form will be accompanied by a copy of the Directive (see above) applicable to the job in question. The applicant should check whether he or she meets the terms of the Directive before completing the application form. To be eligible for a certificate you must normally (but not exclusively) have had managerial or self-employed experience for a number of years in the job concerned. The DTI charges a hefty fee for issuing a certificate and a smaller fee for an update/revision. The charge is to cover the costs of checking and authenticating the information submitted by the applicant. Residents of other EU countries should contact their nearest Chamber of Commerce to ask about the issuance of certificates in the country where they are resident.

The UK National Academic Recognition Information Centre (NARIC) provides information on the comparability of overseas qualifications and can be contacted at ECCTIS 2000 Ltd (Oriel House, Oriel Road, Cheltenham, Glos GL50 1XP; ☎01242-260010; fax 01242-258611; naric@ecctis.co.uk; www.naric.org.uk), runs an enquiry service which provides information and advice on the comparability of international and UK qualifications.

RESIDENCE AND WORK REGULATIONS

UNFORTUNATELY, ITALY'S WHOLEHEARTED ENTHUSIASM for the EU has not diminished or greatly refined the time-consuming morass of bureaucracy required of even EU nationals who wish to work in Italy. If you arrive in Italy with the intention of working, you must apply at the *questura* (police station) for a *ricevuta di Segnalazione di Soggiorno*, which allows you to stay for up to three months looking for work. Upon production of this document and a letter from an employer, you must go back to the police to obtain a *libretto di lavoro*, a form of work authorisation which strictly should not be necessary for EU nationals. However, anyone wishing to work in Italy should be prepared to apply for a *libretto di lavoro* as well as a stay permit (*Permesso di Soggiorno*) if intending to stay and work for longer than three months (Italians need one as well so it is not a form of discrimination against foreigners). One English woman, who was offered a job EFL teaching in Bari, reported that she had to visit three different government offices about eight times in total. Her health card arrived about six months after the wheels were set in motion.

Note that au pairs and academics employed by Italian universities are exempt from obtaining the *libretto di lavoro*. Full information on entry regulations to Italy are given in Chapter Two, *Residence and Entry Regulations*. For anyone considering moving to Rome or its environs, the booklet *Notes on Employment and Residence in the District of the British Embassy, Rome* is available free of charge from the British Embassy (Via XX Settembre 80a, Porta Pia, I-00187 Rome; ☎06-482 5551/5441; fax 06-487 3324). This booklet provides basic information on accommodation, medical care, social clubs and obtaining employment in the Rome area. The US Embassy (via Vittorio Venetto 119/A, 00187 Roma Italy; ☎06-4674 1) also provides similar information for its nationals.

SOURCES OF JOBS

THE MEDIA

National Newspapers and Directories

THE COMBINED EFFECTS of the Single Market and the implementation of the EC Professional Qualifications Directives (see above) have not exactly triggered a flood of trans-continental job recruitment, but mobility has certainly increased and become practicable for an increasing number of EU nationals. UK newspapers carry a growing number of job advertisements from other member states including Italy. Many British newspapers including, *The Times, The Financial Times* and the *Guardian* carry regular job adverts from other European countries. Every Thursday, the Appointments section in *The Times* provides a comprehensive list of opportunities throughout the market place both in Britain and overseas. The *Times Educational Supplement* (published Fridays) and the Education pages of the Tuesday edition of the *Guardian*, carry prolific advertisements for teaching English abroad. The *Guardian* also has a Europe supplement on Fridays, which includes a job section. A specialist fortnightly newspaper *Overseas Jobs Express* (available on subscription (PO Box 22, Brighton BN1 6HX; www.overseasjobsexpress.co.uk) contains articles from a range of working travellers and a substantial jobs section under headings including: Education/TEFL, Hotel and Catering, Information Technology and Trade. In America, the *Wall Street Journal, Washington Post* and other leading newspapers also carry international job listings.

Alternatively, a wide range of casual jobs including secretarial, agricultural, tourism and domestic work, are advertised in the directory *Summer Jobs Abroad*, while *Teaching English Abroad* lists schools worldwide which employ English language teachers each year and *Working in Ski Resorts Europe & North America* includes all the main Italian resorts and tells you how and where to get jobs in them. These publications are available directly from Vacation Work (9 Park End Street, Oxford OX1 1HJ; ☎01865 241978; fax 01865 790885; www.vacationwork.co.uk) as well as bookshops and online booksellers.

International and European Newspapers and Magazines

A number of international English-language newspapers, drawing on journalistic input from around the world, are available in most countries with a sizeable expatriate population. These publications circulate editions across national boundaries and usually carry a modest amount of job advertising. The volume of adverts carried is rising, though the number of such publications has consolidated in recent years. Presently, the newspapers to consult include the *The International Herald Tribune, The Weekly Telegraph* and *The Weekly Guardian* and *Wall Street Journal Europe*.

In addition to the above newspapers, magazines such as *Time, Newsweek, Asiaweek* and *The Economist* are distributed internationally and include adverts for senior employees in various countries, including Italy. International subscriptions are available, though they are expensive. Individual copies can usually be purchased from major bookstores in cities with a sizeable expatriate population. Bookstores at international airports and also main railway stations in large cities where expatriates are resident, often stock English language publications such as those listed above.

There are specialist expatriate magazines such as *Nexus* (Expat Network Ltd., Rose House, 109a South End, Croydon CR0 1BG; ☎020-8760 0469; fax 020-8760 0469; nexus@expatnetwork.com; www.expatnetwork.com), which carry international job adverts and also allow members to include their CV in the members' database.

When living outside of the UK and North America, the newspapers and magazines listed in both the National and International sections above can often be found in the libraries of *The British Council* (www.britishcouncil.org) and cross cultural associations such as the *American Chamber of Commerce* (AmCham) and the *Franco-American Association*, as applicable to the country you are in.

As well as employers advertising in the International and European newspapers, individuals can also place their own adverts for any kind of job, although bilingual secretaries and assistants, marketing managers and other professionally qualified people seeking to relocate abroad are in the greatest demand. Obviously, advertising rates vary but will be several US$ per line, per insertion. For details contact the classified advertising departments of the newspapers at the addresses listed below.

The Financial Times: 1 Southwark Bridge, London SE1 9HL; ☎020-7873-3000.
   The Financial Times is printed in English in the UK, Germany, France, the USA and Japan and distributed worldwide. International appointments appear on Thursdays in all editions.

The Guardian Weekly: 164 Deansgate, Manchester M60 2RR; 020-7713 4111; fax 020-7831 5712. The condensed weekly version of the British daily newspaper.

International Herald Tribune: 63 Long Acre, London WC2E 9JH; ☎020-7836 4802; Appears daily: the IHT international recruitment section appears on Thursdays.

Wall Street Journal: The International Press Centre, 76 Shoe Lane, London EC4; ☎020-7334 0008; online news and subscriptions from www.wsj.com. European edition published in Brussels: Wall Street Journal Europe, Bld. Brand Whitlock 87, 1200 Bruxelles; ☎+32 27411211; www.europe.wsj.com. US subscriptions 1-800-369-2834. The recruitment section which covers appointments and business opportunities worldwide and appears on Tuesdays.

For information on the Italian press, see below and the *Daily Life* chapter, *Media* section. Some Italian newspapers can be obtained in major city newsagents in the UK on the day of publication. Alternatively, try major city reference libraries.

Advertising in Newspapers

An advertisement in an Italian newspaper may produce an offer of employment. Smyth International, 1 Torrington Park, London N12 9GG; 020-8446 6400; www.smyth-international.com deal with *La Stampa* (Turin daily), and other provincial newspapers. The Milan paper *Il Giornale* is published at Via Gaetano Negri 4, 20123 Milan. Note however, that anyone in the UK wishing to insert an advert in the widely-read *Corriere della Sera* should contact the Italian Publishing Group (4 Wendle Street, 131-157 Wandsworth Road, London SW8 2LL; ☎020-7498 2333) who deal exclusively with this publication. It may also be worth advertising your skills and services in the monthly English-language website *The Informer* which has a classified section. Adverts can be placed online and subscriptions to the members' section of *The Informer* website is Euros 49 per year. The Italian American Heritage Foundation website also has extensive links to Italian newspaper websites at: www.iahfsj.org/links.htm.

Italian publications worth looking at include *The Career Book* (usually issued in October by the newspaper *Il Sole 24 Ore* for its subscribers; Redazione Il Sole 24 Ore, Via Lomazzo 52, 20154 Milan; fax 02-3103426; or 02 341062; www.careerbooklavoro.somedia.it.) Also worth checking is the Friday jobs page of the newspaper *Corriere della Sera* and monthly magazines *Campus, Tuttolavoro, Trovalavoro* and *Bolletino del Lavoro*.

Professional and Trade Publications

Professional journals and magazines are another possible source of job vacancies abroad, from British companies wishing to set up offices elsewhere in Europe and foreign firms advertising for staff, e.g. *The Architects' Journal, The Architectural Review, Accountancy, Administrator, Brewing & Distilling International* and *The Bookseller* to name but a few. Anyone in the air transport industry should consult *Flight International* while those employed in the catering trade could try *Caterer and Hotel Keeper* and agricultural workers *Farmers Weekly*. Although published in the UK, some of these magazines are considered world authorities in their field and have a correspondingly wide international readership.

An exhaustive list of trade magazines can be found in media directories such as *Benn's Media* available in major reference libraries. More limited lists can be found in writers directories such as *The Writers Market* (US), *Writers' and Artists' Yearbook* (UK) and *The Writers Handbook* (UK), which are available in major reference libraries and bookstores.

PROFESSIONAL ASSOCIATIONS

PROFESSIONAL ASSOCIATIONS are a useful point of contact for their members with regard to practising elsewhere in the world. Most professional organisations have links with their counterparts around the world and can often provide generic contact details, if not personal contact. During the negotiations involved in finalising the EU mutual recognition of qualifications directives, most professional associations negotiated with their counterparts in other member states and can therefore be much more helpful in providing contacts.

Details of all UK professional associations may be found in the directory *Trade Associations and Professional Bodies of the UK*, available at most UK reference libraries. It is also worth trying to contact the Italian equivalent of UK professional associations – the UK body should be able to provide the address. Alternatively you can consult your trade union for information, as they may have links, however tenuous, with their counterpart organisation in Italy. A list of addresses of the more mainstream professional organisations is given below.

Contact details of US and Canadian professional organisations can be found in a similar fashion – through local libraries and chambers of commerce. Additionally, most professional organisations in North America and the UK have an internet presence and a growing number of Italian ones do too. A simple search using Yahoo! or a similar search engine will generally produce the required results. A comprehensive directory of UK trade associations can be found at www.martex.co.uk/taf. Their US counterparts can be found in the Yahoo!directory:http://dir.yahoo.com/Business_and_Economy/Organizations/ Trade_Associations/.

Useful Addresses

Architecture & Surveying Institute: St Mary House, 15 St Mary Street, Chippenham, Wiltshire; ☎01249-444505; fax 01249-443602; asi@asi.org.uk .

Architects Registration Board for the United Kingdom: 8 Weymouth Street, London W1W 5BU; ☎020-7580 5861; fax 020-7436 5269; www.arb.org.uk.

Association of Professional Music Therapists: Mrs Diana Asbridge, 26 Hamlyn Road, Glastonbury, Somerset, BA6 8HT; tel/fax 01458-834919; APMToffice@aol.com; www.apmt.org.uk.

Biochemical Society: Biochemical Society Membership Office, Commerce Way, Whitehall Industrial Estate, Colchester, Essex CO2 8HP; ☎01206-796351; fax: 01206-799331; www.biochemsoc.org.uk..

British Computer Society: 1 Sandford Street, Swindon SN1 1HJ; ☎01793-417424; fax 01793-480270; www.bcs.org.uk.

British Dietetic Association: 5th Floor, Charles House, 148/9 Great Charles Street, Queensway, Birmingham; B3 3HT; ☎0121-200 8080; fax 0121-200 8081; www.bda.uk.com.

British Medical Association: BMA House, Tavistock Square, London WC1H 9JP;

☎020-7387 4499; fax: 020-7383 6400. The BMA's International Department gives extensive help and advice to its members wishing to work elsewhere in Europe, and to incoming doctors from other countries.

Chartered Institute of Bankers: See Institute of Finacial Services below.

Chartered Institute of Building: Englemere Kings Ride, Ascot, Berks SL5 7TB; ☎01344-630700; fax 01344-630777; www.ciob.org.uk.

Chartered Institute of Building Services Engineers: 222 Balham High Road, Balham, London SW12 9BS; ☎020-8675 5211; fax 020-8675 5449; www.cibse.org.

Chartered Institute of Marketing (CIM): Moor Hall, Cookham, Maidenhead, Berks SL6 9QH; ☎01628-427500; fax 01628-427499; marketing@cim.co.uk; www.cim.co.uk).

Faculty of Advocates: Parliament House, 11 Parliament Square, Edinburgh EH1 1RF; ☎0131-226 5071; www.advocates.org.uk.

General Council of the Bar (The Bar Council): 3 Bedford Row, London WC1R 4DB ☎020-7242 0082; www.barcouncil.org.uk.

General Dental Council: 37 Wimpole

Street, London W1G 8DQ; ☎020-7887 3800; fax 020-7224 3294; www.gdc-uk.org.

General Optical Council: 41 Harley Street, London W1N 2DJ; ☎020-7580 3898; fax 020-7436 3525; www.optical.org.

Institute of Actuaries: Napier House, 4 Worcester Street, Gloucester Green, Oxford OX1 2AW; 01865-268200; fax 01865-268211; www.actuaries.org.uk.

Institute of Biology: 20-22 Queensberry Place, London SW7 2DZ; ☎020-7581 8333; fax 020-7823 9409; www.iob.org.

Institute of Cast Metals Engineers: Bordersley Hall, Alvchurch, Birmingham B48 7QA; ☎01527-596100; fax 01527-596102; www.ibf.org.uk.

Institute of Chartered Accountants in England & Wales: Chartered Accounts' Hall, P O Box 433, Moorgate Place, London EC2P 2BJ; ☎020-7920 8100; fax 020-7920 8547; www.icaew.co.uk. Is able to offer members advice on working within the EU.

Institute of Chartered Foresters: 7A Colme Street, Edinburgh EH3 6AA; ☎0131-225 2705; www.charteredforesters.org

Institute of Chartered Secretaries and Administrators: 16 Park Crescent, London W1N 4AH; ☎020- 7580 4741; fax 020-7323 1132; www.icsa.co.uk.

Institute of Chartered Shipbrokers: London Branch, 3 St Helen's Place, London EC3A 6EJ; ☎020-7628 5559; fax 020-7628 5445; www.ics.org.uk.

The Institution of Chemical Engineers: 165-189 Railway Terrace, Rugby CV21 3HQ; ☎01788-578214; fax 01788-560833; www.icheme.org.

Institute of Civil Engineers: 1 Great George Street, Westminster, London SW1P 3AA; ☎020-7222 7722; fax 020-7222 7500; www.ice.org.uk. Also has an international recruitment agency: Thomas Telford Recruitment Consultancy, Thomas Telford House, 1 Heron Quay, London E14 4JD; Customer Services ☎020-7665 2464; www.t-telford.co.uk.

The Institution of Electrical Engineers: Savoy Place, London, WC2R 0BL; ☎020-7240 1871; fax 020-7240 7735; www.iee.org.uk.

Institute of Financial Services: Administration Centre, IFS House, 4-9 Burgate Lane, Canterbury, Kent CT1 2XJ; ☎01227-762600; fax 01227-763788; www.cib.org.uk.

Institution of Gas Engineers: 21 Portland Place, London W1B 1PY; ☎020-7636 6603; fax 020-7636 6602; www.igaseng.com.

Institute of Marine Engineers: 80 Coleman Street, London EC2R 5BJ; ☎020-7382 2600; fax 020-7382 2670; www.imare.org.uk.

The Institution of Mechanical Engineers, 1 Birdcage Walk, London SW1H 9JJ; ☎020-7222 7899; fax: 020-7222 4557; www.imeche.org.uk.

Institute of Mining and Metallurgy: Danum House, South Parade, Doncaster DN1 2DY; ☎01302-320486; fax 01302-380900; www.imm.org.uk.

Library Association: 7 Ridgmount Street, London WC1E 7AE; ☎020-7255 0500; fax 020-7255 0501; www.la-hq.org.uk.

The Registrar and Chief Executive, United Kingdom Central Council for Nursing, Midwifery and Health Visiting: 23 Portland Place, London W1B 1PZ; ☎020-7637 7181; fax 020-7436 2924; www.ukcc.org.uk.

Royal Aeronautical Society: 4 Hamilton Place, London W1V OBQ; ☎020-7670 4300; fax 020-7670 4309; www.raes.org.uk.

Royal College of Speech and Language Therapists: 2 White Hart Yard, London SE1 1NX; ☎020-7378 1200; fax 020-7403 7254; www.rcslt.org.uk.

Royal Pharmaceutical Society of Great Britain: 1 Lambeth High Street, London SE1 7JN; ☎020-7735 9141; fax 020-7735 7629; www.rpsgb.org.uk.

Royal Town Planning Institute: 41 Botolph Lane, London, EC3R 8DL; ☎020-7929 9494; fax 020-7929 9490; www.rtpi.org.uk.

Royal College of Veterinary Surgeons: Belgravia House, 62-64 Horseferry Road, London SW1P 2AF; ☎020-7222 2001; fax 020-7222 2004; www.rcvs.org.uk.

Society and College of Radiographers: 207 Providence Square, Mill Street, London SE1 2EW; ☎020-7740 7200; fax 020-7740 7204; www.sor.org.

EMPLOYMENT ORGANISATIONS

EURES. THE EUROPEAN EMPLOYMENT SERVICES (EURES) is a computerised, pan-European job information network accessible through Jobcentres that have a specially trained Euroadvisor and through these special advisors you can find out about jobs in Italy. The idea is that you contact the Euroadvisor nearest you in your own country and with their help use the EURES system (which has computer links with job organisations in the countries of the European Economic Area – the EU plus Iceland and Norway), to track down a suitable vacancy in another country. EURES can be used free by employers. Details on the EURES service can be obtained from the Overseas Placing Unit (Level 4, Skills House, 3-7 Holy Green, Off the Moor, Sheffield S1 4AQ; ☎0114 2596051, or from the EURES website: http://europa.eu.int/comm/employment _social/elm/eures/en/index.htm.

At the time of writing there is a total of 7461 vacancies of all types registered on EURES, from unskilled to executive and professional posts; 741 of these vacancies are in Italy. Jobseekers can also search the EURES system online at: www.eures-jobs.com/jobs/en/jobs.jsp.

EURES CV-search (www.eurescv-search.com) allows jobseekers in the European Economic Area to enter CVs into a database that employers can search. At the present time the system is only set up for those looking for work in the IT, Hotels and Restaurant, Healthcare and Air Travel sectors. Italy has 22 Euroadvisors (*euroconsiglieri*) who mainly help Italians wanting to work abroad.

UK Employment Agencies. Contact details of employment agency members of the national organisation, the Recruitment and Employment Confederation (36-38 Mortimer Street, London W1N 7RB; www.rec.uk.com) can be ordered for £3.75 by ringing 0800 320588. The agencies listed deal mainly with specific sectors e.g. electronics, secretarial, accountancy etc., and will only recruit qualified and experienced staff. Alternatively, some 400 recruitment agencies can be located through the *CEPEC Recruitment Guide*, which is available in reference libraries or from the Centre for Professional Employment Counselling (Lilly House, 13 Hanover Square, London W1R 9HD: ☎020-7629 2266) for a fee, plus postage and packing. The *Recruitment Guide* lists agencies which arrange jobs, predominantly for graduates and professionals, within the UK and sometimes abroad.

Recruitment agencies also advertise specific vacancies in the newspapers mentioned above and contacting them about other vacancies they have on their books can also be productive.

Italian Employment Agencies. The state-run *Ufficio di Collocaménto Manodòpera* has lost its monopoly in employment and recruitment and private agencies are now permitted. A complete list of authorised Italian agencies can be found at www.minlavoro.it, the Italian *Ministero del Welfare* website. For those interested in temporary employment, there are also agencies listed in the Italian *Yellow Pages.* It should be borne in mind, however, that there is little point in applying for most of the jobs you will find listed in the resources mentioned above if you are not proficient in Italian.

ONLINE JOB RESOURCES

ONLINE RECRUITMENT AGENCIES are becoming increasingly common and many traditional recruitment agencies now have a web presence where their vacancy lists can be accessed and CVs submitted for consideration. A search using the main search engines such as Yahoo!, Google and Lycos or meta engines such as www.mamma.com and www.dogpile.com will generate many such agencies. There are agencies that recruit for the whole of Europe and also some that specialise in Italy, e.g. www.monsteritalia.it, where you will find thousands of job offers (Italian version available only).

Alternatively, www.recruitaly.it gives access to job postings in English and provides further information on living and working in Italy and the site *Jobs in Italy* also provides useful links and resources at: www.ferreri.freeserve.co.uk/jobsitaly.html. The website www.payaway.co.uk also lists agencies offering work in most areas covered in the *Temporary Work* section below, i.e. Agriculture, Au Pair and Tourism. Finally, *Job Partners* provide a recruitment service for employers around the world and local contact details can be found via their website, www.jobpartners.com.

CHAMBERS OF COMMERCE

THE MAIN FUNCTION of the Italian chambers of commerce (*Camera di Commercio Industria*) is to promote business and trade in their area, but they may well do a sideline in providing information on potential employees to interested companies. The Italian Chamber of Commerce for Great Britain is based at 1 Princes Street, London W1R 8AY, UK; ☎020-7495 8191; fax 020-7495 8194; info@italchamind.org.uk; its Secretary General is Mr. Fabio Corazzo.

Anyone setting up in business or self-employment in Italy has to register with the local chamber of commerce on arrival; there are local and regional chambers of commerce in virtually every town and city. Their main task is to provide enthusiastic support for local industries and companies and, on request, will provide details of these and a list of government incentives for new industry (see the section, *Government Incentives*, in the Business chapter). The British Chamber of Commerce in Milan (Via Dante 12; ☎02-877798; fax 02-86461885; e-mail bcci@britchamitaly.com) actually does this. For a small fee they will lodge your CV on their files for possible employers to see for up to a year; you can also place a classified advertisement both in their monthly newsletter and online. They hold information on member companies and though you have to pay them for the printed version of their directory, all the information is online at their website, www.britchamitaly.com. This site also advertises job vacancies for bilingual staff.

British Chambers of Commerce in Italy.

Bergamo; Mr Arnold Attard (Hon. Area Secretary for Bergamo), c/o British E.L.T., Via Taramelli, 52 - 24121 Bergamo, Italy; tel/fax 035 249150.

Bologna; Mr Roger Warwick (Honorary Regional Secretary for Emilia Romagna), c/o Pyramid, Viale Masini, 20 - 40126 Bologna, Italy; ☎051 254568; fax 051 254948.

Brescia; Ms Julia A. Jones; C.S. International, V.le. della Bornata 42, 25123 Brescia, Italy; ☎030 3366811; fax 030 3366098.

Florence; Maria Grazia Antoci, Viale Milaton 33, 50129 Firenze, Italy; ☎055 4625049; fax 055 486463; mgantoci@videosoft.it.

Gorizia; Mr D. Katan, Via F. Filzi 14, 34132 Trieste, Italy; ☎040 6762322 or ☎040 6762385; fax 040 6762301.

Naples; Roy Boardman, St. Peter's ELC, Riviera di Chiaia 124, 80100 Napoli, Italy; ☎081 683468; fax 081 682721.

Padova ; Ms Christine King, c/o Abbey National Bank, Via Altinate 8, 35121 Padova, Italy; ☎0498 761380; fax 0498 761381.

Pordenone; Mrs Susan Clarke (Hon. Regional Secretary for Friuli Venezia Giulia), c/o Overseas Language Consultancy, Corso Vittorio Emanuele 54, 3170 Pordenone, Italy; tel/fax 0434 29089.

Rome; Mr Andrew Calvin, Via Acherusio 18, 00199 Roma, Italy; ☎06 86206459; fax 06 86383162; acolvin@tin.it.

Taranto; Ms Stefania Lo Cascio, Worldwide Trusts Consultants Srl, Via Nitti 45/a, 74100 Taranto, Italy; ☎0348 3851033 or ☎099 4590880; fax 099 4590809; staff@trustsitaly.com.

Trieste; Prof. John Dodds, Università di Trieste, Via F. Filzi 14, 34132 Trieste, Italy; ☎040 6762322 or ☎040 6762385; fax. 040 6762301; dodds@sslmit.univ.trieste.it.

Turin; Mrs Jocelyn Holmes (Hon. Regional Secretary for Piemonte), c/o Musci & Holmes Architetti, Via Genola 3, 10141 Turin, Italy; tel/fax 011 331216.

Udine; Mr C. J. Taylor, Via del Torso 41/8, 33100 Udine, Italy; tel/fax 0432 600397.

Venezia; Mr Ivor Neil Coward, Lexicon Translations SAS, Via Caneve 77, 30173 Mestre, Italy; ☎0422 780505 or 041 5348005; fax 0422 782821 or 0415349720; lexivor@tin.it.

Verona; Mr Peter Eustace (Hon. Regional Secretary for Veneto), c/o CSA snc - via Pigna 14/a, 37121 Verona, Italy; ☎045 592482; fax 045 597629.

The American Chamber of Commerce is at via Cantu, 20123 Milano, Italy; ☎0286 90661; fax 028057737; amcham@amcham.it; www.amcham.it/English/home.asp. Their website lists job vacancies for those with Italian-US experience and

Italian language skills. The American Chamber of Commerce also offers a business advisory service to its members. The membership directory of the American Chamber of Commerce is only available to their members.

APPLICATION PROCEDURE

TO AVOID DISAPPOINTMENT it is as well to accept that if your speculative letter of employment successfully negotiates the Italian postal system and lands on the desk of the right person, your application is still only at the very earliest stages in the job-hunting process. Remember that the Italians are notoriously bad at answering letters and faxes and that each application will have to be accompanied by copious amounts of persistence and patience, if not goodwill. However, after accepting these drawbacks as inherent in postal applications, proceed with the utmost enthusiasm and determination. The *Directory of Employers* later in this chapter is a good source from which to base a speculative job hunt list. If your Italian is not up to scratch or you prefer to make sure it is perfect, then a translator may be called for. In the UK the Institute of Linguists (Saxon House, 48 Southwark Street, London SE1 1UN; ☎020-7940 3100; 020-7940 3101; www.iol.org.uk) provides a good service of freelance translating, putting callers and visitors to their website in touch with translators who will provide a fluent translation for a fee of approximately £100 per thousand words. Translators can also be found online, for example, www.angloitalian.com. The *inlingua School of Languages* also offer translation services from their schools in the UK and North America and contact details can be found on their websites (www.inlingua.com and www.inlingua.com/usa.html).

Keep your letters formal, clear and polite and to the point; a flood of personal history will not be greeted appreciatively. Always send a CV (resumé) with your application, whether the letter is speculative or in response to an advertised vacancy. For advice on how to compile and write your CV, refer to the publications *The Right Way to Write Your Own CV,* John Clarke (Paper Fronts) and *CVs and Written Applications,* Judy Skeats (Ward Lock). Agencies which prepare CVs for a fee can be found under the heading *Employment Agencies* in the local *Yellow Pages* or online. It would be best to have someone familiar with the Italian employment market, who is also fluent in Italian, prepare your CV to ensure it will be suitable for submitting to Italian employers. After the CV has been written, any abbreviations, etc. which may confuse a foreign reader should be modified. Do not send any original certificates or documents with an enquiry or application as it is extremely unlikely that you will ever see them again.

If you are offered an interview, remember that first impressions and appearances are always important. Whatever the number of interviewers, you will usually find that the meeting is formal as a casual approach to interviews is an Americanism not yet in vogue with most Italian or European employers. As for dress, try to look smart, as the Italians inevitably are. However, it is probably wisest to err on the side of conservatism in your dress, rather than attempting, and more often than not failing, to beat the Italians at their own game (i.e. the notorious *bella figura*, which involves looking one's best at all times). Remember that handshaking is popular throughout Italy with both men and women and that it is polite to shake hands both on arrival and departure. As with any job interview in any country, it is best to find out as much background information as possible about the company and the position for which you have applied in advance of the interview. An interest based on knowledge and hard facts is bound to impress a potential employer.

TEMPORARY WORK

NON-EU NATIONALS will have a greater problem finding temporary work as the employer is taking the risk of employing someone illegally. Most of the information below is therefore only applicable to EU citizens – except the EFL teaching and au-pair sections. Some language schools specifically want North American teachers to teach American-English and many North Americans find teaching jobs every year in Italy. Overseas Teachers Digest (www.overseasdigest.com) provides information for Americans looking to teach abroad and provides numerous links to possible employers. Non-EU citizens can become au-pairs and enter Italy on a cultural or educational visa as long as they attend language classes whilst in the country; further information is in the relevant section below.

AGRICULTURE

CASUAL LABOURING JOBS in Italy are harder to come by than in some other Mediterranean countries. This is because vineyard owners traditionally employ migrant workers from North Africa, Albania, etc. who are prepared to work illegally and for a pittance throughout the duration of the grape harvest (*vendemmia*) each year. Opportunities for grape picking are best in the north west of the country, for example in the vineyards lying south east of Turin in Piedmont, in the north-east in Alto Adige and to the east and west of Verona. The harvest takes place in September and October. There are other possibilities for fruit picking earlier in the year, but again there will be stiff competition for the limited number of jobs available. Strawberries are picked in the region of Emilia Romagna in June and apples from late August in the Alto Adige region and in the Valtellina, which lies between the north of Lake Como and Tirano. Jobs are also available picking grapes and tobacco leaves in Tuscany in September each year.

The Val di Non apple harvest around Cles in the river valley of the Adige, north of Trento, is a mecca for migrant workers and is a veritable cultural melting pot of Italians, East Europeans, Africans, South Americans, et al, and picking begins around 20-25th September for about four to five weeks. Women normally get the sorting jobs and the men earn slightly more picking. The object seems to be to get the harvest gathered in record time, so expect to work ten hours a day with no days off. If lunch and accommodation are provided there is a standard deduction and most farmers eat lunch with their pickers. And yes, Italian workers do sing operatic arias in the orchards while they work.

The International organisation WWOOF (World Wide Opportunities on Organic Farms) has a national organisation in Italy: WWOOF Italia, c/o Bridget Matthews, Via Casavecchia 109, 57022 Castagneto Carducci, Livorno, Italy (wwoofitalia@oliveoil.net; www.wwoof.org/italy). Membership costs €24, €13 of which is for compulsory insurance. Further details of WWOOF International can be obtained from WWOOF in your own country. In the UK send a s.a.e. to WWOOF UK, PO Box 2675, Lewes, East Sussex BN7 1RB. Membership benefits include a bi-monthly newsletter with adverts for helpers in the UK and abroad. You can also buy a *Green Holiday Guide* to Italy (German language only) for €13/£6/US$12 from the European Centre for Eco Agro Tourism (Postbox 10899, 1001 EW Amsterdam, Netherlands; fax: 31-20 463 0594; www.pz.nl/eceat). However, this list is aimed at promoting *agriturismo* (i.e. paying stays on farms) and it is merely a suggestion that you can use it for contacts who might let you work and learn about organic farming in return for keep.

For those with a professional interest in farming, the International Farm Experience Programme (YFC Centre, National Agricultural Centre, Kenilworth, Warwickshire CV8 2LG, UK) arranges courses combining language tuition and work experience on farms for five months beginning in February and July. Five weeks at a language school are followed by four months on a farm. Free board and lodging throughout the language course and wages at local rates while on the farm are provided. Applicants must be aged 18-26 and have at least two years of practical farming experience. Travel costs and insurance are subsidised.

The Italian organisation SCICA – Sezione Circondariale per L'Impiego et il Collocamento (Via Maccani 76 38100 Trento; ☎0461-826433 & 826434) organises agricultural jobs and training placements in the Alps.

AU PAIR

THERE IS ALWAYS A DEMAND for au pairs (known as *alla pari* or *i babysitter* in Italian), and also for qualified nannies. The rules for EU citizens who are au pairing are slightly confused in that they are not in general eligible for a *libretto di lavoro* (see *Residence and Entry Regulations*) but must apply for a stay permit (*permesso di soggiorno*) if they are staying for longer than three months. They must also register at the local registry office (*Ufficio Anagrafe*) which must be done before they can for instance, open a bank account in Italy. Non-EU or EEA nationals are not eligible for a *permesso di soggiorno* and must therefore arrive in Italy with an exchange or cultural visa.

The Almondbury Aupair & Nanny Agency (Damian Kirkwood; tel/fax +44 (0)1288 359 159; fax/ans: +44 (0)207 681 2508; in the USA (419) 844-8497; Damian@aupair-agency.com; www.aupair-agency.com) who arrange au-pair placements in numerous countries say that for an au-pair that comes from outside of the EU, the following documentation is needed to obtain a long stay visa:

- A certificate of enrolment (plus receipt of payment) at any Italian School or College where the au-pair-to-be will be attending a course of Italian language. This school or College must be legally acknowledged (*legalmente riconosciuto*) and the above mentioned certificate must be stamped by the local police. The visa will be issued for the length of time of the enrolment in school.
- A return air ticket.
- Travel assistance insurance and medical insurance.
- A written statement of support signed by the host family which must be stamped by the local police.
- A written agreement between the au-pair-to-be and the host family (which should specify the duration of stay, salary, study benefits, etc.). The above must be stamped by the *Ufficio Provinciale del Lavoro*, together with a permit issued by the local police. In some areas it is sufficient to just have this stamped by the local police.

The au pair visa is granted for study purposes and the age guidelines are 18-30. In general, the conditions of work for an au pair among the affluent Italian middle classes who take them are reasonably good. They get board, lodging and pocket money of €65-€70 per week. Mothers' helps will work longer hours a week and get more money. Au pairs are expected to devote a certain amount of time to their hosts' offspring, to attend a part-time language course at the local school and to be an active member in the family's social milieu. In Italy particularly, au pairs tend to be embraced into the bosom of the host family and to the uninitiated this can be an overpowering and bewildering experience. Most people seem to adapt to the Italians' demonstrative and vociferous ways and whatever else this arrangement may involve, it is unlikely that you will ever feel alienated or lonely in the midst of Italian family life. As the Italians who can afford au pairs tend also to be the ones who can afford luxury holiday villas on the coast, keep your fingers crossed for a trip to the seaside in the holiday month of August and one to the Italian Alps in the skiing season.

The majority of European au pair agencies deal with Italy and so you should have no trouble arranging a job there. At the time of writing au pairs may be required to pay a fee to the agency of up to a maximum of £40 plus VAT once they have accepted a position abroad but this is likely to be abolished later in 2002.

Au pairs who are EU nationals have to visit the local police station (*Questura*) after three months accompanied by a member of the host family who will need to sign that he or she is willing to take responsibility for you. Proof may also be required that you are actually attending a language course. Au pairs are then granted a three-month extension, which must be renewed for a further three months on its expiry. The publication, *The Au Pair and Nanny's Guide to Working Abroad* is an invaluable source for those looking for an au pair job abroad and is available from Vacation Work in Oxford (☎01865-241978; www.vacationwork.co.uk).

North American au-pair agencies who arrange placements in Italy can be found in the list below. Non-EU citizens must obtain a visa before arriving in Italy and a good agency will be able to advise how to obtain this.

Useful Addresses

Useful Websites

International Association of Au Pair Agencies (www.iapa.org): Lists their member agencies online.

Europa Pages has a searchable database of agencies offering placements in Italy: www.europa-pages.com/au-pair.

Agencies in Italy

A.R.C.E: (Attivitá Culturali con l'Estero), via XX Settembre 20, 16121 Genova, Italy; ☎010-583020; fax 010-58309; www.arce@tin.it.

Au Pair International: Via S. Stefano 32, 40125 Bologna, Italy; ☎051-267575; fax 051-236594; www.au-pair-international.com.

Aupairitaly.com: via Demetrio Martinelli, 11/d - 40133 Bologna; ☎051-383466; info@aupairitaly.com, www.aupairitaly.com.

EUR Au Pair: via Ghibellina 96r - 50122, 50122 Firenze (FI); ☎055-242181; fax 055-241722.

Intermediate: Via Bramante 13, 00153 Rome; ☎06-5747444; fax 06-5730057 4; www.intermediateonline.com.

Sunrise Associazione Culturale: Viale Principessa Mafalda 14, 90149 Palermo, Sicily; tel/fax 091-454870.

Agencies in the UK

Abbey Au Pairs: 8 Boulnois Avenue, Parkstone, Poole, Dorset BN14 9NX; tel/fax 01202-732922.

Academy Au Pair & Nanny Agency: 42 Milsted Road, Rainham, Kent ME8 6SU; tel/fax 01634-310808; www.academyagency.co.uk.

Angels International Au Pair Agency:, 31 Bushfield Crescent, Edgware, Middlesex HA8 8XQ; ☎020-8958 7002; fax 020-8958 7000.

Anglo Pair Agency: 40 Wavertree Road, Streatham Hill, London SW2 3SP; ☎020-8674 3605; fax 020-8674 1264; www.anglo.pair@btinternet.com.

A-One Au-Pairs & Nannies: 216 The Commercial Centre, Picket Piece, Andover, Hants SP11 6RU; ☎01264-332500; fax 01264-362050; www.aupairsetc.co.uk.

The Au Pair Agency: 231 Hale Lane, Edgware, Middlesex HA8 9QF; ☎020-8958 1750; fax 020-8958 5261; www.aupairagency.com.

English-Italian Agency; 69 Woodside, Wimbledon SW9 7AF; ☎020-8946 5728; partner agency in Turin: The English Agency, Via Pigafetta 48, 10129 Turin; tel/fax 011-597458.

Agencies in North America

Accord Cultural Exchange: 750 La Playa, San Francisco, CA 94121, USA; ☎415-386 6203; fax 415-386 0240; www.cognitext.com.

Au Pair in Europe: PO Box 68056, Blakely Postal Outlet, Hamilton, Ontario, Canada L8M 3M7; ☎905-545 6305; 905-544 4121; www.princeent.com/aupair/.

InterExchange Inc., Au Pair USA Programme, 13th Floor, 161 Sixth Avenue, New York, NY 10013, USA; ☎212-924 0446; fax 212-924 0575; www.interexchange.org.

Le Monde Au Pair: 7 rue de la Commune Ouest, Bureau 204, Montréal, Québec H2Y 2C5, Canada; ☎514-281 3045; fax 514-281 1525.

Scotia Personnel Ltd: 6045 Chery Street, Halifax, Nova Scotia B3H 2K4, Canada; ☎902-422 1455; fax 902-423 6840; www.scotia-personnel-ltd.com.

World Wide Au Pair & Nanny, 2886 Davison St, Oceanside, NY 11672, USA; tel/fax 516-764 7528; www.worldwideaupair.com.

TEACHING ENGLISH AS A FOREIGN LANGUAGE

ITALY IS ONE OF A NUMBER of European countries that has a steady demand for Teachers of English as a foreign language: this demand has increased greatly over the last five years as the popularity of the internet has increased. There are hundreds of language schools in Italy as any *pagine gialle* (yellow pages) will confirm, and between them they employ thousands of teachers. Moreover, it is not just the inhabitants of the large and sophisticated cities of Rome, Florence and Milan who long to learn English. Small towns in Sicily and Sardinia, in the Dolomites and along the Adriatic all have more than their fair share of private language schools and thus offer a variety of teaching opportunities. As you might surmise from the above range and distribution of schools, there is some variation of standards. At the elite end there are the schools which are AISLI (Associazione Italiana Scuole di Lingua Inglese) members; AISLI, c/o Cambridge Centre of English in Modena, Via Campanella 16, 41100 Modena. AISLI has very strict regulations and its schools are ultra-respectable. However, it would be a mistake to assume AISLI represents all the best schools; for instance neither the British Institute in Florence, nor International House in Rome is a member.

However, just because there are hundreds of schools does not mean jobs are that easy to come by. In some cases supply outstrips demand and it can be difficult to get anything other than short-term contracts and freelance work as the cost to employers of full-time employees is prohibitive. The best way of finding private teaching jobs on the spot is to head for any of the 31 university towns and put up notices that you are offering conversation lessons. Since all Italian university students have to take some type of English course, many are eager to be taught by a native speaker. For other teaching work, it is worth looking in English language papers such as the *Daily American* and the Italian newspapers, *Messaggero in Rome* or *La Pulce* in Florence for adverts. For speculative applications you will find a list of language schools listed under *Scuole di Lingue* in the Italian Yellow Pages; the best time to apply to these schools is September/October time or just after Christmas. Do keep in mind, however, that your chances are much improved if you have some kind of TEFL qualification, either the Cambridge CELTA or Trinity TESOL certificates or a shorter TEFL training course. Below are listed some addresses for training courses in the UK, the US and Italy.

If you do not have any teaching qualifications it is still possible to talk your way into a job, bearing in mind, however, that competition tends to be keenest in Rome, Florence and Venice, so non-qualified job-seekers would be advised to avoid the major cities. However, reports suggest that the number of schools willing to employ unqualified teachers is declining so private conversation lessons are probably a better bet. As mentioned above, the publication, *Teaching English Abroad* (Vacation Work, £12.95) is an invaluable source of reference for anyone considering teaching in Italy. Also, try the Education section of the *Guardian* on Tuesdays, the *Times Educational Supplement* on Fridays and the fortnightly *Overseas Jobs Express* , all of which are regular sources of TEFL jobs. The weekly *Times Education Supplement*, better known as the TES, has weekly job listings including overseas appointments, which it also posts online along with useful articles at: www.tes.co.uk.

In the US the equivalent is the bi-monthly TIE (The International Educator) that includes both TEFL and regular K-12 vacancies at mostly American schools around the world. TIE vacancies are posted online, but can be viewed by subscribers only. Subscriptions giving immediate access can be bought online at: www.tieonline.com.

One of the most comprehensive resources for EFL teachers is *Dave's ESL Café* (www.eslcafe.com) which provides extensive listings and information. Other online job sites include www.tefl.net, www.eslworldwide.com (38 institutions with vacancies in Italy at the time of writing), www.joyjobs.com (subscription costs $40), www.iteachnet.com and www.intlschools-k12.com. The *European Council of International School* (www.ecis.org), *International Schools Services* (www.iss.edu) and *Search Associates* (www.search-associates.com & www.search-associates.co.uk) who specialise in teacher placement at K-12 International Schools (see below) will also have a very few EFL vacancies in their job listings. The website www.wwteach.com has extensive information, advice and links for those considering going abroad to teach, all provided by an experienced international teacher.

The standard teaching wage in Italy is not high and EFL teachers should not expect to receive subsidised or free accommodation, though some help may be given in finding somewhere to live.

TEFL Schools in Italy:

Associazione Italiana Scuole di Lingue: (Association of Italian Language Schools) Maintain their database online at: www.eaquals.org/aisli/.

A.C.L.E.: via Roma, 54, 18038 San Remo (Liguria); tel/fax 0184-506070; info@acle.org; www.acle.org. Requires teachers for summer camps.

British Institutes: Via Leopardi, 8, 20123 Milan; ☎02-4390041; fax 0 2 - 4 3 9 0 0 3 1 ; www.britishinstitutes.org.

British s.r.l.: Via XX Settembre 12, 16121 Genoa; ☎010-593591/562621; fax 010 562621.

Byron Language Development: via Sicilia, 125, 00187 Roma; ☎06 4828556; fax 06 4744987; www.byronschool.it.

Cambridge Centre of English: Via Campanella 16, 41100 Modena; ☎059-241004; fax 059-224238; www.cambridgecentre.com. Member of AISLI (see above).

The Cambridge School: Via Mercanti 36, 84100 Salerno; ☎089-228942; fax 089-252523.

CLM-BELL (Centro di Lingue Moderne/Bell Educational Trust): Via Pozzo 30, 38100 Trento; ☎0461-981733; fax 0461 981687. Member of AISLI.

The English Centre: Via P Paoli 34, 07100 Sassari, Sardinia; ☎079-232154; fax 079 232180. Member of AISLI.

Lord Byron College: Via Sparano 102, 70121 Bari; ☎080-5232686; fax 0 8 0 - 5 2 4 1 3 4 9 ; www.lordbyroncollege.com. Eight-month renewable contracts.

Modern English Study Centre: Via Borgonuovo 14, 40125 Bologna; ☎051-227523; fax 051-225314; www.modern-english.com.

Oxford School of English: Administrative office: Via S. Pertini 14, Mirano, 30035 Venice; ☎041-5702355; fax 041-5702390; www.oxforditalia.it.

Regency School: Via dell'Arcivescovado 7, 10121 Turin; ☎011-562 7456; fax 011-541845; www.regency.it

Wall Street Institutes: (www.wallstreetinstitute.com). Has about 50 Italian franchise schools that are listed on their website.

TEFL Training in the UK:

In addition to the addresses below many technical colleges and universities offer TEFL courses on a part-time or full-time basis; further information can be found from the colleges themselves.

Bell Teacher Training Institute: 1 Redcross Lane, Cambridge CB2 2QX; ☎01223-212333. Four weeks (130 hours). Also part-time courses (Tues and Thurs evenings) October to June. Six full time courses per year. Can advise on host families.

Berlitz (UK) Ltd: 9-13 Grosvenor Street, London W1A 3BZ; ☎020-7915 0909; fax 020-7915 0222. Does not run TEFL courses but compulsory method training for its own method lasting one to two weeks. This can be taken in the country in which the employee is successfully interviewed rather than in the country where they will be working.

inlingua Training Courses: Rodney Lodge, Rodney Road, Cheltenham, Glos GL50 1JF; ☎01242-250493; fax 01242-253181. Five weeks Trinity Certificate in Cheltenham.

International House: 106 Piccadilly, London W1 9FL; ☎020-7518 6999. Cambridge Certificate offered

throughout the year.

TEFL Training in the US:

Boston Language Institute, 648 Beacon St, Boston, MA 02215; ☎877-998 3500; fax 617-262 3595; www.teflcertificate.com. Intensive 4-week TEFL Certificate courses.

International House Teacher Training USA, 200 SW Market Street, Suite 111, Portland, OR 97201; ☎503-224 1960; fax 503-224 2041; www.ih-usa.com. Full-time Cambridge certificate courses.

St. Giles Language Teaching Center, One Hallidie Plaza, Suite 350, San Francisco, CA 94102; ☎415-788 3552; fax 415-788 1923; www.stgiles-usa.com. Full-time four-week Cambridge Certificate courses.

Transitions Abroad magazine provides information on TEFL training in the US and has links from its website; www.transitionsabroad.com.

Transworld Schools, 701 Sutter Street, 2nd Floor, San Francisco, CA 94109; ☎888-588 8335; fax 415-928 0261; www.transworldschools.com. Comprehensive Certificate in TESOL.

TEFL Training in Italy

Taking a course in Italy allows non-EU citizens to build up contacts in Italy that may lead to a job; some addresses are listed below. Via Lingua (www.vialingua.net) amongst others offers 4 week courses in Florence and Rome for €1,500 throughout the year. Many of the websites listed above that list EFL vacancies will also provide links to EFL training course providers. There are also online TEFL courses such as the one at: www.teacher-training.net and www.onlinetefl.com.

The Cambridge School: Via San Rocchetto 3, 37121 Verona; ☎045-800 3154; fax 045-8014900. Part time courses January-June.

International House – Palermo: Via Gaetano Daita 29, 90139 Palermo; ☎091-584954; fax 091-323965. Full time CELTA course.
International House – Rome: Viale Manzoni 22, 00185 Rome; ☎06-704 76 894; fax 06-704 97 842; www.ihromamz.it. Both full time and semi-intensive courses offered.

TEACHING IN PRIMARY AND SECONDARY (K-12) SCHOOLS

ONE EFFECT OF SO MANY foreigners living in Italy is the large number of International and National Curriculum schools dotted around the country providing an education for the children of expatriate families. The schools offer a variety of curricula including English National Curriculum, American Curriculum, International Curriculum and various other national curriculum schools including French, German, Japanese and Swiss. They will recruit staff experienced in teaching their national curriculum, which means that American schools will sponsor experienced US teachers to work in Italy.

These schools employ experienced and qualified teachers in all the subjects and specialisms required for good private schools. Methods of recruitment vary from school to school and a direct application works for some while others recruit through job fairs and recruitment agencies. The main international schools in Italy can be found in the directories on the websites of the European Council of International Schools (www.ecis.org), International Schools Services (www.iss.edu), the International Baccalaureate Organisation (www.ibo.org) and the Council of Independent British Schools in the European Community (www.cobisec.org).

Many schools will recruit their teachers both at job fairs in Europe and North America and through adverts in the education press. The main recruitment fairs are organised by the European Council of International Schools (www.ecis.org), International Schools Services (www.iss.edu), Search Associates (www.search-associates.com) and Carney Sandoe & Associates (www.carneysandoe.com).

In addition to the vacancies listed on the websites of the organisations mentioned above, the *Times Education Supplement* (www.tes.co.uk), *The International Educator* (www.tieonline), Nord Anglia (www.nordanglia.com) and QTS Worldwide (www.qts-worldwide.com) contain advertisements for teaching vacancies around the world.

TOURISM

ITALY'S BUZZING TOURIST INDUSTRY is a major source of employment providing jobs for six to seven per cent of the population. It is often difficult for foreigners to gain access to this source of work since even the so-called menial jobs available in major resorts in other European countries have a readily available pool of impeccably turned out, well-trained, multi-lingual locals. This can be rather frustrating if you have set your heart on working in, and gaining an insider's knowledge of Florence, Venice, Rome, Pisa, etc. An alternative is to work for a foreign tour company. Even this is problematic owing to restrictions on the employment of non-Italians in the industry. Some companies have exploited a legal loophole and called themselves art and cultural associations in order to employ non-Italians. The main tourist areas apart from the cities are the coastal resorts of Rimini and Pescara (on the Adriatic), Portofino and San Remo on the Italian Riviera, the island of Capri and Sorrento and Amalfi (south of Naples). However, finding any kind of work in tourism is going to be difficult. Your chances improve if you speak German. There is an agency which specialises in vacancies in the tourist industry in northern Italy (Agentur Messner, Stadelgasse 9, 39042 Brixen; tel/fax 471 80 12 22).

If your knowledge of Italian fails to get you a job with a local employer, your skill may be more valued as a campsite courier with one of the major British camping holiday organisers such as Canvas Holidays – though this will only really be an option for Brits. You can also try Italian-run campsites and holiday villages run by Club Valtur (the Italian Club Med) which have a large staff to run the on-site restaurants, bars and shops. The two main campsites in Rome (the Tiber and the Flamignio) take on English help before the season begins in the early summer of each year. If you have a background in the hotel trade or childcare you could try Forte's village in southern Sardinia which caters largely for families.

The book *Working in Tourism* (Vacation Work) provides useful advice and information on finding work in the tourism sector throughout Europe. Also, the Association of British Travel Agents (ABTA) website (www.abtanet.com) contains contact details for their members.

British tour operators/campsite companies operating in Italy

Canvas Holidays Ltd: East Port House, 12 East Port, Dunfermline, Fife KY12 7JG; ☎01383-629018; recruitment@canvas.co.uk; www.canvasholidays.com. Campsite couriers April to end of September. Applications can be made via their website.

Club Med: Recruitment Dept., Club Med London, 115 Hammersmith Road, London W14 0QH; www.clubmed.com. Has two villages in Sicily and two in Sardinia and another three in mainland Italy. Information on jobs available and the application procedure are available on the website.

Eurocamp plc: Recruitment through Holidaybreak Camping, Overseas Recruitment Department; ☎01606 787522; www.holidaybreakjobs.com/pages/jobsabroad.cfm. Has about 40 sites dotted around Italy on the Ligurian coast, in the Dolomites, on the Adriatic Coast, Sardinia, Amalfi Peninsula and Tuscany.

Garoto Tours: 020-7430 1378; www.garoto.com. Small operator, occasionally employs office staff to meet and greet and who can speak Italian.

Haven Europe: 1 Park Lane, P O Box 216, Hemel Hempstead HP2 4GJ. Campsite couriers and children's staff for campsites.

Mark Warner: All kinds of staff (managers, accountants, receptionists, watersports instructors, nannies, handypersons etc) for beachclubs in Capo Testa on the northern Sardinian coast and Punta Licosa, about two hours south of Naples. Application forms available online at their website: www.markwarner-recruitment.co.uk/apply.html.

Venue Holidays: 21 Christchurch Road, Ashford, Kent TN23 7XD. Employs summer season reps at campsites on the Venetian Riviera. To apply for overseas jobs, telephone 01233-629950 or email jobs@venueholidays.co.uk.

Italian Employers and Job Finding Organisations:

Some useful addresses in Italy are listed below: for other potentially useful addresses see the list of tourism organisations at www.comune.fe.it/giovani/animazione.htm and www.jobonline.it. You will usually have to be Italian-speaking to deal with them and, as for almost all temporary jobs in the tourism industry, being on the spot in Italy would greatly increase your chances of gaining employment. Approaching hotels and bars directly, especially those catering to foreign tourists and expatriates, is also likely to increase your chances of employment

Alberghi Consorziati: 61032 Fano; ☎0721-827376. A consortium of hotels that recruits summer workers for the establishments along the beach resort of Fano (near Pesaro).

Associazione Albergatori di Rimini: Viale Baldini 14, 47037 Rimini; fax 0541-56519. Organisation which recruits seasonal staff for Adriatic hotels.

Associazione Pesarese Albergatori: 61100 Pesaro; ☎0721-67959.

Associazione Balneare Azienda Turismo: ☎0733-811600.

Associazione Bagnini di Numana e Sirolo, 60026 Numana Ancona; ☎0721-827376.

Blue Hotels SRL: Via Porto Portese 22, 25010 San Felice di Benaco, Brescia; ☎0365-559900; www.bluhotels.it. Hotel chain with establishments in Lake Garda, Sardinia, Umbria, Arezzo, Tuscany and Lazio.

Centro per l'impiego are regional offices with information on seasonal hotel and agricultural work:

Agenzia del Lavoro – Centro per l'impiego di Trento, Via Maccani 76, 38100 Trento; ☎0461-496189/90; www.agenzialavoro.tn.it.

Centro per l'impiego di Fiera di Primiero, Via Fiume 10, 38054 Fiera di Primiero, Trento; ☎0439-762232. Hotel work in the Alps.

Centro per l'impiego di Riva del Garda, via Vannetti 2, 38066 Riva del Garda; ☎0464-552130. Hotel work on lake Garda.

Centro per l'impiego di Cavalese, Via Bronzetti, 38033 Cavalese, Turin; ☎0462-340204. Hotel and agricultural work in the Alps.

Centro per l'impiego di Tione, Via Damiano Chiesa 1, 38079 Tione, Trento; ☎0465-32113. Hotel and agricultural working holidays in the Alps.

Club Mediterranee Servizio Risorse Umane: Largo Corsia dei Servi 11, 20122 Milan; ☎02-77861; fax 02 76014518; www.clubmed.com. Worldwide organisation has villages in Italy including Sardinia. UK applicants should contact the London address for Club Med in the above list.

DIEFFE Animation: Corso Vittorio Emanuele 749, 80122 Naples; ☎ 081-665479; www.dieffegroup.com. Organisation that recruits personnel for tourist villages and cruise ships on the Tyrrhenian coast (Naples).

Hotel Giardinetto, Via Provinciale 1, Pettenasco; ☎0323-89118; fax 0323-89219;www.hotelgiardinetto@ti.it; recruits for three hotels on the Lago d'Orta.

Grand Hotel Cesenatico: Piazza A Costa, 1, 47042 Cesenatico, Forli; ☎ 0547-80012; www.grandhotel.cesenatico.fo.it. International tourist Hotel on the coast between Ravenna and Rimini recruits summer staff.

Hotel Cavallino d'Oro: 39040 Castelrotto (BZ) Sudtirolo; ☎0471-706337; fax 0471-707172; www.cavallino.it. Hotel in picturesque town in the Dolomite mountains. All year round resort.

Valtur S.P.A. Risorse Umane: Via Milano 42, 00184 Rome; ☎06-4821000; www.valtur.it. Tour operator that runs a series of tourist villages on Italy's Mediterranean coast. Employs couriers, etc.

TABLE 13	JOBS GLOSSARY
aiutocuochi/aiuto-cucin	assistant chef/kitchen assistant
baristi	bar persons
camerieri/e di sala	waiters/resses
cameriere di piano	chambermaids
commessi/e	shop assistants
cuochi	chefs
lavapiatti	washer-upper
portieri	porters

Winter Resorts

The winter playgrounds of Italy in the Alps, Dolomites and Apennines offer on-the-spot opportunities. Many of the jobs are part-time and do not pay well, but if they come with free accommodation and a ski pass at least you can improve your skiing technique for free at famous resorts like Cortina and Courmayeur. The Veneto region of Italy is a good area to target as it is within easy reach of the eastern Dolomites and boasts a number of ski resorts, including Cortina d'Ampezzo (near Belluno), Asiago, Canarei, Alleghe and Santo Stefano di Codore. Other resorts include La Villa, San Cassiano, Pedraces, Corvara and Colfosco in the province of Bolzano. The winter season lasts from Christmas to Easter and most mountain resorts also have a summer season (mainly July and August). Remember that jobs in ski resorts do get snatched up very quickly and the earlier you apply the more likely you are to get a job; Mark Warner told us that they recommend people to apply as early as June for the winter season. If you speak Italian you can call round the resorts in person.

Note that if you work for an Italian employer you are likely to work much longer hours than if you work for a British tour company: some addresses are given below. For more detailed information on working in winter resorts, *Working In Ski Resorts* is available from Vacation Work Publications.

Equity Total Travel: Dukes Lane House, 47 Middle Street, Brighton, East Sussex BN1 1AL; ☎01273-886878; fax 01273-203212. Goes to 19 resorts in Italy.

Interski: Acorn Park, St. Peter's Way, Mansfield, Notts NG18 1EX; ☎01623-456333; fax 01623-456353; www.interski.co.uk. School group organiser that employs up to 250 ski instructors for the resorts of Courmayeur, Aosta/Pila and La Thuile.

PGL Ski Europe: Alton Court, Penyard Lane, Ross-on-Wye, Herefordshire HR9 5GL; ☎01989-764211; fax 01989-765451; www.pgl.co.uk/personnel/index.html.   Organises

school travel groups to Italy.

Italian Job Finding Organisations:

Agenzia del Lavoro sede del Centro per l'impiego (Valle di Non): Via C.A. Martini, 28, Cles; ☎04-63421372; fax 04-63424710.

Agenzia del Lavoro sede del Centro per l'Impiego (Valle di Fassa): Via Milano, Pozza di Fassa; tel/fax 04-62763102.

Agenzia del Lavoro sede del Centro per l'Impiego (Valle di Fiemme): Via Bronzetti 8/A, Cavalese; tel/fax 04-62340204.

For other potentially useful addresses, see list of tourism organisations at www.jobonline.it.

VOLUNTARY WORK

THERE ARE MANY ORGANISATIONS that accept volunteers, mostly during the summer months, to work on various and diverse projects. It is not uncommon for voluntary projects to request some form of payment from volunteers to cover administration cost, food, accommodation and other costs.

More orgainsations offering all types of voluntary work are listed in *The International Directory of Voluntary Work* (£11.95), which is obtainable from www.vacationwork.co.uk. The book *Green Volunteers* (Euro16.01) covers opportunities in the field of nature conservation; it is available worldwide from www.greenvol.com or in the UK from www.vacationwork.co.uk.

Abruzzo National Park: Viale Tito Livio 12, 00136 Rome; ☎06-3540 3331; fax 06-3540 3253; post@pna.it. Volunteers carry out work protecting flora and fauna in an outpost of the Abruzzo National Park. Further details available from park offices: Pescasseroli (☎0863-1955) and Villetta Barrea (☎0864-9102; fax 0864-9132).

Archeoclub d'Italia: Via Sicilia 235, 00187 Rome; ☎06-4288 1821; fax 06-4288 1810; www.archeoclubitalia.it. Can provide information about archaeological work camps.

Brown Bears, Central Italy: CTS, Via A. Vesalio 6, 00161 Rome; ☎06-4411 1471; fax 06-4411 1401; ww.cts.it. Volunteers needed to help researchers in the Abruzzo National Park, the only habitat of a sub-species of Brown Bear. Volunteers must be able to walk for long periods during the day.

Communita' di Agape: Centro Ecumenico, 10060 Prali (Torino); ☎0121-807514; fax 0121-807690. This organisation recruits volunteers to work alongside the permanent staff to help run this ecumenical centre for national and international meetings. Applicants should be at least 18 years old and be available to work for a minimum of one month over the summer. Knowledge of Italian would be an advantage; board and lodging is provided.

CTS-Centro Turistico Studentesco e Giovanile: Via Nazionale 66, 00184 Rome; tel-06 4679317; fax-06 4679252; ctsambi@mbox.vol.it; www.cts.vol.it/). The largest Italian youth association, CTS organises research activities and expeditions which use paying volunteers to work in the field and fund different projects carried out by scientists. Some of the projects are in Italy in the Alps, Apennines and National Parks. Membership is required to join the expeditions. Further details from the above.

Emmaus: Via Castelnuovo 21/B, Segretariato Campi Lavoro, c/o Parr, 59100 Prato; ☎0574-541104; fax 055-6503458. Social and community work camps. At the time of press www.emmaus-international.org is aiming to list all Emmaus groups online including those in Italy.

Europe Conservation in Italy: Via Bertini 34, 20154 Milan; ☎02-33103344; fax 02-33104068. Volunteers are needed to work on archaeological excavations for a minimum of two weeks between July and September – six hours per day, six days per week. Board and accommodation are available for approximately £140 per week. Previous archaeological experience is desirable. Placements involve lectures and excursions but no fares or wages are paid.

Kalat Project: Information from ARCHEOCLUB, Progetto Kalat, c/o Banca di Credito Cooperativo, Sen. P.Grammatico, Via Amendola, 91027 Paceco, TP; ☎0923-558077; fax 0923-557642;www.infocom.it/kalat/. Environmental and archaeological camps in summer during July and August.

Legambiente: Via Salaria 403, 00199 Rome; ☎06-862681; fax 06-86218474; www.legambiente.com. Non-profit organisation. Volunteer opportunities include work camps, currently these are: restoration and protection camps on small islands off Sicily, bear research project in the Apennines, underwater archaeology and ecology in Sicily, etc.

LIPU (Lega Italiana Protezione Uccelli): Via Trento 49, 43100 Parma; ☎0521-273034; fax 0521-273419; www.lipu.it. The Italian equivalent of the RSPB publishes a list (in Italian) of their programme of summer working holidays protecting birds. Camps last one or two weeks and cost from €130 per week.

La Sabranenque, Centre International, rue de la Tour de l'Oume, 30290 Saint Victor la Coste, France (+33 4-66 500505; www.sabranenque.com). French-based organisation uses voluntary labour to restore villages and monuments in Altamura (inland from Bari in Southern Italy) and Gnallo (Northern Italy). The cost of participation is £180 for three weeks in July/August.

Mani Tese: P. le Gambara 7/9, 20146 Milan; ☎02-407 5165; fax 02-4812296; www.manitese.it. Collects and recycles objects for profit to finance department projects. Their summer projects include a study of development issues for which a knowledge of Italian is necessary.

Mediterranean Fin Whale Programme: Tethys Research Institute c/o Aquario Civico, Viale Gadio 2, 20121 Milan; ☎02-72001947; fax 02-72001946; www.tethys.org. Volunteers to assist with study of Fin Whales during the summer in the western Ligurian Sea and off Corsica. Volunteers must be able to swim and their tasks are varied from helping run the camp to collating data and observing.

OIKOS Via Paola Renzi 55, 00128 Rome; ☎06-5080280; www.oikos.org/ecology/volunteer.htm. Environmental organisation that has, since 1979, organised work camps to work on ecological projects to the south west of Rome.

Organizzazione Internazionale Nuova Acropoli: Piaza Regina Margherita 7, 67100 l'Aquila; ☎08-6261051; fax 08-6262860; http://space.tin.it/associazioni/ruqbr. Environmental protection organisation that organises various projects in Italy. Information, in Italian only, on their website.

WWF Italia: Ufficio Campi, Via Canzio 15, 20131 Milan; ☎02-2056 9505; fax 02-2056 9246; www.wwf.it. Publishes a list of annual *campi* (work camps) in magazine form and online – in Italian only.

ASPECTS OF EMPLOYMENT

SALARIES

EACH INDUSTRY IN ITALY has a national labour contract stipulating minimum wage (set every three years) and salary levels. However, workers in the North would never dream of being offered (let alone accepting) work paid at the minimum wage level and it is only in the most depressed areas of the Mezzogiorno where the minimum wage is a working reality. A major bone of contention between employers and unions continues to be Italy's adherence to the *scala mobile* when negotiating salary levels. Although the *scala mobile*, whereby wages are indexed to inflation, no longer passes on 100% of inflation but instead around 47% of the official inflation rate, the principle remains and the unions are reluctant to forgo it.

Although Italian salaries have a reputation for being lower than the European norm for individual jobs, many Italians hold a second or third salaried job, so increasing their take home pay dramatically. Managerial jobs (*dirigenti*) in particular are well paid with managing directors, marketing, personnel and financial executives and other senior employees earning wages comparable to anywhere in Europe, though this is likely to be lower than in the USA. Middle level staff will earn slightly less than a UK employee (much less than a US employee) and office staff and manual workers (*operai*) a lot less than UK employees. These guidelines will, however, depend on the area and individual qualifications. In southern Italy all of these salary rates will be significantly lower than in the north.

Peculiar to some West European countries (but not the UK) and some countries in the Far East is the practice of employers distributing from one to a maximum of four extra payrolls each year. All employees are entitled to an additional month's remuneration (the so-called 13th month) payable in December, though the collective bargaining contracts for certain sectors provide for additional payments. For example, in banking, monthly salaries are paid 16 times a year and, in the petroleum industry, 15 times. In commerce, a 14th month salary is payable in June of each year. These extra payments unsurprisingly comprise one of the greatest perks for UK and North American nationals when working abroad. Remember, however, that the base annual salary offered by the employer is usually divided by fourteen, fifteen or sixteen, rather than twelve so any feeling of extra wealth is unfortunately illusory.

WORKING CONDITIONS

THE STANDARD WORKING week is 40 hours with a legal maximum of 48 hours. Overtime cannot be demanded of any employee and is paid at a rate of between 130% and 150% of the normal hourly rate, depending on the number of hours worked and whether it is on a weekend or holiday. However, many unions do not permit overtime and are not convinced either that the proposed 35-hour week (which is supposed to create more jobs), is at all a good thing. This suggestion followed the initiative set by France, which has already implemented the idea. Having seen the French operate the system, where people are often expected to do the same work in less time, the Italians will probably not be too keen to adopt the system themselves.

Italian business hours vary from the Mediterranean working day of 9am-1pm and 3pm-7pm (maintained particularly in the south) to the more familiar 9-5 working day, followed by most of the larger companies and institutions. As in France, most Italian businesses simply close down for the entire month of August as the country takes its month-long summer holiday. Every employee is entitled to an annual holiday of between five and six weeks, depending on the length of service, in addition to the ten statutory days of holiday (see *Daily Life Holidays*) which are celebrated nationally.

HIDDEN JOBS

THERE ARE ABOUT 24,000,000 individuals who are working in Italy and of these approximately one sixth, or almost four million of them, are working black (*lavoro nero*). In other words they are unrecorded and do not pay tax or social security payments. This unofficial workforce comprises housewives, retired people, the 'unemployed' (those on redundancy funds and work mobility schemes), students, and people who already have another job. Having two jobs, but only declaring one, is more common in the north whereas in the south, illegal work is virtually a permanent form of employment. The result of such a huge percentage of illegal workers is a boon to the Italian economy and general prosperity, as companies and businesses have benefited from irregular workers boosting their productivity and profits, while not having to pay the heavy social security costs.

PENSIONS

ONE OF THE REFORMS that made Italy ready for the Euro was an assault on Italian pensions which until 1997 represented the highest percentage of GDP (14%) when compared to France, Germany, the UK and Ireland. At one point in the last decade the number of pensioners had slightly outnumbered workers at 1.03 pensioners per worker. One of the main problems tackled by the reforms was the number of people receiving pensions in Italy before reaching the maximum retirement age. Included in this was the fact that civil servants had the right to receive a pension after 16 years service.

Reforms have been making private sector workers ineligible for a long service pension until they are 57 years old with a minimum of 35 years of contributions. Public sector pensions are being brought into line with private ones gradually over a period of years until by 2004 they will have the same age and period of contributions limits.

BUSINESS ETIQUETTE

ANYONE USED TO NORTHERN EUROPEAN or North American business practices will find the Italian way of doing things somewhat less aggressive. Contrary to what you may be used to, the Italians consider it uncivilised to race through a deal in one day and positively barbaric to hustle at a working lunch. Like in France, working lunches in Italy are as much to see if you are someone that they want to work with as a time to do any actual business. Instead, once you realise that business is likely to be indivisible from pleasure, and produce a flurry of lunch and dinner invitations, at which you should use as much of the Italian you have succeeded in mastering, you are going to do better at business the Italian way than you think. The down side of this business mixed with pleasure scenario is that you may not see as much of your spouse and family as you were used to – which is probably why the French and the Italians take so many holidays and the whole of August off.

Although seemingly relaxed and easy going, most Italian offices and all business procedures are far more intensely hierarchical than Britons and North Americans are used to. This is largely because of the Italian's status-conscious psyche and to err on the side of safety it is often wise to adopt the blanket title of Signor or Signora, rather than breach the familiarity of Christian names.

TRADE UNIONS

ITALY'S FOUR MAIN TRADE UNIONS (*sindacati*) are grouped by political identity rather than profession. The CGIL, *Confederazione Generale del Lavoro* is predominantly Communist with a Socialist minority faction, while the UIL, *Unione Italiana del Lavoro* has a strong affiliation with the Socialists. The CISL, *Confederazione Italiana Sindacati del Lavoro*, is Christian Democrat while the CISNAL is affiliated with the right wing Italian social movement. There are also trade unions formed on the basis of an industry or sector of economic activity, mainly in the public sector and transportation industry. The most important of these are the General Confederations of Industry, Commerce and Agriculture. Although harbouring a history of radicalism and turbulence during the post-war decades of the 50's and 60's, the 80's saw a taming of the Italian trade unions to some of the most peaceable and compliant in Europe.

Union membership is not compulsory in Italy and membership figures have fluctuated considerably from 60% membership at the union's most militant post-war period in 1947 to an all time low of 33% membership in 1967. However, after the UK, Italy remains the most strongly unionised country in Europe.

The unions tend to work through a cycle of relative peace (with the exception of sporadic strikes on such national issues as housing, schools, unemployment, etc.) until the negotiation for the renewal of the two or three yearly labour contracts (*il rinnovo del contratto*) comes around. Then whole sectors of different industries are protesting simultaneously during the arduous negotiation process. The situation is not eased by the frequency with which *La Confindustria* (the Italian employers' confederation, the equivalent of the CBI in the UK) deliberately allows the contract expiry dates to overrun and so gain bargaining power over the unions, whose workers are technically without employment contracts during this interim period.

WOMEN IN WORK

STATISTICS CONCERNING THE FEMALE working population in Italy show that with a roughly identical female population to the UK, slightly fewer (just over 40%) women work overall. The position of women in the Italian work place is ambiguous. Italian females have yet to penetrate the highest and most elite echelons of Italy's political and business establishments; as yet there is no Italian equivalent of France's Edith Cresson, Britain's Margaret Thatcher or America's Madeleine Albright. However, increasingly, women are reaching the forefront of the major professions (journalism, medicine, law and architecture in particular) and commanding the respect that their influential positions warrant. Moreover, the Italian social services are not geared to the working mother; there is a serious shortage of free nursery schools and of company and state-funded crèches. Ironically then, it is often only those who can afford babysitters and private nursery school fees who are able to have a career or even work outside the home if they wish to. Many Italian women go further and say that they have to choose between a career and children because of the lack of care facilities.

Depending on who you speak to, Italian male chauvinism is a resilient dinosaur that working women still have to contend with, or Italian men are still gentlemen who protect and provide for their women. Many of these old-fashioned Latin prejudices are connected to the woman's perceived role within the family.

Italy has a law entitled 'Positive action for the achievement of male-female equality at work' (*Azioni positive per la realizzazione della parità uomo donna nel lavoro*). This was designed to remove all obstacles and give women free access to professions and types of work where they were under-represented and introduced the concept of indirect discrimination, where discrimination is unseen but evidenced by the facts. If a woman were to bring a case against an employer, the onus would be on the employer to demonstrate that there was no discrimination and not the other way around. It also allowed for the setting up of a series of organisations to oversee the administration of the law.

However, judges who rule that a slap on the bottom is not harassment, as long as it is a one-off and lacks sexual connotations (as happened in January 2001) do not help judicial protection of women harassed in the workplace! Similarly, the appeal court ruled in 1999 that a woman could not be raped if she was wearing tight jeans, as their removal required consent.

Also in 1991, a special law (number 215) was passed aimed at helping women to start their own businesses. Further information can be obtained from local chambers of commerce, regional co-operatives and artisan associations and *Centri Bic* (Business Innovation Centres).

Useful Addresses for Women

Differenza Donna: listing of regional offices at www.fpcgil.it/aree_att/donne/donneind.htm. Women's organisation providing help and advice to working women suffering harassment and abuse.

Telefono Rosa: viale Mazzini 73, 00195 Rome; ☎06-375 18261/2; fax 06-375 18289; www.telefonrosa.org. Monday to Friday from 10am to 1pm and 4pm to 7pm. Women's association that can offer advice to working women on subjects such as sexual discrimination and harassment, offices in various Italian cities.

Ufficio Speciale della formazione Professionale: These are located in most areas and can be found via the Chamber of Commerce. Provide professional training courses for women, regardless of age, designed to provide the skills that employers are looking for.

Further details can be obtained from the above address. The courses are designed for Italians and will therefore be conducted in Italian.

Contacts for business start-ups by women:

Impresa Femminile Singolare: c/o Federlazio viale Libano 62 Rome; ☎06-549121; www.federlazio.it.

La Societa per l'Imprenditorialita Giovanile: via Mascagni, 160 Rome; ☎06-862641.

Sentiero Impresa: Providing online advice on finance, e commerce and business: www.sentieroimpresa.it.

Women, job, feminism: website providing advice and information in Italian: www.gnomiz.com/nexus/argcon00/donne01.htm.

BUSINESS AND INDUSTRY REPORT

THE 1980'S SAW A DECADE of enormous economic and industrial success for Italy. After entering the decade with the highest strike record in the West, lame-duck industries and layer upon layer of ill-concealed political corruption, Italy succeeded in emerging from them as the capitalist world's fifth strongest economy, poised to overtake France and rise into fourth position. However, the successes of the manufacturing industry during this time belied an ominous lack of any overall economic policy and a national debt greater than the country's GDP, with a budget deficit running at over 12%. By mid-1990 to 1991 Italy's recession marked the end of one of the longest and most prosperous periods of expansion ever experienced by the industrialised economies since the reconstruction years following the Second World War. In 1993-94 the recession was still biting with rising unemployment (25% in the south). However, in addition to the political upheaval in the late 1990s that saw the ignominious demise of the Christian Democrats in a sea of corruption allegations, an economic upheaval took place as Italy tightened its welfare belt ready for joining the single currency. There is still high unemployment, but this has shown a downward trend in recent years. Unfortunately for Italy, the general world economic slowdown that started in 2001 is expected to affect its growth and budget plans; as Silvio Berlusconi admitted in the autumn of 2001 when actual tax revenues fell below estimated income.

High-tech industries in Italy have grown greatly in recent years due to increased demand and to the availability of skilled labour. Fast-growing sectors include telecommunications, electrical appliances and the machine tool (industrial robots) industry. Within the service sector, business services and financial services and insurance companies in particular are expanding. Further information on the Italian business scenario is provided in the chapter *Starting a Business*. Many of the multinational companies which dominate Italian industry provide good potential for well skilled job hunters. These companies are to be found predominantly in the motor vehicles (Fiat, Ford, Renault) and electrical appliances (Merloni, Zanussi, Electrolux) sectors.

The level of state-run industry in Italy has gone down quickly from being the highest in the EU, thanks to a massive sell off in recent years that has brought deregulation in that most dynamic of sectors, telecommunications. There is still however a large state interest in a variety of industries, especially those which are considered of strategic importance, such as raw materials, transport, defence, power generation, telecommunications and banks. Istituto per la Ricostruzione Industriale (IRI) is Europe's largest single company (excluding oil companies) and directly or indirectly employs huge numbers of people and controls hundreds of companies, including three major banks, RAI (the radio and television network), Alitalia (airways) and companies belonging to groups such as Finsder (steel), Finmeccanica (engineering), Fincantieri (shipbuilding) and Telecom Italia (electronics). Istituto Ente Nazionale per Idrocarboni's (ENI) interests include oil, raw and derived chemicals, petrochemicals, mining, energy engineering and services, textiles and financing. It has a share in some 285 companies, employing around 100,000 people. Finally, Ente Participazioni & Finanziamento Industria Manifattureriera (EFIM) has shares in 137 companies employing 60,000 workers. Its subsidiaries include aluminium, glass, food, engineering, transport and railways, aircraft and diesel engines companies. Although state-controlled industry includes many well-managed and technologically advanced concerns, it is suffering from huge accumulated debts and the effects of political interference and mismanagement in past years. The origins of all three mega-companies date back to the years following the Second World War, when the state intervened to rescue many companies with the proposed objective of selling them back into the private sector once they had been restructured and revitalised. This, however, rarely happened. Recently, some companies have been sold back into the private sector, though the government often holds a 'golden share' that basically means it still own more than 50% of the company.

Small businesses have dominated Italian industry over the last decade, and comprise one of its most distinctive features. Only 19% of the workforce is employed in companies which have more than 500 staff and over 59% of the manufacturing workforce is employed in companies where the total number of workers is less than 100. By contrast, these percentages for Britain and Germany are nearly a complete reverse. At the last count there were approximately three million registered small businesses functioning in Italy. Thus, small businesses are responsible for a large share of industrial output, especially in sectors where size is not a strategic feature, e.g. the retail trade, clothing and furniture and other areas requiring not large investments but substantial entrepreneurial ability. Most businesses in Italy are owned by a family or a partnership and this is typically true of farms, most retail and service establishments and many small manufacturing concerns. Gaps in the market exist (e.g. health food shops, DIY outlets, fast food, small garages) and are there to be taken advantage of by expatriates with hands-on experience of the relevant market in their own country. See the Chapter, *Starting a Business* for more ideas for new businesses. Although it will take perseverance to find a gap and to establish a presence in the Italian market, once you have made contacts and established your foothold the rewards, both financial and in terms of job satisfaction, can be immense. Of course fluency in Italian is a prerequisite for most of theses opportunities.

The widely-held belief that the whole of the Mezzogiorno is an area lacking potential for industrial development and to be avoided at all costs on account of Mafia infestation is mistaken. Admittedly, some areas in the far south, e.g. parts of Sicily and Calabria, are not ideal areas for industrial investment, dominated as they are by organised crime and hampered by a ludicrously inadequate system of infrastructure, communications and transport. However, some areas of the south – the mountain region of Abruzzi, Puglia and parts of Molise – have factories which function as efficiently as in the north, while benefiting from impressive government tax and credit incentives.

Finally, the opportunities of the single market are being taken very seriously by Italy (as her wholehearted endorsement of the Euro shows), even if her observance of EU directives is not quite so assiduous. Italy has been one of the most frequent offenders in the European Court for non-implementation of European directives – though France is also a major defaulter it rarely seems to get taken to court over it. However, harmonising trade will probably be a lot easier for Italy than harmonising banking standards and practices which still lag behind as do financial services providing private pensions and life assurance.

The following section provides an alphabetical guide to the most important Italian industries. The current prosperity or otherwise of each industry is discussed with a view to its employment and business potential for the expatriate. The most powerful companies in each sector have been listed wherever possible and the Italian contact addresses for these and many other Italian and international companies can be found in the *Directory of Major Employers* at the end of this chapter.

AEROSPACE

THE AIRCRAFT AND DEFENCE ELECTRONICS GROUP, Alenia, was formed in December 1990 from the merger of the Selenia electronics and Aeritalia aircraft subsidiaries of IRI and is Italy's leading aerospace group. Italy has joined the UK, Germany and Spain in participation in the Eurofighter programme. However, despite general buoyancy at the time of press there is cause for gloom in the defence business owing to a decline in other orders from the military services as defence budgets continue to shrink. Funding difficulties for the Italian air force have put a ceiling on the number of Tornado jets being purchased and there are doubts about how many other aircraft will be needed.

Bright spots on the industry's horizon include aerospace electronics, concentrated in the former Selenia group, which continues to flourish. Alenia in particular has also expanded on the space side. Combined with Aerospatiale and Alcatel Espace of France, it spent has spent millions of dollars on a stake in Space Systems/Loral, the satellites business controlled by Loral, the US defence group.

On the commercial aviation front, Alitalia the national carrier is seeking a state subsidy to finance its reorganisation plan. However, dubious management practices have resulted in a delay in the subsidy going through and the airline is the subject of investigations. As the airline industry suffers the after-effects of the September 11 terrorist attacks in the US and experts talk about consolidation of the numerous European airlines into three or four large groups, Alitalia's future does not look rosy. The profitable small airline, Air Dolomiti, like many low-cost European airlines is likely to continue its recent successes.

AGRICULTURE

ITALY HAS A TOTAL LAND AREA of 30,127,874 hectares of which 24% is classified as mountainous (i.e. above 600m or 700m according to region). Forty-five percent is hill land and the remaining 31% is plain. Average rainfall is 43 inches in the north, 37 inches in the centre and 33 inches in the south. There are more than 3,200,000 agricultural holdings, with an average farm owning 7.2 hectares of land of which 4.8 hectares is usable. The main agricultural area is the large fertile Po Valley, which is responsible for about 40% of Italy's total grain production. Other important, though less fertile plains are on the Tyrrhenian coast from Pisa down towards Naples and the coastal plains in Puglia.

About 8% of Italians work in agriculture which is considerably higher than the EU average of 2% which means that there is no shortage of experienced workers for agricultural enterprises. About half of the value of Italy's total agricultural output is derived from Mediterranean produce grown largely in the southern regions: wine, olive oil, and especially fruit and vegetables; Italy is the most prolific grower of fruit and vegetables in Europe. The remainder of Italy's agricultural output is farmed in the north and mostly comprises meat, dairy products and cereals. Farms in the south tend to be smaller, more labour intensive and much less fertile than those in the north. Additionally, the level of mechanisation and investment is lower in the south, communications are relatively poor and marketing less developed. Agricultural contribution towards the GDP fluctuates but represents about 7% on an average year. Sugar beet, grapes for wine and maize are the three largest agricultural crops in Italy, while sheep, pigs and cattle are the most profitable forms of livestock. Of those working in agriculture, approximately 63% are self employed and 35% are women. However, the interest in agriculture and the opportunities offered within it have declined and Italy's youth are now opting increasingly for the more attractive conditions offered by industry.

Italian farmers have embraced organic farming much more than other European countries and consequently organic produce in Italy is often no more expensive than chemically fertilised food. A number of expatriates have bought and now operate vineyards in Italy, combining business and pleasure in an Italian idyll.

THE AUTOMOTIVE INDUSTRY

THE ITALIAN AUTOMOTIVE INDUSTRY is led by Fiat of Turin, which has dominated Italy's home market for the last decade. The success of this mega-corporation, the largest in the private sector, is mainly due to the popularity of their new models because of the dramatic improvement in quality and styling. Other major manufacturers include the Fiat subsidiaries of Lancia, Alfa Romeo and high class makes, which account for only minimal shares of the market, such as Maserati, Ferarri and Lamborghini. Fiat's current primacy is a far cry from 1991 when Fiat laid off between 20,000 and 50,000 workers for one week each month when foreign competition and the recession dampened demand within the Italian market.

Japanese-badged cars (many of which are constructed in Europe) have begun, for the first time, to pose a threatening presence in the Italian market. Ford and Renault have also made vast inroads into the Italian market.

Piaggio and Greave's of India formed a joint venture to produce the three-wheeled 'Ape' in a new plant at Baramati.

The DIY sector has been the centre of increased interest, with the number of outlets selling parts and accessories growing. As Italy has the world's highest number of cars per thousand inhabitants (533 against the US's 469) this market has great potential for growth.

CHEMICALS

THE OUTLOOK FOR THE ITALIAN chemicals sector is not a rosy one. If the industry is to catch up with its principal rivals and to be a competitive international force it will have to carry out large-scale structural reforms or suffer the alternative of continued decline or being taken over. The chemicals sector has always been subject to political manipulations and has suffered directly as a result of this. Moreover, the industry has moved against international trends by becoming more rather than less state-controlled and by relying heavily on the domestic market for sales and plant location. The industry is now dominated by the chemicals subsidiary of the state-controlled ENI, EniChem. In an effort to turn around its poor economic situation, EniChem had to weather a strong union protest as it closed some of its plants in the south and cut some 4,500 jobs from its 50,000 strong workforce. Almost 55% of new investment in the chemical industry is in the south, Sardinia and Sicily.

However, EniChem still represents a significant percentage of world chemical production and a larger percentage of European production. The industry employs approximately 230,000 workers and the other major chemicals force, the privately-owned Montedison company is currently in a stronger position than its larger and more powerful rival. Major foreign multinationals with a strong presence in the Italian industry include Unilever, Esso, Dupont, BASF, Ciba Geigy, Hoescht, ICI, Henkel and Alusuisse.

The highly successful Menarini group makes over 40% of its sales abroad and has spent heavily to develop foreign interests. The group's current priority is to develop a market in the UK. Many small and medium sized companies also flourish in this sector; 60% of Italian chemicals companies employ less than 50 staff.

CLOTHING AND TEXTILES

ITALY IS ONE OF THE WORLD'S LARGEST textile and clothing producers but now, with increasingly strong competition from low-cost producer countries (notably, Portugal, Romania and certain countries in the Far East) and a turndown in the home market, Italy is striving to maintain its position and reputation within the market. Biella and Prato in northern Italy are the two centres of the Italian textile trade. Some of the most powerful Italian textile companies include Marzotto, Montefibre, Gommatex, Snia-fibra, Lanerossi and Legier Industria Tessile. However, after nearly three decades of spectacular growth the industry is facing its first crisis. During the 90s a number of well-known family-run concerns had to look to outside investors to survive – some families had to concede control in order to survive at all. The number of textile companies has fallen by many thousands from a peak of 17,000 and employment levels have dropped to fraction of the all-time high of 60,000 jobs in the 1980's. In an effort to cut costs, the industry employs an immigrant and largely illegal work force (mostly Chinese and North African).

The unpredictability of the fashion business is partly responsible for these cutbacks, combined with the small size of the majority of the companies which means that financial structures are weak. Moreover, as mentioned above, the Portuguese textile industry has emerged over the last decade as a major competitor, and more recently Romania and a number of Asian producers as well. Today a large percentage of activity is still concerned with recycling textiles and producing for the mass market. Roughly half of total productivity is taken up with supplying the ready-to-wear business and department stores; while the remaining 15% focuses on the production of upmarket fashion garments. However, the textiles industry is under no serious threat of extinction and some of its greatest supporters even argue that the decline in the number of companies during the last five years is a part of a dynamic process whereby the industry is being strengthened and modernised.

Italian designers are also struggling to find a new focus. A centuries-old artisan tradition in working endless variations of fabric and leather, added to extensive recent research on novel ways of treating or developing various fabrics, allows Italian designers to adopt a unique look which constantly eludes and frustrates foreign designers. However, as competition from new rivals (e.g. USA, Germany and Japan) grows more intense and the pressure is maintained from traditional rivals (e.g. France), Italian designers are exploring all available avenues in order to survive and prosper; market flotation, expansion into other manufacturing fields via franchises – even the financial market. Some of the largest Italian clothing manufacturers of international renown are Benetton, Max Mara, Stefanel, Miroglio Tessile, Linea Sprint and Confezioni di Matelica. The top Italian fashion designers include Valentino, Versace, Armani, Ferre, Trussardi, Krizia, Enrico Coveri, Laura Biagiotti, Missoni and Mario Valentino.

COMPUTERS

THE ITALIAN COMPUTER INDUSTRY, in line with the industry worldwide, has experienced dramatic fluctuations in orders and profits over the last few years. Olivetti, the champion of Italy's computer industry, has suffered serious difficulties over the years and has been looking to find a new direction to increase its profit and performance. Olivetti has moved some of its production plants to cheaper plants in Singapore and Mexico amidst an inevitable fury of protest from trade unionists and politicians alike. Olivetti plans to try to build the order-invoking and profit-building government links enjoyed by the French and German computer industries with their respective governments.

A potential growth area for the industry in Italy is in software and services, where margins remain relatively high. Finsiel, the software subsidiary of the IRI and the main agent for the Italian public sector in software development is another powerful force in the Italian computer industry.

ELECTRICAL HOUSEHOLD APPLIANCES

Italy's white goods sector counts among one of the country's greatest successes in terms of innovation, productivity, quality and sheer financial success. At its peak, Italy was responsible for approximately 40% of total European production of electrical appliances – as is obvious if you walk around any European showroom admiring the rows of sleek washing machines and dryers sporting 'Made in Italy' tags. The success of the industry is not only due to low labour costs. Innovative thinking and personal leadership by the industry's giants e.g. Lino Zanussi and the Fumagalli brothers (from Candy), were responsible for the industry's meteoric rise to fame and success in the 1950's and 1960's. The industry's export market is thriving and exports represent nearly three quarters of the market. In particular, the Eastern European market is one which presents future potential for Italian exports. Italy's white goods producers have sold hundreds of thousands of appliances to former eastern bloc countries and are well placed to sell more. The home market is also thriving, helped by the Italians' propensity (by British standards anyway) to feverishly change their entire kitchen armoury with great regularity.

The industry's largest companies include Merloni (the largest Italian-owned company in the industry whose brands include Ariston, Indesit and Colston), Zanussi (now owned by the Swedish Electrolux group), Elettrodomestici, Ocean, Rancilio, Framec and Nilox.

FOOD AND BEVERAGES

Although Italy is traditionally regarded as being an agricultural country self sufficient in foodstuffs, food and agricultural produce account for the largest percentage of Italy's import bill and this percentage seems to be increasing. The average Italian family spends around 30% of its income each year on food. The following unlikely assortment of food products are recognised as potential growth areas in the Italian retail market: health food, breakfast cereals, high quality biscuits, processed sliced cheese, pork, mayonnaise and beer. The general trend of this industry is one of increased profitability achieved through the application of high technology production methods and the adoption of high-quality advertising campaigns. Olivetti, IBP (Buitoni Perugina), Gardini, Barilla, Galbani, Sagit, Ferrero and Parmalat are some of the largest Italian food companies. European and American multinationals have also made large inroads into the Italian market. The main Italian beverage companies include Martini & Rossi I.V.L.A.S., Fransesci Cinzano and Gio Butoni.

The change in eating and drinking habits of Italian is seen best in the drinks market – beer consumption has grown so much that wine producers have to resort to advertising their product.

HIGH TECHNOLOGY

Italy features well in various high technology sectors e.g. robotics, radar systems and aerospace. Fiat's Comau subsidiary makes industrial robots which are used worldwide (General Motors is a major client), as well as in Italy where they have successfully automated much of the Fiat auto production line and the gigantic Benetton warehouse stock systems. Italy's hi-fi industry is fairly buoyant – Brionvega radios, Seleco TV's and Autovax car stereos all have as good a name as imports from Northern Europe or Japan, as does the entire Olivetti office equipment range.

For non-EU citizens this is one of the best sectors to look for employment as there is a great shortage in skilled workers in Italy and throughout Europe.

HOUSING AND CONSTRUCTION

In recent years high interest rates and strict legislation on rents and building permits have troubled the construction sector. The result has been an unsatisfied demand for both rental property and accommodation for outright purchase and a parallel proliferation of illegal building work. However, subsidies are available to facilitate access to finance and thereby encourage construction activity.

As foreigners continue to buy old Italian property for renovation, there will be a continued demand for skilled workers who can restore and rebuild old property and also speak English.

IRON AND STEEL

Industrial development in Italy is a very recent phenomenon and the iron and steel industry only dates back as far as 1958. This was when new ventures mushroomed while existing industries underwent a solid period of consolidation and marked a boom period in the iron and steel industry which lasted until the arrival of 1974 and recession. The industry has never really returned to its former heights although steel-pipemaking is doing well and the Marcegaglia group announced at the end of 1997 that it will be building a new 500 billion lire factory for pipes and steel plate at Ravenna. In 1993 the European Commission elected to cut the EU's capacity for hot steel production by subsidising shut-downs. In Italy this resulted in a 43.8% reduction in capacity up to 1996. Generally speaking, however, there has been a shift in focus away from the manufacturing to the service sectors in industry, Italy's current fastest-growing sectors are all steel users e.g. the machine tool, automobile, industrial equipment and household electrical appliance sectors. Italian iron and steel foundries have invested heavily lire in plant and equipment to help fend off increasing competition from outside Italy.

IT SECTOR

ITALY'S IT SECTOR is one of its biggest success stories and demand for IT specialists has outstripped supply for many years. Based mainly in the north where companies has easy access to European market, IT companies actively recruit specialist employees from abroad, including from outside the EU, via the internet.

MACHINE TOOL INDUSTRY

DESPITE A SLIGHT DOWNWARD trend in the home market shared with the majority of Italian industries during the 1990s, the machine tool sector continues to thrive and Italy successfully in ousted the USA from its position as fourth largest machine tool producer in the world. The machine tools industry is comprised mainly of small-sized industries (the watchword of Italian industry) which are able to meet the requirements and adjustments of individual demand; about 85% of the industry's 450 firms have payrolls of less than 100 workers. Especially successful are the metal-bending equipment firm Pedrazzoli and the food-processing machine firm, Braibanti. The industry is represented by the national machine tools, robot and automation manufacturers' association, UCIMU. The association's membership of nearly 220 companies accounts for about 80% of total industry-wide turnover. The industry's particular stronghold is its export market which it is expanding slowly, especially in Germany, France, the US and Russia. UCIMU considers that Italian machine tool makers are well positioned in Europe, particularly in the German, Spanish and French markets. In addition, the industry has good sales networks in Portugal, Switzerland, Eastern Europe and Russia.

MINING

ITALY IS POORLY ENDOWED WITH MINERAL RESOURCES, although sizeable quantities of pyrites, lead, zinc, magnesium, bauxite and coal are mined. Europe's only significant deposits of sulphur are found in Sicily, but extraction is uneconomic. Output of metallic materials has been in long-term decline, although surveying is now being intensified. Domestic coal production accounts for less than 10% of total consumption of coal.

OIL AND GAS

ENI'S TWO DISTRIBUTION SUBSIDIARIES are Agip Petroli and IP, which together hold 48.5% of the Italian market. Agip and IP have 7,730 outlets and 4,760 respectively. The largest non-Italian oil company is Esso, followed by MonteShell (a conglomerate of the privately-owned, home-grown Montedison and Royal Dutch Shell) and Mobil, while the largest Italian concerns are Erg and Api. All non-Italian oil companies used to have to follow the rigid regulatory framework laid down for all ENI state subsidiaries which set limits on the opening and closing times of service stations and any changes of services a service station could introduce, but these restrictions have, however, been liberalised and opening hours extended in recent years.

REGIONAL EMPLOYMENT GUIDE

IN CHAPTER ONE, *General Introduction*, the main cities and regions of Italy were discussed with a view to residence. In this section, the same regions and major cities are covered, but this time with a view to the employment prospects available in the major industries in each area. The information provided will give some idea of the industries which are dominant and the types of jobs which are most readily available in each area.

LOMBARDY, EMILIA-ROMAGNA, TRENTINO-ALTO ADIGE

UNLIKE MOST OF NORTHERN ITALY, which was predominantly agricultural until the end of the Second World War, Lombardy boasts an industrial history which dates back to the nineteenth century. Although Rome attracts many foreign business people and professionals as the country's capital, Milan, the regional capital of Lombardy, functions as the true economic and financial centre of Italy. A major trading and manufacturing centre for centuries, Milan has maintained a business tradition placing it at the forefront of the European business scene. The income that Milan generates is responsible for a sizeable percentage of the Italian gross industrial product and employs a similarly disproportionate percentage of the Italian workforce. Greater Milan alone, with a population of more than four million, has more than 70,000 industrial units employing more than a million people. The most important of the confusingly wide range of industries to be found in Milan include steel, heavy engineering, machine tools, transport equipment, chemicals, oil refining, plastics, textiles, clothing and shoes, electronics and domestic appliances. The food industry as a whole is especially strong in Milan and throughout the entire region. Milan also home to Agusta, the Italian helicopter manufacturer.

The industrial importance of Emilia-Romagna has escalated over the last fifty odd years. At one time solely agricultural, the region, particularly in and around Bologna and Modena, has become extremely influential industrially, particularly in the areas of light engineering, food processing and ceramics. The city of Modena is now estimated to have the highest per capita income in Italy while the 3.9 million citizens of the region as a whole have come to enjoy the second highest per capita incomes in Italy. The number of expatriate in the Modena area is demonstrated by the opening an continued expansion of the International School of Modena. With an unemployment rate of 3.8% set against a national average around 9.2%, the region has the rare problem of facing a shortage of labour. The region boasts 45,000 highly successful small and medium-sized businesses operating in agriculture and food products, industry and tourism. Modena's contribution is in the form of farm machinery, luxury sports cars and Tetra Pak cartons. Bologna is famous for its electronics, packaging and mechanical industries while Forli is an important fruit and vegetable processing industry. Ravenna is an important port as well as being the home town of the Ferruzzi Group which has a whole range of interests from oil seed, cement and sugar production to a controlling interest in one of Italy's largest chemical companies, Montedison. The total group turnover rivals that of the Fiat group.

Trentino-Alto Adige, the alpine area to the north of Verona, has succeeded in implementing a miracle of long-term planning and efficient administration over the past two decades. The largely German-speaking population enjoys a wide-ranging regional autonomy from Rome and its mountain farming population is actually increasing and prospering while everywhere else in Europe such populations are in decline and the indigenous farming population leaves its homes in droves. The Trentino-Alto Adige area is often favoured by large German and Japanese companies setting up in Italy, both for its northern European mentality and its easy accessibility and efficient infrastructure. The highly developed infrastructure of the area includes an efficient motorway system, the Munich-Verona railway line and a gas piping system which covers almost all the industrial development zones of the region. Being close to Austria, Slovenia and therefore much of Eastern Europe it is well placed to attract further inward investment.

This region also offers highly attractive tax and investment incentives which, though less weighty than those offered in the south, can be approved by the efficient local bureaucracy in a very short period, often in little more than three months. Incentives include significant tax concessions, cheap land, subsidised infrastructure development and training courses with the prestigious University of Trento.

Together the three regions produce around half of Italy's gross industrial production. A large portion of this derives from the small and medium-sized manufacturers that abound in Italian industry. Statistics on the size of registered firms show that the great majority of firms employ under 50 people.

Useful Information

Milan: Linate Airport is 7km from downtown Milan. Malpensa Airport is located 50km from the city. Information about both airports can be obtained from ☎02-7485220 and www.sea-aeroportimilano.it/Eng/. Both airports are served by shuttle buses (Malpensa – 02-58583185; Linate – STAM ☎02-717106, STAB ☎035-318472, Air Pullman ☎02-4009 9260) to/from Milano Centrale Railway Station and Malpensa is also served by train from Milan Central and Milan Garibaldi stations. A shuttle service between Linate and Malpensa is also operated by STAM, STAB and Air Pullman.

Milan tourist information, Galleria di Testa Stazione Centrale FF.SS., CAP 20124; ☎02-7252 4360/370.

British Chamber of Commerce, Bergamo; Mr Arnold Attard (Hon. Area Secretary for Bergamo), c/o British E.L.T., Via Taramelli, 52, 24121 Bergamo, Italy; tel/fax 035-249150.

British Chamber of Commerce, Bologna; Mr Roger Warwick (Honorary Regional Secretary for Emilia Romagna), c/o Pyramid, Viale Masini, 20, 40126 Bologna, Italy; ☎051-254568; fax 051-254948.

British Chamber of Commerce, Brescia; Ms Julia A. Jones; C.S. International, V.le. della Bornata 42, 25123 Brescia, Italy; ☎030-3366811; fax 030-3366098.

PIEDMONT AND AOSTA

PIEDMONT FORMS ITALY'S MAIN INDUSTRIAL and commercial heartland and the Valle d'Aosta, although not a major international trading market, is important as a tourist area and attracts many millions of visitors each year, chiefly in the winter months during the ski season. The Valle d'Aosta also exports over 75% of its annual production of electricity to meet the industrial demands of nearby Piedmont. As Italy lacks indigenous sources of fossil fuels, substantial investment to achieve a further increase in the hydro-electric generating capacity of the region is planned.

The region of Piedmont boasts a wealth of distinct, diverse and prosperous commercial features within its six provinces. From the Fiat-based automobile industry of Turin to Olivetti computers at Ivrea, textiles in Biella, wine, soft fruits and agricultural produce from Cuneo, Asti and Vercelli and light precision engineering in Alessandria and Novara, the area is richly endowed as a source of potential wealth. Piedmont has succeeded in motivating its industries through a level of automation and technological innovation that necessitates a labour force of only 1.8 million – less than 9% of the Italian total. Turin is however moving away from its almost exclusive industrial base towards finance, service and technology. The area encompassing the cities of Turin, Ivrea and Novara has been designated Italy's 'Technocity' to signify the wide range of new industries developed in the region i.e. robotics, aerospace, telecommunications, computers, bioengineering and new materials. The Technocity is responsible for much of the national production of robots, computers and by far the majority of its aerospace products.

Notable industrial corporations located in the Technocity area include Aeritalia (aerospace and aviation), SKF (ball and roller bearings), Microtechnica (aviation and space research), Prima Industria, Bisiach and Carm (robotics), BICC/CEAT (cabling) and Pirelli (tyres). As far as the other major provincial towns are concerned, Biella is a prime textile centre processing wool products. Ivrea is the home of Olivetti, famous for its office machinery and communications products while the province of Cuneo is one of the largest market gardening areas of northern Italy. The soil and climatic conditions that exist here are ideal for the cultivation of a wide range of vegetables and soft fruits while Alba and Asti are renowned for their high-quality wines, especially the effervescent Asti Spumante. As part of Technocity, Novara is notable for its hi-tech, precision engineering companies, many of which serve the industrial needs of Milan. Alessandria and Valenza are famous for their jewellery trade while Vercelli is noted for its rice and maize cultivation.

Useful Information

Turin: International Airport (☎011 5676 361/2; www.turin-airport.com) is located 16 kms/10 miles north of the city centre. Shuttle buses (☎011-30 00 611) and train services (☎011-691 0000; www.satti.it) operate to the city centre. A bus service to Aosta (☎0165-262 027) is also available.

Turin tourist information, Via Viotti, 2, CAP 10128; ☎011-5541111; fax 011-5541122; www.regione.piemonte.it/turismo.

British Chamber of Commerce, Turin; Mrs Jocelyn Holmes (Hon. Regional Secretary for Piemonte), c/o Musci & Holmes Architetti, Via Genola 3, 10141 Turin, Italy; tel/fax 011-331216.

LIGURIA

LIGURIA ESSENTIALLY FORMS THE ITALIAN RIVIERA. Genoa saw the start of the industrial revolution in Italy, albeit almost a century after Britain's. The region produced the first motor car, the first military field tank and the first aeroplane. The region's traditional wealth stems from its steel, port handling and ship building industries in the port city of Genoa as well as from the tourist industry in the whole region. However, all of these sectors are now in difficulty and perhaps this history of success has also bred a dangerous complacency among the inhabitants of Liguria and the region has slipped behind others in attracting and creating high-tech industries and new investment.

Investment in the port facilities is aimed at boosting capacity for container handling, ferry activities and improving handling of a still active oil and petrochemicals sector. This investment will compensate for some of the thousands of jobs to be lost due to the decline of the steel industry and may signify a general revival in the regions fortunes. The ship building facility of Fincantieri, has also borne heavy financial losses like much of the worlds shipbuilders due to a cutback in military budgets and competition from the Far East. Tourism, once the main money-spinner of the whole region, has also declined and the current major downturn in tourism will exacerbate the problem. Visitors to the region are mostly Italians rather than foreigners. The fact that the Italian Riviera has to some extent lost its fashionable reputation of the past and is seen as expensive compared to Spain and Turkey, has further reduced the number of visitors to the region.

However, on the more positive side of life, Genoa offers a high quality of life – often ranked head of Milan, Rome and Turin. The purchasing power of the local population is high, boosted by a large number of wealthy people who are in retirement or who own holiday homes in the region. Although there have been some disappointments in overall economic performance, this can be attributed mainly to the poor performance of state sector industries, and regional GDP is almost in line with the national average.

The established oil and associated petrochemicals industries are located in and around Genoa and the small industries sector is also strong. Interestingly, a large percentage of businesses registered with the Genoa Chamber of Commerce are run by women. Finally, the highly developed infrastructure of the area includes an efficient motorway system, the Munich-Verona railway line and a gas piping system which covers almost all the industrial development zones of the region.

VENETO AND FRIULI-VENEZIA GIULIA

THE CONCENTRATION OF ECONOMIC activity is not entirely limited to the north-western regions of Italy. In the past 25 years the Veneto region in Italy's north-east has become one of Italy's most successful business regions, especially with small to medium-sized companies producing high quality, hand-crafted goods such as shoes, clothes, spectacle frames, medical equipment and mechanical components. This is the territory of Benetton, Stefanel and Carrera Jeans. Other commercial activities include speciality cakes and foods, printing and publishing, natural stone, wine, banking, light and heavy engineering, advertising, consultancy and research. Verona is the area's commercial hub and is strategically placed to take advantage of the good communications to central Europe and the Balkans now that they are beginning to settle into post-war peace. Verona is also home to Italy's third largest exhibition centre. Verona focuses on pharmaceuticals, transport, engineering and publishing, while Vicenza is famous for its tanning, textiles, industrial jewellery, ceramics and steel and mechanical engineering. Names of international stature in the area include Benetton in the Treviso province, the Vicenza-based Marzotto (the biggest wool manufacturer in Europe). This region was largely agricultural until after the Second World War, the main exceptions being the textile, jewellery, tanning and ceramic manufacturing industries around Vicenza which date back to the eighteenth century. Treviso specialises in textiles, sportswear, ceramics and mechanical engineering and

Venice in glass, heavy industry and fishing. Padua is known for mechanical engineering, finance and services distribution

The Friuli region is made more attractive to potential investors by the various financial and tax incentives offered here by the Government. However, most likely due to the area's somewhat isolated position geographically, investments by foreign and Italian companies were slow to build up but are now booming. Ironically, the area's position tucked into the north-east corner of Italy was traditionally its downfall, but now makes it its biggest advantage in years to come with its strategic closeness to the rapidly changing economies of Eastern Europe and the Balkans. At the very least it is well-placed to profit from the through traffic that will have to transit the area. The industrial area of Porto Marghera in the Venice lagoon was established in the 1920's and shipbuilding takes place along the coast near Trieste. However, now these traditional, large industries are at least equalled in importance by a firmament of young medium and small enterprises, producing an extensive range of capital and consumer goods. Belluno is noted for its spectacle manufacturing industry and Pordenone for its white goods and steel engineering sectors; Zanussi have a large base in Pordenone. Pordenone is the main town in the province of the same name and is a dynamic economic and cultural centre. There is an annual international business Fair (*fiera*) held in September and throughout the year there are many other events based around various sectors: machine tools, horticulture, food and catering, electronics and hi-fi, optical equipment, design and more. Significant trends in the region include a much stronger decrease in the number of agricultural workers than the national average and a much higher rate of increase in industrial workers. Thus, the economic outlook is rosy and industrialists and traders, aware of the blossoming of opportunities that the EU has brought, are ready to collaborate with British firms.

Useful Information

Venice: Marco Polo Airport (☎041-541 6397; www.veniceairport.it) is 13km north of Venezia and direct transfers are available by boat (Motorboat Service – ☎041-541 5180; water taxis – ☎041-541 5184), bus (041-541 5180) and taxi.

Venezia tourist information, Santa Lucia (Stazione Ferroviaria), CAP 30122; ☎041-529 8711; fax 041-523 0399.

Vicenza tourist information, Stazione FF.SS., CAP 36100; ☎04-4454 0355.

British Chamber of Commerce, Trieste; Prof. John Dodds, Università di Trieste, Via F. Filzi 14, 34132 Trieste, Italy; ☎040-6762322 or ☎040-6762385; fax 040-6762301; dodds@sslmit.univ.trieste.it.

British Chamber of Commerce, Pordenone; Mrs Susan Clarke (Hon. Regional Secretary for Friuli Venezia Giulia), c/o Overseas Language Consultancy, Corso Vittorio Emanuele 54, 3170 Pordenone, Italy; tel/fax 0434-29089.

British Chamber of Commerce, Gorizia; Mr D. Katan, Via F. Filzi 14, 34132 Trieste, Italy; ☎040-6762322 or ☎040-6762385; fax 040-6762301.

British Chamber of Commerce, Verona; Mr Peter Eustace (Hon. Regional Secretary for Veneto), c/o CSA snc – via Pigna 14/a, 37121 Verona, Italy; ☎045-592482; fax 045-597629.

British Chamber of Commerce, Venezia; Mr Ivor Neil Coward, Lexicon Trans-

lations SAS, Via Caneve 77, 30173 Mestre, Italy; ☎0422-780505 or 041-5348005; fax 0422-782821 or 041-5349720; lexivor@tin.it.
British Chamber of Commerce, Padova ; Ms Christine King, c/o Abbey National Bank, Via Altinate 8, 35121

Padova, Italy; ☎0498-761380; fax 0498-761381.
British Chamber of Commerce, Udine; Mr C. J. Taylor, Via del Torso 41/8, 33100 Udine, Italy; tel/fax 0432-600397.

TUSCANY, UMBRIA & LE MARCHE

ABOUT 57% OF THE TOTAL POPULATION of these three regions is concentrated in Tuscany, of which Florence is the much-famed and tourist saturated capital. Close to Florence, at Prato, is the centre of the largest textile area in Italy which involves some thousand companies and nearby at Santa Croce sull'Arno is Italy's largest tanning industry which supplies the local shoe and leather industry. Other important industrial areas include Pisa, Lucca (home to a large paper-making industry), Livorno (which boasts the main Italian container port) and Empoli (renowned for its glass and pottery). Other important industries in Tuscany include steelworks, electronics, furniture, medical equipment and the famous Chianti wine and olive oil as well as Carrara marble. Umbria, home to approximately 23% of the regional population, is mainly agricultural although important steelworks exist at Terni and ceramic production near Perugia. Le Marche is again predominantly agricultural although the prospering Merloni group (producer of white goods) is based in this area.

Also important are the needs of the large numbers of foreigners who own homes in the region.

Useful Information

Florence: Florence airport tends to just receive regional flights as the nearby mountains prevent larger planes from landing. Passengers for Florence normally go to the larger Pisa airport.

Pisa: Aeroporto Galileo Galilei (050-500707; www.pisa-airport.com) is only 20km from Lucca and Livorno and 80km from Florence. Trains run directly to Pisa airport from Firenze SMN station and it is possible to check in at the air terminal inside on platform 5. Compagnia Pisana Trasporti (www.cpt.pisa.it) run regular buses to and from central Pisa. Tickets for buses and trains can be bought from the information office in the arrivals hall. Car rentals are available through the major companies such as Hertz, Avis, Euoprcar, Sixt and Thrifty.

Firenze, tourist information, Piazza Stazione, 4, CAP 50121; ☎05-521 2245; fax 05-5238 1226.

Pisa tourist information, Via Pietro Nenni, 24, 56124 Pisa; ☎050-929777; fax 050 929764.

Florence; Maria Grazia Antoci, Viale Milaton 33, 50129 Firenze, Italy; ☎055-4625049; fax 055-486463; mgantoci@videosoft.it.

LAZIO, ABRUZZO AND MOLISE

THIS AREA IS SIGNIFICANT FOR the strong presence of service industries, especially Lazio. The three regions of Lazio, Abruzzo and Molise together account for around 10% of the GNP and slightly more of the total national expenditure on goods and services. Rome, besides being the administrative and governmental capital of Italy is also home to the main offices of the state holding companies, IRI, ENI, and EFIM. The head offices of the main Italian banks are also found in Rome, in cosy proximity to the majority of state agencies and public utilities e.g. RAI, the state television company; ENEL, the national electricity board; CNR, the national research council; the Italian State Railways and the Southern Italian Economic Development Board (Agenzia per la Promzione dello Sviluppo des Mezzogiorno). Industrial activity in the capital is low in comparison with the service industries. However, a number of towns near the capital have become centres of intensive industrial production e.g. Frosinone, Latina, Aprilla, Pomezia, Civita Castellana and Rieti which specialise in the electronics, telecommunications, light engineering, pharmaceutical and chemical industries.

Useful Information

Rome: Leonardo da Vinci International Airport (☎06-65953640; www.adr.it), at Fiumicino, is located 35 km/22 miles from the city center. A taxi ride takes approximately 40 minutes. Regular trains run from Termini Station and Tiburtina Station (☎848-888088). A night service shuttle bus (☎800-431784) runs between Tiburtina and the International terminal. Ciampino Airport (☎06-794941) is 20 minutes from the centre of Rome and a Bus service connects the Airport to Ciampino railway station and Anagnina underground station, which have frequent connections to the centre of Rome.

Roma tourist information, Via Parigi, 5, CAP 00185, ☎06 488 991; fax 06 481 9316.

British Chamber of Commerce, Rome; Mr Andrew Calvin, Via Acherusio 18, 00199 Roma, Italy; ☎06-86206459; fax 06-86383162; acolvin@tin.it.

THE SOUTHERN ITALIAN MAINLAND

THE FOUR SOUTHERN REGIONS of the Italian mainland are Campania, Puglia, Basilicata and Calabria. The total working population is around 4 million and unemployment is high, well over 20% in some parts.

Calabria and Basilicata, comprising approximately 20% of the area's population, are relatively undeveloped with few industries and remain largely dependent on agriculture and a growing tourism industry. Campania has the largest concentration of industry in the south and this region's economic growth has been only slightly below the national average over the last few years. Campania's main interests include traditional industries such as food processing, canning, tanning and leatherwork, ship building and steel railway rolling stock and chemicals, but also more advanced and potentially prosperous sectors such as aerospace, electronics, telecommunications and motor vehicles. The latter are the areas in which there has been the greatest amount of new investment in recent years, largely by the major national companies. The older industries, and particularly the myriad small artisan-type industries which abound in the Naples area, have however, been slow to invest in new technology and risk being left behind by their international rivals.

In Puglia, the highest concentration of population is around Bari, which also has a high concentration of relatively small but energetic industries and every year the *Fiera del Levante* is held, while in Foggia, there is an agricultural fair. Taranto is a major steel production centre, with a number of ancillary industries but had to cut back production to meet EU directives, which did not help the local economy as other industrial regions in Europe found with same EU directive. The main agricultural products of the region are hard wheat, wine, olive oil, chestnuts and hazelnuts, tomatoes, vegetables and fruit (citrus fruits and kiwi fruit in particular). Agriculture accounts for around 20% of the total local gross product and around half the population still depends directly or indirectly on agriculture for a living. Though the number of people directly engaged in agriculture is declining, land holdings still remain relatively small. The average per capita income in the south is official much lower than in the north and the disparity in wealth between the north and south are widening – though this low level should be considered in the context of the large black economy of the region. To demonstrate the size of the black economy, there is no lack of money in the south and a large consumer market exists for luxury items. There are approximately 4,000 wholesalers and 99,000 retailers in Campania; 4,500 wholesalers and 42,000 retailers in Calabria and 700 wholesalers and 11,000 retailers in Basilicata.

Useful Information

Naples: A 15 minute drive from the centre of Naples, there are bus connections between *Aeroporto Internazionale di Napoli* (☎081-789 6259; www.gesac.it) and Piazza Garibaldi (Azienda Napoletana Mobilità – ANM, ☎081-763 2177) or Piazza Municipio (CLP, ☎081-531 1706).

Bari tourist information, Piazza Moro, 32/A, CAP 70122; ☎080-5242244.

British Chamber of Commerce, Naples; Roy Boardman, St. Peter's ELC, Riviera di Chiaia 124, 80100 Napoli, Italy; ☎081-683468; fax 081-682721.

British Chamber of Commerce, Taranto; Ms Stefania Lo Cascio, Worldwide Trusts Consultants Srl, Via Nitti 45/a, 74100 Taranto, Italy; ☎0348-3851033 or ☎099-4590880; fax 099-4590809; staff@trustsitaly.com.

DIRECTORY OF MAJOR EMPLOYERS

Additional employers and employers in certain fields can be found through the online Italian Yellow Pages, Chamber of Commerce Directories and internet search engines.

Accountants

Coopers & Lybrand Spa: Via delle Quattre Fontane 15, 00184 Rome; ☎06-4818565; fax 06-48146365.

Deloitte and Touche Spa: Palazzo Carducci, Via Olona 2, 20123 Milano; ☎02-88011; fax 02-433440.

KPMG Peat Marwick Fides Snc.: Via Vittor Pisani 25, 20121 Milano; ☎02-67631; fax 02-67632278.

Pricewaterhouse Coopers Spa: Corso Europa 2, 20122 Milan; ☎02-77851; fax 02-7785240.

Reconta Ernst & Young SaS di Bruno Gimpel: Via Torino, 68, 20123 Milano; ☎02-722121; fax 02-72212037.

Advertising Agencies

CiTieS Holdings Srl, Via dell'Artigianato 2, 20044 Bernareggio, Milan.; ☎03 96900570; fax 03 96901201.

Saatchi & Saatchi Spa, C.so Monforte, 52, 20122 Milano – (Mi); ☎02 77011; fax 2781196.

Aerospace Manufacturers and Suppliers

Aerea S.p.A., Via Cefalonia, 18, 20156 Milano (MI); ☎02 33 4831; fax 02 3340 2676.

Aermacchi S.p.A., Via Ing. P.Foresio, 1, 21040 Venegono Superiore (VA); ☎03 3181 3111; fax 03 3182 7595; www.aermacchi.it.

Agusta S.p,a,, Via G. Agusta, 520, 21017 Cascina Costa (VA); ☎03 3122 9111; fax 03 3122 2595; www.agusta.it.

Alenia Aeronautica, Un'Azienda Finmeccanica, Via Giulio Vincenzo Bona, 85, 00156 Roma; ☎06 417231; fax 06 411 4439; www.aleniaerospazio.com.

Alstom Ferroviaria S.p.a., Via Fosse Ardeatine, 120, 20099 Sesto S. Giovanni (MI); ☎02 2442 3211; fax 02 244 23400; www.alstom.com.

Avionteriors S.p.A., Via Appia Km. 66,400, 04013 Tor Tre Ponti (LT); ☎07 73 6891; fax 07 73 631546; www.avioninteriors.it.

Bonetti Aircraft Supports S.r.l., Via Sottoripa 1/a, 16124 Genova; ☎01023 501; fax 010235 0222.

Elettronica S.p.a., Via Tiburtina Valeria Km 13, 700, 00131 Roma; ☎06 41541; fax 06 415 4924.

Galileo Avionica S.p.a., Via di S. Alessandro, 10, 00131 Roma; ☎06 418 831; fax 06 4188 3800.

GSE - Ground Support Equipment S.r.l., Viale del Vignola, 44, 00196 Roma; ☎06 322 2877; fax 06 361 1715; www.g-s-e.it.

Lital S.p.a., Via Pontina Km 27, 800, 00040 Pomezia (RM); ☎06 911 921; fax 06 912 2517.

Logic S.p.a., (Gruppo Aeronautica Macchi), Via Brescia, 29, 20063 Cernusco Sul Naviglio (MI); ☎02 922 4401; fax 029210 2528; www.aermacchi.it.

Mecaer Meccanica Aeronautica S.p.a., Via per Arona, 46, 28021 Borgomanero (NO); ☎03 2283 7173; fax 03 2284 4081; www.mecaer.it.

Moreggia S.p.a., Via Bardonecchia, 77/10, 10139 Torino; ☎011 385 5635; fax 011 4028436; www.moreggia.com.

Piaggio Aeroindustries S.p.a., Via Cibrario, 4, 16154 Genova Sestri; ☎010 64811; fax 010 6481234.

Secondo Mona S.p.a., (Aircraft equipment), Via Carlo Del Prete, 1, 21019 Somma Lombardo (VA); ☎0331 756111; fax 0331 252334; www.secondomona.com.

Airline and Associated Companies

BAA Italia, BAA GESAC – Capodichino Airport, 80014 Napoli – (Na); ☎081 7896528; fax 081 7896201.

bmi british midland c/o SAS, Via Albricci 7, 20122 Milano – (Mi); ☎0272435211; fax 0272021945.

British Airways Plc., Corso Italia, 8, 20122 Milano – (MI); ☎02 724161; fax 02 8055806.

Buzz c/o B. & D.P. Srl, Piazza Bertarelli, 1, 20122 Milano – (Mi); ☎02 72022466; fax 0272020162.

Cathay Pacific Airways Limited, Via Barberini, 3, 00187 Roma – (RM); ☎06 4820703; fax 06 4741297.

Gandalf Airlines Spa, Via Aeroporto 13, 24050 Orio al Serio – (Bg); ☎035 4595011; fax 035 4595083.

Go Fly Ltd, Enterprise House, Stansted Airport, Stansted, Essex CM24 1SB, UK; ☎+44 (0)1279 666333; fax +44 (0)1279 681762.

Banks

Banca Popolare di Novara Scrl, Via Quintino Sella 5, 28100 Novara – (No); ☎0321 662736; fax 0321 662017.

Banca Toscana Spa, Via Pancaldo 4, 50127 Firenze – (FI); ☎055 4391374; fax 055 4360061; www.bancatoscana.it.

Banca Woolwich Spa, Via Pantano, 13, 20122 Milano – (MI); ☎02 584881; fax 02 58488511.

Barclays Bank Plc (Corporate clients only), Via Moscova, 18 20121 Milano

– (MI); ☎02 63721; fax 02 63722925.

Credito Emiliano Spa, Vicolo Santa Margherita, 20121 Milano – (MI); ☎02 88131; fax 02 8813340; www.redem.it.

Credito Italiano Spa, Via Arsenale, 23, 10121 Torino – (To); ☎011 57131; fax 011 57131.

HSBC Bank Plc, Via Santa Maria alla Porta 2, 20123 Milano – (Mi); ☎02 724371; fax 02 72437402.

Ing Barings (Italia) Srl, Via Brera, 3, 20121 Milano – (MI); ☎02 809271; fax 02 809007; www.ing-barings.com.

National Westminster Bank, Via F.Turati, 16/18, 20121 Milano – (MI); ☎02 6251; fax 02 6572869.

Robert Fleming Sim Spa, Via Manzoni, 12, 20100 Milano – (Mi); ☎02 760361; fax 02 76008107.

SBC Warburg Dillon Read, Italia SIM Spa: Via Santa Maria Segreta 6, 20123 Milano; ☎02-725271; fax 02-72527773.

UBS Warburg (Italia) Sim Spa, Via Santa Margherita 16, 20121 Milano – (MI); ☎02 725271; fax 02 72527772.

Chemicals and Pharmaceuticals

Chr. Lechler & Figlio Succ.ri S.p.a., Via Cecilio 17, 22100 Como (CO), ☎03 1586211; fax 03 1586206; www.lechler.it.

Nuncas Italia S.p.a., Via G.di Vittorio, 43, 20017 Rho (Mi); ☎02 9317961; fax 02 93179630; www.nuncas.it.

Reckitt & Benckiser Italia S.p.a., Via Lamedusa, 11A, 20141 Milano (MI); ☎02 844751; fax 02 8464810; www.reckitt.com.

Segix Italia Srl, Via del Mare 36; 00040 Pomezia; ☎06 911 801; Fax 06 912 2882. Manufacturer of pharmaceutical products.

Unilever Italia S.p.a., Via N. Bonnet

10, 20154 Milano (MI); ☎02 623380; fax 02 6552310; recruitment.milan@unilever.com; www.unilever.com.

Clothing and Textiles

Coats Cucirini S.p.a., Via Vespucci, 2, 20124 Milano (MI) ☎02 636151; fax 02 659 6509. Also: Viale della Costituzione, Isola A/3, 80143 Napoli (NA); ☎081 562 5004; fax 081 562 5200; www.tamtamitalia.com/coats/.

Samar S.p.a., Via M. Libertà 68, 13874 Mottalciata (Bi); ☎0161 872111; fax 0161 857782; www.samar.it.

Techwear S.p.a. (Production and world-wide distribution licencee of Gian-franco Ferre' Men's Underwear and Homewear), Via Vivaio 11, 20122 Milano (Mi); ☎02 7733 0150; fax 02 7733 0155; www.gianfrancoferre.com.

Construction and Contracting

J & A Consultants Italia Snc, Piazza San Fedele, 4, 20121 Milano (Mi); ☎02 869 15041/2/3; fax 02 8901 1120; info@jacons.com.

Turner & Townsend Project Management Italia, Corso Monforte 39, 20122 Milano (Mi); ☎02 7639 4760; fax 02 7639 9973; www.turnerandtownsend.com.

Estate Agents & Relocation Services

Bonaparte Spa, Via Clerici 11, 20121 Milano – (Mi); ☎02 8855161; fax 02 88551660; www.bonaparte.it.

CB Richard Ellis Spa, Via dei Giardini, 4, 20121 Milano – (MI); ☎02 6556701; fax 02 65567050; www.cbrichardellis.com.

Eres Srl – European Real Estate Service, Via Urbano III, 2, 20123 Milano – (Mi); ☎02 89408373; fax 02 89408413.

Healey & Baker, Via Turati, 25, 20121 Milano – (MI); ☎02 637991; fax 02 653254; www.healey-baker.com.

Immobiliare Internazionale Mina Mothadi Broszio, Residenza Sagittario T2, Milano 220090 Segrate – (Mi); ☎02 2640582; fax 02 26410393.

Jones Lang LaSalle Spa, Via Durini, 28, 20122 Milano – (MI); ☎02 776971; fax 0277697232.

Property International Srl, (Estate & Relo-cation Agent), Via Correggio, 55, 20149 Milano – (MI); ☎02 4980092; fax 02 48194170.

Vigano' Giorgio Srl, Via Maggiolini, 2, 20122 Milano – (Mi); ☎02 76003914; fax 02 783618.

Electronics and Computing

3G Electronics S.r.l., Via Boncompagni, 3b, 20139 Milano (MI); ☎02 539 0441; fax 02 569 0243; www.3gvideogroup.it; www.3gelectronics.it.

Ariete S.p.a., Via Toscana 57A/B, 59100 Macrolotto, Prato (Po); ☎054 5281; fax 054 528400; www.ariete.net.

Arteleta International S.r.l.: Via Pelizza da Volpedo, 57, Postbox 26, 20092 Cinissello Balsamo; ☎660 1541; fax 02 612 2573.

BBJ S.r.l., Piazza Sicilia 6, 20146 Milano (Mi); ☎02 3650 4650; fax 02 3650 4662; www.bbj.it.

Comestero Sistemi S.r.l. Via Bolzano, 1/E, 20059 Vimercate (Mi); ☎039 625 091; fax 039 667479; www.comestero.com.

Control Techniques Spa: Via Brodolini 7, 20089 Rozzano, Milano; ☎02 575 751; fax 02 5751 2858. Electronic speed and position controls.

Easynet Italia S.p.a. Viale Fulvio Testi 7, 20159 Milano (MI); ☎02 3030 1500; fax 02 3030 1590; www.it.easynet.net.

Human Technology S.r.l., Viale Masini, 4, 40100 Bologna (BO); ☎051 254 988; fax 051 244 208; info@humantechnology.it; www.humantechnology.it.

Kontron Instruments Spa: 25, v. Madonna degli Angeli, 84019 Vietri Sul Mare (SA), Campania; ☎08 976 1488. Electromedical equipment.

Rigel Engineering S.r.l., Piazza Attias, 21/C, 57125 Livorno; ☎0586 210222; fax 0586 210255; www.rigel.li.it.

Tecnimex S.r.l., Via A. Corti, 28, 20133 Milano (MI); ☎02 7063 5924; fax 02 7060 0412; www.tecnimex.it.

Vision Engineering Ltd Italia, Via Roma 72, 20037 Paderno Dugnano (Mi); ☎02 9904 9973; fax 02 9904 9973.

Financial and Business Services

American Express Bank Ltd., Piazza San Babila 3, 20122 Milano – (Mi); ☎02 77901 – 800651520; fax 02 7790582.

Invesco Europe Ltd., Via Cordusio, 2, 20100 Milano – (Mi); ☎02 880741; fax 02 88074391.

Norton Rose, Via Visconti di Modrone 21, 20122 Milano – (Mi); ☎02 799144; fax 02 77331538.

Reuters Italia Spa., V.le Fulvio Testi, 280, 20126 Milano – (Mi); ☎02 661291; fax 02 66101498.

Rothschild J., Via E. Panzacchi, 6, 20123 Milano – (Mi); ☎02 72002111; fax 02 8693727.

St. James International (Offshore services), Via Lazzaretto, 6, 20124 Milano – (Mi); ☎02 29516108; fax 02 2914615; www.stjamesinternational.com.

Thomas Cook Italia Ltd., Viale Marche, 54, 00187 Roma – (Rm); ☎06 48782316; fax 06 48782330.

Towers Perrin Group, Via Pontaccio, 10, 20121 Milano – (MI); ☎02 863921;

fax 02 809753; www.towers.com.

Scottish Equitable Italia Srl., Via Turati, 9, 20121 Milano – (MI); ☎02 655821; fax 02 65582500.

Insurance Services

Commercial Union Italia Spa., Viale Abruzzi 94, 20131 Milano – (MI); ☎ 0227751; fax 02 2775204.

Generali Assicurazioni Spa, Piazza Duca degli Abruzzi, 2, 34132 Trieste – (TS); ☎040 671111; fax 040 671600.

Lloyd Italico Assicurazioni Spa., Via Fieschi 9, 16121 Genova – (GE); ☎010 53801; fax 010 541221.

Lloyd's of London, Via Sigieri, 14, 20135 Milano – (MI); ☎02 55193121; fax 02 55193107; www.lloyds.it.

Marsh Spa, Pal.Carducci, Via Olona, 2, 20123 Milano – (MI); ☎02 485381; fax 02 48538300; www.marsh.com.

Marsh Spa, Via Cavour, 1, 10123 Torino – (To); ☎011 565471.

Royal & Sun Alliance Assicurazioni, Via Martin Piaggio, 1, 16122 Genova – (GE); ☎010 83301; fax 010 884989; www.rsa-ass.it.

Royal International Insurance Holdings Ltd., Via F.lli Gracchi, 30/32, 20092 Cinisello Balsamo – (Mi); ☎02 660791; fax 02 66011760; www.royal.it.

SAI – Società Assicuratrice Industriale Spa, Corso Galileo Galilei, 12, 10126 Torino – (TO); ☎011 6657111; fax 011 6657685.

Lawyers

Ashurst Morris Crisp Studio Legale Associato, Via Finocchiaro Aprile 14, 20124 Milano – (Mi); ☎02 620227225; fax 02 620227226.

Colvin Andrew, Via Acherusio, 18, 00199 Roma – (Rm); ☎06 86206459; fax 06 86383162.

Grimaldi e Clifford Chance, Via Clerici, 7, 20121 Milano – (Mi); ☎02 806341; fax 02 80634200; www.cliffordchance.com.

Lovells Studio Legale, Via F.lli Gabba 3, 20121 Milano – (Mi); ☎02 7202521; fax 02 72025252; www.lovells.com.

Simmons & Simmons Grippo, C.so Vittorio Emanuele, 1, 20122 Milano – (MI); ☎02 725051; fax 02 72505505.

Studio Legale Associato Freshfields, Via dei Giardini, 7, 20121 Milano – (Mi); ☎02 625301; fax 02 62530800; www.freshfields.com.

Worldwide Trusts Consultants Srl, Via Nitti, 45/a, 74100 Taranto – (Ta); ☎099 4590880; fax 099 4590809.

Management Consultants

Andersen Spa, Via Della Moscova, 3, 20121 Milano – (MI); ☎02 290371; fax 02 6572876.

ASI Consulting Italy Srl, C.so Venezia 16, 20121 Milano – (Mi); ☎02 76003138; fax 02 795659; www.asigroup.net.

Beavan C.P. Christopher, Via Leopardi, 21, 20123 Milano – (MI); ☎02 4815369 fax 02 48108133.

O'Donnell & Associates Srl, Via Stradon 5, 35010 Borgoricco – (Pd); ☎049 9336275; fax 049 9338847; www.odas.it.

Management Recruitment Consultants

Chayo & Partners Executive Search, Viale Bianca Maria 10, 20129 Milano – (Mi); ☎02 5460499; fax 02 55186540.

DPA Srl, Corso Magenta 56, 20123 Milano – (Mi); ☎02 48020668; fax 02 48020540.

Egon Zehnder International Spa, Piazza Meda, 3, 20122 Milano – (MI); ☎02 770791; fax 02 76021063.

MacCormick Hamilton International Italia

Srl, Via Conservatorio, 17, 20122 Milano – (Mi); ☎02 7742171; fax 02 76012379.

Mindoor Srl, Via Santa Maria Segreta 7/9, 20123 Milano – (Mi); ☎02 45485800; fax 02 45485188; www.mindoor.com.

Nicholson International Italia Srl, Via Cino del Duca 5, 20122 Milano – (Mi); ☎02 7722961; fax 02 798349; www.nicholsonintl.com.

RRA Srl, Via A.Appiani, 7, 20121 Milano – (MI); ☎02 6231121; fax 02 6552837; www.russellreynolds.com.

Manufacturers and Equipment Suppliers

Audco Italiana S.r.l., (Hydraulic equipment), Via D. Cucchiari, 30, 20155 Milano (MI); ☎02 317241/2; fax 02 313464.

Fiat S.p.a., Via Nizza, 250, 10126 Torino; ☎011 686 1111; fax 011 686 1723; www.fiat.com.

Hodara Utensili S.p.a., Viale Lombardia, 16, 20090 Buccinasco (MI); ☎02 457721; fax 02 48842783; info@hodara.it; www.hodara.it.

Indemar S.r.l., Via Guido Rossa, 40, 16012 Busalla (GE); ☎010 9641927; fax 01 09641920; info@indemar.com; www.indemar.com.

JCB S.p.a., Via Enrico Fermi, 16, 20090 Assago, Milan (MI); ☎02 48866401; fax 02 488 0378; www.jcbitalia.com.

Sede SCALA S.r.l., (Home interiors manufacturer), Via Caboto 18/20, Zona Ind. Ranaro, 46046 Villanova Di Reggiolo (RE); ☎0522 973112; fax 0522 974016; www.scalasrl.com.

Sistema Compositi S.p.a., Via Casilina Km. 57, 500, 03018 Paliano (FR); ☎07 7553 8511; fax 07 7553 8158; www.sistemacompositi.com.

SKF Industrie S.p.a., Via Dante Alighieri, 6, 10069 Villar Perosa (TO); ☎0121 312111; fax 0121 514304; www.skf.it.

Special Metals Services S.p.a., Via Assunta, 59, 20054 Nova Milanese (MI); ☎0362 4941; fax 0362494224; www.specialmetals.com/europe.htm.

Metal Sud S.r.l., Via Nazionale Appia - Località Crisci, 81021 Arienzo (CE); ☎08 2380 5397; fax 08 2380 5089.

Oil and Pharmaceuticals

B.P.Italia Spa, Milano Fiori Palazzo E/5-Strada 6, 20090 Assago – (MI); ☎02 822741; fax 02 57500709.

British Gas Italia Spa: Piazza Cavour 2, 20121 Milano; ☎02-777941; fax 02-77794440.

Enterprise Oil Italiana Spa, Via dei Due Macelli, 66, 00187 Roma – (RM); ☎06 699561; fax 06 69956600.

Glaxo Wellcome Spa, Via A. Fleming, 2, 37135 Verona – (VR); ☎045 9218111; fax 04

59218388; www.glaxowellcome.co.uk.

Smithkline Beecham Spa, Via Zambeletti, 20021 Baranzate di Bollate – (MI); ☎02 38061; fax 02 38200536.

Unilever Italia Spa: Via N Bonnet 10, 20154 Milano; ☎02-623380; fax 02-6552310.

Miscellaneous

Cable and Wireless Spa: via Ferrante Aporti, 26, 20125 Milano; ☎02-268181; fax 02-26141504.

Christie's of London: Piazza Navona 114, 00186 Rome; ☎06-6872787; fax 06-6893080.

P & O Container Europe Srl Strada 4, Palazzo A, Scala 7, 20090 Assago, Milano; ☎02-575681; fax 02-57512614.

STARTING A BUSINESS

CHAPTER SUMMARY

○ There are over 3 million small businesses in Italy: some 300,000 new ones set up each year, but many of these fail.

○ There is official encouragement for new businesses but it can be difficult to raise finance and there is much red tape to be faced.

○ Help for prospective businessmen can be obtained from the British Department of Trade and Industry, the British or American Chambers of Commerce in Milan and elsewhere, and the network of Euro Info Centres established by the European Union.

○ Although the north of Italy is the most dynamic business region there are various state incentives for those considering investing in the south.

○ Raising money can be difficult as British banks will not provide start-up loans for Italian businesses, and even if an Italian bank can be persuaded to help the interest rates will be high.

○ An individual setting up in business in Italy must establish a proper business structure, for which professional advice is essential.

○ Possible fruitful types of business to establish include health food stores, car repair, estate agencies; doctors and dentists may do particularly well in areas where there are numbers of other expatriates.

○ The Italian tax system is complex, and so expert fiscal advise is essential for the self-employed.

THE SINGLE EUROPEAN MARKET has made Europeans from EU countries increasingly aware of the possibility of starting a business in another Community country and the close historical and family links of many North Americans with Italy has made many of them consider doing so too. The experience can be a rewarding one for those who have the appropriate skills and know how, and who are also aware of the support and resources that are at their disposal and that are often needed. There are, however, many challenges in starting a business and many more (mainly bureaucratic and cultural) that only manifest themselves when doing so in a foreign country.

Before setting up your own business in a foreign country it will undoubtedly have helped to gain experience in running a business in your own country, or running someone else's abroad, first. Many entrepreneurs have already had a successful business or professional career working for someone else when they set out on their own and this experience is even more useful when setting up in a foreign country.

The possibilities in Italy, if not limitless, are certainly as wide-ranging and in some areas (e.g. financial services, consulting and high quality consumer goods) are more promising than they are in Britain and the US where there is already much competition. Self-employment as a medical or dental practitioner, artist, writer, mechanic, manufacturer, retailer, personal trainer or farmer are just some of the successes notched up so far.

Italy is the land of the small business and there are over three million of them. Estimates put the number of new enterprises started annually at an astonishing 300,000, though the number of failures is also high. This explosion of Italian entrepreneurial activity is linked to the difficulty in finding an employer willing to offer long-term job security, so skilled workers have opted to go into business for themselves, whether they have an aptitude for the chosen business or not. It is therefore small wonder that this exceptional volume of entrepreneurial activity leads to a high failure rate. Studies show that the majority of Italian businesses fold in the first five years of their existence. In fact in some recent years the number of firms that ceased activity has exceeded the number newly registered.

Part of the reason for this historic high failure rate is that while Italy encourages people to set up in business, the necessary support structures including bank finance and even training for potential entrepreneurs is lacking. Another problem is the bureaucratic assault course to be negotiated before nailing up a nameplate, emblazoning a logo or even opening a shop. Getting finance may not be that easy either as many Italian banks have had a policy of not lending to any but well established businesses. There has been some recent progress on bank support for start-ups and banks are now permitted to lend in the medium-term for commercial projects (though application are certain to be strenuously scrutinised). Some banks, notably Credito Italliano have a corporate finance and mergers and acquisitions department.

Evidently, the process of setting up an Italian business is not for the faint-hearted. Problems that you might encounter getting a business up and running in your own country are heightened in a foreign country where you have to cope with unfamiliar bureaucracy, culture, language and business practices, as well as find customers with similarly unfamiliar characteristics.

To sum up, Italy offers two extremes to the prospective foreign entrepreneur. On the one hand Italians are some of the world's best business people and are excellent to deal with. On the other hand, Italy's red tape is one of the world's worst. Depending on the area, it can take up to a year, and cost thousands of pounds spent on various fees, trips to Rome and the town where you will be based, to complete all the formalities, many of which seem tediously repetitive. No wonder that some foreigners take the headache out of the process by employing one of the increasing number of professional advisors and relocation agencies, the majority of which are based in Milan, where some boast of having you up and running in 40 days. The services offered by each vary from helping to form a network of contacts to completing the formalities necessary to start trading, and from complete corporate relocation (including finding accommodation for foreign executives and arranging domestic telephone, gas and electricity connections) to helping find offices and staff for your business.

As already mentioned, it would be unthinkable to attempt going into business in Italy without learning the language, mainly because being a commercial success in Italy probably relies more on socialising than in most other countries. The ability to communicate in Italian is therefore imperative for anyone contemplating an Italian business venture. In addition to speaking Italian, as when starting a business in any country it is also important when starting a business in Italy to:

- Have a sound business plan.
- Carry out an in depth feasibility study on the practicalities of running your proposed business in the area you are considering.
- Have a thorough knowledge and experience of the type of business you are intending to run.
- Have the personal stamina and determination and the capacity to the handle risk of losing everything.
- *Pensare in grande, cominciare in piccolo* (think big, start small).

The following sections outline the various processes involved in setting up different types of businesses.

PROCEDURES INVOLVED IN STARTING A NEW BUSINESS

THE PREDICAMENT FACING FOREIGNERS who wish to operate a business in Italy is whether to acquire an existing business or launch their own and there are compelling arguments for both options. Taking over an existing concern avoids the bureaucracy involved in setting up from scratch. On the other hand it is often difficult to ascertain with certainty the exact financial state or standing of the package you are acquiring. If the package includes staff, then Italy's protective labour laws may make a shake up, or dismissal of staff extremely difficult. On balance there is probably more to be said in favour of starting up an entirely new business.

Preparation from Scratch

Before launching yourself into the necessary formalities for setting up a business in Italy, exhaustive preparation is essential. For instance thorough research should enable you to determine accurately whether a proposed business has a reasonable prospect of succeeding. This often means finding a gap in the market that the Italians have not yet exploited. A prime example of niche-making is that of Abbey National, which having noted the lack of an Italian equivalent of building societies, is now happily ensconced in northern Italy and has ten branches selling mortgages to Italians. Other financial areas include private pension providers and car insurance, which are likely to expand hugely in Italy with recent financial deregulation. There is also scope in providing all these services for the expatriates (see *Ideas for New Businesses* below).

Preparation is not only about spotting a gap in the market. Other considerations include whether or not the prospective business person or organisation feels that the Italians will be able to relate to them. The best way of finding out is undoubtedly to spend as much time there as possible, on holidays, business prospecting trips etc. making friends and useful contacts who will form your network of advisors and allies if and when you finally decide to take the plunge. Many entrepreneurs who have already successfully negotiated the bureaucracy say that, initially, advice from the DTI in London, the British (or American) Chamber of Commerce in Milan, proved invaluable.

Another starting point for those thinking of setting up business in Italy is the Italian Chamber of Commerce for Great Britain (296 Regent Street, London W1; ☎020-7495 8191; www.italchamind.org.uk) which exists to promote two-way trade between Britain and Italy and to promote UK investment in Italy. They can supply a list of British firms operating in Italy and can also provide contact addresses in Italy and information on Italian government incentive schemes. The notorious inertia of the Italian Government in promoting Italy as an international business zone is only too evident in dealings with their representatives in Britain, so do not be put off. The most productive groundwork will undoubtedly be that carried out in Italy itself. Foreigners who have located their market pitch in Italy report that growth is usually meteoric, such is the buoyancy of the Italian market. There are numerous Italian Chambers of Commerce in North America and they can be located through www.italchambers.net and www.italbiz.net.

Special Contact. *The Intertrust Group* (2 Babmaes Street, London SW1Y 6NT, England; www.intertrustgroup.com) are based in London and provide legal, accounting and tax advice for international clients with companies in multiple jurisdictions. They predominantly work with investment, holding, royalty, real property and finance companies through their offices in a number of countries.

Euro Info Centres (EICs)

One of the first steps before moving to Europe to start doing business is a visit to one of the network of Euro Info Centres established in 1987 by the European Commission. There are now hundreds of EICs in fifteen European countries and more around the world. The Info Centres are linked directly to the European Commission's databases and are an up-to-date source of information on European standards, EU initiatives for small businesses, and new opportunities arising from the single market. By linking up with other Centres throughout Europe, information about national and local opportunities and regulations can be obtained. The cost of services is partly borne by the European Union and partly by the client.

A list of the UK EICs is below and many of them can be contacted by email through http://europa.eu.int/comm/enterprise/networks/eic/eic_uk.html. A directory of all EICs in Europe and around the world can be found at: http://europa.eu.int/business/en/advice/eics/index.html,

Belfast: EIC, Ledu House, Upper Galwally, Belfast BT8 4TB; ☎01232-491031; fax 01232-691432.

Birmingham: European Business Centre, 75 Harborne Road, Edgbaston B15 3DH; ☎0121-455 0268; fax 0121-455 8670.

Bradford: West Yorkshire Euro Info Centre, Mercury House, 2nd Floor, 4 Manchester Road, Bradford BD5 0QL; ☎01274-754262.

Bristol: EIC, Business Link West, 16 Clifton Park, Clifton, BS8 3BY; ☎01179-737373; fax 01179-745365.

Cardiff: Wales Euro Info Building, UWCC Guest Building, P O Box 430, CF1 3XT; ☎02920 229525; fax 0290-229740.

Exeter: EIC Southwest, Exeter Enterprises Ltd. Reed Hall, University of Exeter EX4 4QR; ☎01392-214085; fax 01392-264375.

Glasgow: EIC Ltd., ☎0141-228 2793.

EIC: Brynmor Jones Library, University of Hull, Cottingham Road, HU6 7RX; ☎01482-465940; fax 01482-466488.

Inverness: EIC North of Scotland, 20 Bridge Street, Inverness IV1 1QR; ☎01463-702560; fax 01463-715600.

Leicester: Leicester EIC, 10 York Road, Leicester LE1 5TS; ☎0116-2559944; fax 0116-2553470.

Liverpool: EIC North West, Liverpool Central Libraries, William Brown Street, Liverpool L3 8EW; ☎0151-298 1928; fax 0151-207 1342.

London I: EIC 33 Queen Street, London EC4R 1AP; ☎020-7489 1992; fax 020-7489 0391.

Manchester: Manchester EIC, Churchgate House, 56 Oxford Street, Manchester M60 7BL; ☎0161-237 4020; fax 0161-236 9945.

Newcastle-Upon-Tyne: EIC, Great North House, Sandyford Road, Newcastle-upon-Tyne NE1 8ND; ☎0191-2610026; fax 0191-2221774.

Norwich: EIC East Anglia, 112 Barrack Street, Norwich NR3 1UB; ☎0345 023144; fax 01603-633032.

Nottingham: EIC, 309 Haydn Road, Nottingham NG5 1DG; ☎0115-9624624; fax 0115-9856612.

Slough: Thames Valley Euro Centre, Commerce House 2-6 Bath Road, Berks, SL1 3SB; ☎01753-577877; fax 01753-524644.

Southampton: Southern Area Euro Info Centre, Civic Centre, Southampton SO14 7LW; ☎02380-832866; 02380-231714.

Staffordshire: Staffordshire European Business Centre, Commerce House, Festival Park, Stafford ST1 5BE;

☎01782-202222; fax 01782-274394.
Telford: Shropshire and Staffordshire EIC: Trevithick House, Stafford Park 4, Telford TF3 3BA; ☎01952-208213.

Useful Addresses

British Chamber of Commerce for Italy: Via Camperio 9, Milan. ☎02-877798/8056094; fax 02-86461885; www.britchamitaly.com.

Direzione Generale della Produzione Industriale: Via Molise 2, 00100 Rome, Italy; ☎010-39 6 47051.

Export Market Information Centre (EMIC): Kingsgate House, 66-74 Victoria Street, London SW1E 6SW; ☎020-7215 5444/5; fax 020-7215 4231; e-mail: (EMIC@xpd3.dti.gov.uk). Statistics, directories, market research reports, mail order catalogues, country profiles etc.

Italian Chamber of Commerce for Great Britain: 296 Regent Street, London W1; ☎020-7637 3153; fax 020-7436 6037.

Accountancy Firms: Anyone planning to start a business in Italy would be advised to seek the advice of accountancy firms in Britain which have branches in Italy. A list of international accountancy firms with offices in Italy can be found in the list of *Major Employers* in the *Employment* chapter.

Chambers of Commerce in Italy

In the initial stages of setting up a business in Italy you will probably be dealing with the British Chamber of Commerce in Milan (☎02-877798; bcci@britchamitaly.com; www.britchamitaly.com) or the American Chamber of Commerce (☎02 8690661; amcham@amcham.it; www.amcham.it. The chamber can provide you with contacts, make introductions and advise on offices if you need a physical base in Italy.

In addition to all its other services the British Chamber of Commerce for Italy produces *Britaly*, an online newsletter available to subscribers. It also prints:

Focus on Italy: the guide to business and pleasure in Italy with facts, figures, articles contacts and information on doing business in Italy.

Speak to the World: an annual brochure of the Chamber's English Language Consultancy Service. It has a print run of about 5,000 copies.

Trade Directory and Members' Handbook: is a bi-annual publication which lists all chamber members and is now on-line on their website (www.britchamitaly.com). Print run of some 1,500 copies.

To advertise in any of the above you can phone (02-877798) or fax (02-86461885) or email bcci@britchamitaly.com.

The branches of the British Chamber of Commerce throughout Italy (listed under *Chambers of Commerce* in the *Employment* chapter above) will be able to provide local advice and information for prospective entrepreneurs.

The Italian Chamber of Commerce in Milan (via Meravigli, 12-20124 MI, Italy; www.mi.camcom.it) is the main one in Italy and they may refer you to a local chamber of commerce (*camera di commercio*), of which there are over 100 throughout Italy, to complete your paperwork. Local Chambers of Commerce can be found through the Yellow Pages (www.paginegialle.it) or from overseas branches of the Italian Chambers of Commerce. The website of the Chamber of Commerce has links to various investment authorities in Italy who may be able to assist with financing and other incentives. During the 1990's the chambers of commerce were reformed and given a totally independent status in their role of supporting and promoting business interests for their area.

CHOOSING AN AREA

IN ADDITION to market research and preparing the ground, one also has to choose an area. As mentioned, northern Italy is the most dynamic business region of Italy . This does not mean however that the Mezzogiorno should be totally ignored. Generous incentives have resulted in a rush of both foreign and Italian companies to the south. However, the deep south (Naples to Sicily) is traditionally the least-favoured region because of mafia activity and poor infrastructure.

The type of business envisaged will also have a bearing on the choice of area. Some foreigners find themselves partly or wholly dependent on other expatriates for clientele, while others will rely on Italian consumers and yet others on an international clientele. Medical and dental practitioners prefer the Milan area where there are an estimated 30,000 expatriates. For the Lombardy region as a whole the number is probably triple that. Those in the real estate business could find themselves based in the north, Rome, Tuscany or Umbria.

USEFUL RESOURCES

The Economist Survey: Available from The Economist Shop, 15 Regent Street, London SW1Y 4LR; ☎020-7839 1921; www.economist.com/surveys/.
English Yellow Pages: These are nothing to do with British Telecom. They are a source guide for the English-speaking foreign community in Rome, but with supplements for Florence, Milan, Naples, Genoa, Palermo and Catania. Available from international bookshops and news-stands in the above three cities and also online at: www.intoitaly.it.
Financial Times Surveys: From time to time the Financial Times produces surveys of business in different areas of Italy or on Italian industry as a whole and publishes them in the paper. To obtain a copy of a specific issue first call the Readers' Enquiry Service, ☎020-7873 4211, to find the date of publication and then call the back issues department on 01988 -402221 to place an order.
The Informer: Buroservice SNC, Via Tigli 2, 20020 Milan; ☎02-93581477; fax 02-93580280; www.informer.it. An online magazine aimed at expatriates in Italy. Provides regular updates on changes in the legislation regarding tax, businesses etc. plus the best ways to tackle the bureaucracy. Subscription costs Euro 49 per annum.
The Italian Business Review: Founded in 1967. Published monthly (except August) by

The Italian Business Review Inc., European address: Suite 693, 2 Old Bromp-
ton Road, London SW7 3DQ; ☎020-7413 9554; fax 020-7581 4445. Subscription US $510 annually. Comprehensive reporting of Italian business news and
a good way to keep in touch with developments in Italy; includes forecasts and
indicators and focus and analysis sections.
Opportunities for Investment and Joint Ventures in Southern Italy: published by IASM (see
below), Via Ariosto 24, Milano; ☎02-481 76 36.
Wanted in Rome: (www.wantedinrome.com) An online magazine aimed at the expatriate community. Has a large classified advertisement section listing accommodation, jobs and other services needed by expats.

RAISING FINANCE

THOSE CONTEMPLATING OPENING a business in Italy should note that
UK banks in Britain will not be able to provide start-up loans in cases where
the prospective proprietor intends to be resident abroad. As already mentioned
Italian banks are unlikely to lend money to small businesses for start-ups, and
in any case, the interest rates are prohibitive. The obvious way for prospective
proprietors to raise money is by selling their UK home. If this proves insufficient
then it should be possible to raise a mortgage on an Italian property. Abbey
National and the Woolwich Building Society have opened offices in Milan (see
Mortgages in the *Setting up Home* chapter).
  Alternatively one could investigate the potential of the Italian government
business incentive schemes (see below).

Investment Incentives

If raising finance is a problem, it may be worth investigating whether or not your
proposed business could benefit from a government or EU incentive programme.
Government schemes are heavily biased in favour of the Mezzogiorno (the
provinces south of Rome, and Sicily and Sardinia), however certain small islands
and specially designated zones in Tuscany, Umbria and the north of Italy also
come with inducement packages, albeit less munificent ones. The government
agency that handles new investment (ie. new businesses) in the Mezzogiorno is
the Istituto Assistenza Sviluppo Mezzogiorno (Agency for the Promotion and
Development of Southern Italy) known as IASM, the head office of which is in
Rome. There are also regional IASM offices in Brussels, Milan, Turin, Verona,
Bologna and in the towns of southern Italy. The main development agency
Sviluppo Italia can be contacted in +39 06 421 60939/43/54 and it now has
a website, www.sviluppoitalia.it. The British Chamber of Commerce in Milan
(☎02-877798) can also put you in touch with local offices.

Tax Incentives: Certain of the employer's social security contributions are
refunded in the case of new investments.

Non-tax incentives: The governent also offers grants and low-interest loans up to the level of 70% to 75% of total investment. For joint ventures, regional and state agencies in the Mezzogiorno will put up half the share capital and then give the private partner the option to buy out the state's shares when the company is over the start-up period. Small and medium-sized businesses valued at not more than about 30,000 Euros are entitled to loans at 10.3% interest (lower in the south). The maximum loan is 2,000,000 million Euros.

Research and technological assistance: All businesses engaged in research projects 60% based in Italy are eligible for incentive grants subject to government approval.

Specific Activity Incentives: Companies engaged in certain types of business activities are eligible for grants throughout Italy:

Agriculture	Shipping yards and ship repairs
Cinema	Waste Disposal
Machine Tools	Publishing
Trading companies (retail and wholesale)	Mining
Aircraft	Energy Saving
Publishing	Hotel and Catering
Maritime Fishing	Handicrafts

European Union Incentives: Europeans carrying out business activities in Italy are entitled to grants and soft loans under aid programmes operated by the EU. The main programmes are:

The European Regional Development Fund: the ERDF exists to redress regional imbalances within the EU.

European Social Fund: aims to facilitate employment of workers through increasing their mobility.

European Agricultural Fund: aims to improve agricultural structures.

The New Union Instrument for Borrowing and Lending: The purpose of the NCIBL is to furnish loans for investment projects that contribute to the greater convergence and integration of the economic policies of the EU member states.

Other EU incentives are obtainable for the coal and steel industries and research and technology development.

RELOCATION AGENCIES AND BUSINESS SERVICES

INSPIRED BY AN INCREASING awareness of the business potential of Italy but deterred by the awfulness of the red tape, newcomers can turn to a relocation or business assistance agency. There is an expanding number of such agencies, particularly in the north and Rome, which can help aspiring business people not only with commercial contacts and guidance through the formidable procedures for setting up, but also the equally frustrating domestic problems of finding somewhere to live and arranging connections to the utilities, telephone, internet etc. In addition to the addresses provided below, a list of such agencies can be obtained from the British Chamber of Commerce for Italy (Via Camperio 9, 20123 Milan; ☎02-877798; www.britchamitaly.com – directory online) and The English Yellow Pages at www.intoitaly.it.

Useful Addresses

At Home, Specialty Relocation and Real Estate Services, via Bisagno 28, 00199 Rome; ☎06 86398549; fax 06 8606244; www.at-home-italy.com.

CORE (Cocchini Relocation S.r.L., Via Sirtori 13, 20129 Milan; ☎+39 02 29512793; fax +39 02 29513075. Relocation services (securing of documents, school registration etc.) and location of homes and offices for individuals and businesses. Agents also in Rome, Florence, Turin, Genoa and Venice.

Crown Relocations, V. Salaria 161 - 00016 - Monterotondo , Rome, ☎06 90085244; fax 06 90085060; www.crownrelo.com.

Global Relocation Solutions, via Cornaggia 10, 20123 Milan; ☎02 85141; fax 02 72212915: Rome Office, via G.B. Vico 9, 00196 Rome; ☎06 3609631; fax 06 36096363; www.globalrelocationsolutions.it.

International Relocation Management, Res. Cedri 611, 20080 Basiglio; ☎02 90785503; fax 02 90785503.

Milligan & Milligan Rentals, via degli Alfani 68, 50121 Florence; ☎055 268256; fax 055 268260; www.italy-rentals.com.

Property International, Via Correggio 55, 20149 Milan; ☎02-49 80 092; fax 02-48 19 41 70; also Rome office at Viale Aventino 79; ☎06 47 43 170; fax 06-57 43 182. Provides a wide range of services from rentals and sales of residential and commercial property to obtaining the necessary documentation for an expatriate to live and work in Italy.

Relocation Italy, via Montenero Sabino 21/c B/3, 00131 Rome; ☎06 41294697; fax 06 41294692; info@relocation-italy.com; www.relocation-italy.com. Also with offices in Milan, Palermo, Catania, Naples, Florence, Bologna and Genoa.

Studio Papperini: 114 Via Ugo Ojetti, 00137 Rome; ☎06-86895810; fax 06-86896516. Comprehensive relocation service headed by Giovanni Papperini, a solicitor specialising in immigration and nationality law. Based in Rome, but with offices in Milan, Naples, Genoa, Palermo, Florence, Bologna and Catania. Offers a pre-move service and cost effective, tailor-made package to suit employer or employee.

Turin Relocation, via Daneo 20, 10135 Turin; ☎011 3035504; www.turinrelocation.com.

Business Services & Business Consultants:

Abacus Serviced Offices Worldwide, ☎ 07074-847882; fax 01483-200221; enquiries@serviced-offices-europe.com; www.serviced-offices-europe.com, searchable online database of available offices.

English Yellow Pages, www.intoitaly.it has an extensive list of service providers.

British Chamber of Commerce in Italy, online database of service providers at: www.britchamitaly.com.

CSA snc: Via Pigna 14/A, 37121 Verona; ☎045-592482; fax 045-597629. CSA provides a full range of commercial services from set-up and relocation to providing essential contacts throughout northern Italy and is a member of the British Chamber of Commerce in Milan.

Regus Business Centre Srl: Via Torino 2, 20123 Milano; ☎02-725461; fax 02-72546400; www.regus.com. Fully furnished offices at five locations in Milan and four in Rome, contact detail can be found on their website.

BUSINESS STRUCTURES

IN ORDER TO operate commercially in Italy, an individual or a company must have a recognized Italian business structure. The equivalent of a UK Limited Liability company is a *Societa per Azioni* or SpA. Individuals may prefer a simpler entity, the *Societa di responsibilita limitada* (SrL), or the simplest, *Societa in Accommodita Semplice* (SAS). The formalities of setting up a business structure are normally entrusted to a legal or fiscal advisor. Large international accountants such as PricewaterhouseCoopers, Andersen, KPMG, Ernst & Young etc. who have offices in Italy will sometimes recommend local consultants. Alternatively, the British Chamber of Commerce in Milan will be able to suggest ways of locating possible advisors.

The different business entities and the steps required to form them are as follows:

SpA. An SpA roughly corresponds to a UK Plc. To create an SpA specific information regarding the company, its shareholders and directors must be incorporated into a public deed. Before an SpA can be formed two thirds of the capital must be underwritten by at least two of the shareholders and deposited with the Banca d'Italia until the company is officially registered unless there is a sole shareholder in which case the entire capital is required. Within 30 days of incorporating the company memorandum (*Atto Costitutivo*) and Articles of Association/Statutes (*Statuto*), they must be submitted to the registrar at the local Chamber of Commerce. After ascertaining that the necessary legal requirements have been fulfilled, the court will enter the company in the business register. Following incorporation, it is necessary to apply immediately for a VAT number (*numero di partita IVA*). You will also be given a company number (*numero REA*) and company register details (*registro imprese*).

In order to be quoted on the stock exchange an SpA must have a minimum capital of around €105,000. Stock exchange flotation is not however compulsory once this level of capital is reached. Once an SpA has gone public it is required to submit its accounts to outside auditors. Formation procedures for an SpA are very costly: an SpA with capital of €260,000 will cost approximately €16,000.

Srl. An Srl is a private (limited liability) company. The procedures for an Srl are similar to an SpA. The minimum authorized capital is €10,000. Liability is limited to the paid-up company capital. The capital contribution of a participant in an Srl is referred to as a quota. Unlike SpAs, Srls are not required to appoint an outside auditor if their capital is less €50,000.

Partnerships. Partnerships of various kinds are suitable for the self-employed as the setting up procedures are less complicated and there are no minimum capital requirements as there are for companies and corporations. The main disadvantage of partnerships is that participants are personally liable for company debts. The types of partnership structures are:

Societa in nome collettivo (Snc): A general partnership with unlimited liability, (ie. all the partners are liable for the debts of the partnership).

Societa in accomandita semplice (Sas): An incorporated partnership in which the main partners' liability is without limit.

Societa in accomandita per Azioni (SapA): A partnership in which the liability of individual participants is restricted by agreement to the amount of their capital input.

All partnerships have to be incorporated in a deed which gives details of the partners including their duties and responsibilities, and the aims of the partnership. The registration procedure is the same as for an SpA.

There is a minimum limit of two partners, but no maximum. Companies, including Italian companies may be partners. Partnerships are required to keep a company journal and an inventory register, with invoices of all purchases and copies of all correspondence sent and received. There is no legal requirement for an audit.

Sole Proprietor: A sole proprietor has to register within 30 days with the business registry of the town where his or her business is located – i.e. with the registrar at the local Chamber of Commerce. Sole proprietorship is disadvantageous for tax reasons (see *Taxation* below).

Accountancy Addresses

Andersen Spa: Via della Moscova 3, 20121 Milano; ☎02-290371; fax 026572876.

Coopers & Lybrand Spa: Via delle Quattre Fontane 15, 00184 Rome; ☎06-4818565; fax 06-48146365.

Deloitte and Touche Spa: Palazzo Carducci, Via Olona 2, 20123 Milano; ☎02-88011; fax 02-433440.

KPMG Peat Marwick Fides Snc.: Via Vittor Pisani 25, 20121 Milano; ☎02-67631; fax 02-67632278.

PricewaterhouseCoopers Spa: Corso Europa 2, 20122 Milan; ☎02-77851; fax 02-7785240.

Reconta Ernst & Young SaS di Bruno Gimpel: Via Torino, 68, 20123 Milano; ☎02-722121; fax 02-72212037.

IDEAS FOR NEW BUSINESSES

UNLIKE SPAIN AND PORTUGAL where the majority of expatriates are concentrated in specific areas of the country, in Italy they are more widely dispersed. This makes it difficult to start up bars, restaurants, shops etc. that are largely dependent on expatriate patronage. As already mentioned, the Italians are avid, but very discerning consumers, so competition in the food and other retail businesses is likely to be keen, and in the case of fashion, unbeatable. It is for this reason that newcomers may feel happier taking over an established and profitable business through which new products can be gradually introduced on a trial-run basis. This can be a less risky way of creating a new business ie. by introducing new products with existing ones rather than starting from scratch.

Some ideas that have proved successful so far include: running a characterful, luxury guesthouse/hotel, offering cookery or painting courses in Tuscany, Umbria, Puglia and anywhere picturesque, also other types of holiday, horse-riding, cycling, walking etc., running an English book/video shop or one selling typically English products that the Italians will buy perhaps combined with an English tea shop or restaurant.

By European standards the majority of Italian businesses are on a small scale employing fewer than 100 staff; only 19% of the workforce are employed in companies with over 500 workers. This means there is no shortage of small commercial concerns available in the in the market place.

Doctors and Dentists

An area where foreigners are likely to succeed, sometimes beyond their wildest dreams, is in the professions where their training, particularly in the medical and dental fields, is acknowledged to be vastly superior to those acquired by the vast majority of their Italian colleagues. Italians and expatriates alike prefer to trust their health and teeth to private practitioners, despite the enormous fees charged, rather than suffer the often abysmal public health and dental services. Under EU reciprocity regulations, doctors' and dentists' qualifications obtained in one EU country are recognized throughout the EU. There is therefore little difficulty for foreigners establishing a lucrative niche in private healthcare, once the initial, bureaucratic procedures have been dealt with.

Estate Agents

One professional that is in short supply in Italy is the estate agent. There are relatively few Italian estate agents and they deal mainly in city property. Although there are also a few British estate agents their clientele is almost exclusively British. There is definitely a gap in the market for estate agents to sell to Italians. Now that currency restrictions have been abolished in Italy, Italians are also beginning to buy up property in France, Spain, Portugal etc. and it would certainly be worth the while of estate agents with international contacts looking into this area of business.

Food

Health food is becoming increasingly popular in Italy and there is potential here for frozen and prepacked diet meals and other health foods.The other food area that has become a craze amongst young Italians is *il fast food*. American hamburger joints are doing a roaring trade. For all their culinary skills, the Italians are not particulary good at fast food preparation and so at the moment, this is an outsiders' market.

Restaurants are another possibility although it will have to be something exotic to the Italians, for instance Indian or Thai restaurants and be in a big city where tastes are cosmopolitan. Another food-related area is food-travel, where tourists come to sample real Italian food, shop in the markets and learn to cook the food for themselves.

The Garage Trade

There are no national chains of car repair centres in Italy and the trade is dominated by thousands of small, family-run businesses specializing in supplying services to the motorist: mechanical maintenance (*auto riparatori*), body shops (*carrozzieri*) and tyre supply and maintenance (*gommisti*). Such businesses are supplied by small local wholesalers who supply individual businesses with minimal quantities of parts.

Wine Producer

It is the dream of many expatriates to be the proprietor of a vineyard but often they do not know where to begin and what it involves. In fact being the owner can be the easiest part and it is very common practice in Italy to sub-contract production (crop maintenance, harvesting, wine-making, bottling, labelling) in part or in full which is fine if all you want is to see your name on a wine label but not if you want to try to make a profit. Unless you are an experienced viticulturist you will probably need some outside help while you learn more about the art of wine-growing.

One company which specialises in properties with vineyards in the unspoilt Piedmont region is Piedmont Properties, the British trading agent for the Azienda Agricola Ute de Vargas. The eponymous Ute is a retired opera diva who has lived in Italy for 30 years and owned and run a successful vineyard in Piedmont since 1987. She has been marketing property, especially vineyards, in the region since 1989. The UK and USA marketing operations can be contacted online at www.piedmontproperties.com or telephone 01344-624096. Prices start at £60,000 for a small (1.5 hectare) vineyard on its own, and from £120,000 for a small vineyard with a period farmhouse.

See also *Appendix I, Personal Case Histories, John Matta*.

Other

Other foreign professionals who have located a demand for their services in Italy, and who have set up successful businesses include lawyers qualified in international law, accountants, veterinarians, landscape gardeners and house restorers.

Exporters

Areas of high demand for imports into Italy include high quality paper products and stationary, meat, electro-medical equipment (with technical support services) and security systems. The Italy Desk of the Overseas Trade Services of the Department of Trade and Industry (DTI) in London (Kingsgate House, 66-74 Victoria Street, London SW1E 6SW; ☎020-7215 4385; fax 020-7215 4711; www.tradedepartment.gov.uk) and the regional Business Link offices (see below) provide help and information specifically for exporters in a number of ways. They are able to provide basic market information, commission status reports on specific companies and find suitable representatives for UK firms as well as giving current information on tariff rates and import procedures. Fees are charged for most of these services. Although this service will only be of use to those considering exporting to Italy, the DTI also publishes several booklets focused on Italy including *Italy Trade Brief* and *Italy, an Overseas Trade Supplement*. It can also advise small businesses thinking of venturing into Italy. All of these publications are available free of charge from the DTI by calling the above number and asking for the Italy Desk.

In addition, the Trade Partners UK Library at Room 150, First Floor, Ashdown House, 123 Victoria Street, London SW1; ☎020-7215 5444; www.tradepartners.gov.uk) is worth a visit for anyone researching into business opportunities in Italy. The library boasts a mine of statistical information and business and industry reports as well as an extensive supply of the Italian *Yellow Pages*. The library is open from 9.30am-5.30pm Monday to Friday and visitors may use the library at any time within these hours (you will have to sign in with a business address), although students are mysteriously required to make appointments in advance.

An alternative to the DTI's Italy Desk in London are the Business Link offices set up around the country as one-stop-shops for businesses. They can also advise on exporting to other countries including Italy. To find your nearest, look up Business Link in the telephone directory.

RUNNING A BUSINESS

Employing Staff

EMPLOYER AND EMPLOYEE relations in Italy are controlled by a mass of social and labour legislation, parts of which may vary according to the employer's principal industrial activity and the work status of the employee. The three main categories of staff are *dirigenti* (managers), *impiegati* (white-collar staff) *and operai* (workmen/women). Depending on their category, conditions of employment, including the level of employer/employee social security deductions, minimum salary, holiday allowance and minimum advance notice of dismissal, retirement and death benefits, will vary.

Successful small companies run by foreigners in Italy are unanimous in exhorting newcomers to take enormous care in the selection of staff. The Italian labour laws are significantly more protective towards employees than in other EU countries like Britain, and a small employer can be ruined by his or her virtual inability to dismiss inefficient staff.

Workers' rights. Italian workers' rights are guaranteed by Law number 300 of 20 May 1970. They are as follows:

- Freedom of opinion.
- The installation of audiovisual equipment is not permitted for checking workers' activities.
- Employers are not permitted to check on a worker's fitness to work.
- Personnel searches of unskilled workers may only be made by automatic selection systems and must respect the dignity and privacy of the worker.
- Disciplinary action is only permitted under laid-down procedures.
- Opinion surveys by employers are not permitted.
- Employees may ascertain that safety regulations are being adhered to.
- Employees may not be downgraded; no worker may be transferred from one unit to another, except for proven technical, organizational or production reasons.
- Workers have the right to form and join unions and carry on union activities on work premises.
- The courts may reinstate a worker judged to have been unfairly dismissed.
- Companies may not suppress union activity.

Trades Union: Apart from the major trade unions (see Chapter Six, *Employment*) which are unified into political rather than work-type categories, there are others which spring from a particular industry or sector of activity. Working hours lost through strikes have halved since 1984 thanks to Italy's economic boom which has brought prosperity to a large number of Italians. Nowadays, strikes are most likely to occur in the public sector and transportation industries. The continuing influence of Italy's trade union movement should not be underestimated at worker level although its powers have declined considerably since the 1970's. Workers are not obliged to belong to a union and an estimated 70% are non-unionized.

Employer Associations: Most of the employers' associations were set up in the aftermath of the First World War. The four main ones are: The General Confederation of Agriculture (Confagricoltura), The General Confederation of Commerce (Confcommercio) and The Confederation of Small Firms (Confabi). These Associations represent their members in discussions with the government; tax evasion is a regular subject on the agenda.

Employee Training. There is no obligation for employers to provide employee training programmes but they may enhance the employer's activity. As an incentive to employers to engage young people, the 1986 Contract of Training and Work was passed. Under this, employees of less than 30 years of age can be engaged for a period of two years on normal salary rates but with minimal social security contributions. After two years the employer may confirm or terminate the contract with no further obligation.

Wages and Salaries. For each Italian industry there is a national minimum wage and salary scale. However most employers are obliged to pay way above the mininum, except in the most deprived regions. In common with many other European countries employees are entitled to an additional month's salary ('the thirteenth month'), payable in December. In commercial industries it is also customary to pay a further additional month's salary in June.

Social Security Contributions. The government social security system provides old age and disability pensions, sickness and unemployment benefits, healthcare and medical treatment. As the quality of public health service is extremely variable, most employees opt for private treatment. Nevertheless social security and welfare contributions are obligatory on the part of the employee and employer, the latter paying the major share of the employee contributions.

Paid Holidays: In addition to a statutory annual vacation, variable between five and six weeks according to the employer's activity, and the employee's category and length of service, staff are entitled to the ten statutory public holidays (see Chapter Four, *Daily Life*). Women are entitled to five month's paid maternity leave beginning in the last two months of pregnancy.

Taxation

The scale of Italian tax evasion practised by businesses and individuals makes other Europeans look like amateurs and has already been dealt with in the *Daily Life* chapter. For the foreign business person the temptation to follow the Italian example is great, but probably not worth it, as the Italian tax authorities are likely to be far from lenient with foreign tax dodgers.

When contemplating setting up in business abroad some professionals consider opting for sole proprietor or freelance status. However, from a tax point of view this can be a handicap since you are taxed at source, usually at an excessive rate, which obliges you to claim rebate from the tax authorities; a process which can take several years by which time bankruptcy may well have occurred.

Once a business structure has been registered in Italy, the company becomes liable for Italian taxes. Unlike the UK, the fiscal year for companies can begin or end on any date in a period not exceeding twelve months. However since it is easy to overlook the dates when tax instalments fall due and thus become liable for a 15% surcharge plus 9% interest charges per annum, it may be advisable to stick to the calendar year ie. 1 January to 31 December which is easily remembered.

Each corporation must file an annual tax return on Form 760, giving company results. The tax return must be accompanied by a balance sheet, a report from the statutory auditors (*sindaci*) and the directors' reports and resolutions approving the accompanying financial statements. The tax return covers both Corporate

Income Tax and Local Income Tax (see below). The main company taxes are:

Imposta sul Reddito delle Personne Giuridiche (IRPEG). IRPEG, or Corporation Income Tax, is levied on corporations at the fixed rate of 36%. Note that the Mezzogiorno is a tax-free zone for newly established companies. Other company tax-free zones abut on Livigno, Trieste and Gorizia.

Partnerships will either pay IRPEG, or in some cases personal (IRPEF) income tax.

IRAP a local income tax payable by businesses as well as individuals: it is levied at the base rate of 4.25%.

Imposta sul Valore Aggiunto (IVA). The Italian equivalent of VAT is charged at the standard rate of 20%. Other rates 4% and 10%. The area of VAT exemptions can cause complications for businesses. Certain types of supply, principally services, are VAT exempt. As far as companies are concerned this means means that no VAT is charged on output; correspondingly no input deductions may be made. The main categories of exemption are sales and leasing of both land and buildings (except newly constructed buildings and leasing of buildings used as fixed assets by a business), insurance, banking and financial services, certain health services and education.

The payment and collection of VAT is separate from other taxation. Traders are required to produce monthly computations of the VAT payable and the VAT receivable. If the balance is in favour of the payable this must be paid to the tax authority by the twentieth day of the following month. If the balance is in favour of the trader, the amount is carried forward to be offset against future payable amounts. If, at the end of the calendar year, the balance still shows in the trader's favour the amount may be reclaimed from the authorities.

For small businesses with a turnover of less than €180,000 there is a simpler administrative procedure.

Imposta Comunale sugli Immobili (ICI): An annual tax on the value of property that varies from 0.4% to 0.65%.

Tassa di Concessione Governativa. This is a company registration tax introduced   payable on June 30th and every year thereafter. The tax varies according to the capital and legal entity of the company.

Accountancy Advice

Owing to the complexity of the Italian tax system it is essential to have expert fiscal advice: see the list of accountants under *Business Structures*, above.

APPENDICES

PERSONAL CASE HISTORIES

FURTHER READING

APPENDIX 1
PERSONAL CASE HISTORIES

SARAH RASMER

AS AN EXPAT EXPECTING to spend only a few years in Italy, life is very different to that experienced by a retiree in Tuscany and the experience will be very different to someone who speaks Italian and has decided to relocate to Italy to start a business. Sarah Rasmer, an American, accompanied her partner to Ferrara in northern Italy and has the following comments and advice to pass on to those who follow her to Ferrara, or Italy. We asked her:

How important is speaking the language?
It has been essential for us to study Italian as few people speak English in Ferrara. My husband must speak Italian at work, and was surprised that some people he works with do not speak in Italian, but in the local dialect. We find Italians to be very friendly, they have gone way out of their way to help us, even before we could speak any Italian.

What is the most infuriating part of living in Italy?:
The most frustrating thing that I have found about living in Italy has been the Italian bureaucracy system. We were advised to hire a translator to go with us when obtaining the necessary paperwork when we first arrived. We are very glad we followed this advice, as it took away some of the frustration involved due to our lack of Italian at the time. One thing that has been a source of confusion for me when dealing with the bureaucracy is that I took my husband's name when I got married. Italian women keep their maiden names when they marry and every

office where I had to get paperwork assumed I did the same. It has been easier for me to use my maiden name on my paperwork, because they didn't understand when I tried to explain it to them.

Did you find it hard to acclimatise to Italian working hours?:

Business hours are improving, but can still be frustrating. Many government offices are only open for a few hours in the mornings. It is always a good idea to call ahead to check business hours. Banks are open from 8:30-12:30 or 1pm and again between 3 and 4pm. Most shops are open from 9am through tp 12:30 or 1:00 pm, and open again from 3:30 or 4 to 7pm (4:30 or 5-7:30/8pm in summer). Each city designates one morning or afternoon a week that the shops close, Ferrara's is Thursday afternoons. Small, family run businesses close for funerals and vacations; they will leave a note on their door to notify their customers. Most businesses close for at least a couple of weeks in August. Many shops are opening on Sunday afternoons; and some do not close for lunch. All *Tabacchi* shops, which sell various items like stamps and prepaid phone cards in addition to cigarettes, remain open for lunch. There are two large shopping centres outside of Ferrara, which have large grocery stores. These stores are called *supermercato* and they have the best selection and prices for groceries. They also carry household items like appliances and clothes. There are fruit and vegetable shops in most neighbourhoods in the city where they pick out the produce for you, so it is best to find one you like and frequent it as they give the best selection to regular customers.

How did you find motoring in Italy?:

Buying a car was more complicated than we expected. We were able to buy a used car from a dealer and dealers offer warranties with used cars. The dealer seemed reluctant to sell us a car at first, even though my husband's colleague, who also speaks English, was friends with the owner and accompanied us. They told us that there is more paperwork for them to fill out because we are foreigners. They were also concerned with the fact that we are here on a temporary basis. My husband's employer had to call the dealer to 'put in a good word' for us. We were only able to finance the car for 18 months, I think because we told them we were going to be here for 2-3 years. The whole process took several weeks, but we did manage to buy the car we wanted in the end! We were advised to buy either German or Italian made cars because they are the easiest to resell, diesels are also popular.

Many streets in the historic centres of cities are closed to traffic except for taxis and buses. We live on such a street and had to get permission to drive on it, and can only drive on part of the street.

Have you found any Italian websites particularly useful?:

The website I use most is the Italian railway's website: www.fs-on-line.com. This is the best place to find current train schedules and you can also look up the fare. It is now possible to purchase train tickets online, but only for tickets that have reservations and that depart between the hours of 6:30-11:30pm. Ferrara's train station is not a full service station, so sometimes it is easier to purchase tickets at a travel agent; the website above lists authorised travel agents.

For good information about shopping and factory outlets see: www.made-in-italy.com. The International Women's Forum is a group located in Bologna for international women who speak English; their website is www.iwfbologna.org. They also provide a job bank for members.

GEORGINA GORDON-HAM (JINKS)

GEORGINA HAS AN ITALIAN-FRENCH MOTHER and an English father and so, apart from being trilingual from an early age she has always had familial links with Italy, and some of her schooling took place there. After finishing a PhD in Languages at the University of Rome in 1975 she did a Postgraduate course in translating and interpreting at the University of Westminster. For six years she was the permanent staff translator/interpreter for the ENI Group (Italy's National Petroleum Board). She is a Member of the Institute of Translating and Interpreting and the Institute of Journalists, London and has been a freelance translator/interpreter/journalist since 1982. She has lived in Italy for about 20 years and her husband who is English, is in the IT business. We asked her:

How do you find the Italian red-tape?
It is very irritating. For instance the *Permesso di soggiorno* has to be renewed every five years even if you have lived in Italy for 20 years. However belonging to the European Union has caused some improvements. Things do move a bit faster.

I suppose you had a head-start setting up in business with your connections?
Well yes, but you still have to work very hard at it, especially the international marketing aspect. To be taken seriously you should also become a member of the Chamber of Commerce and belong to a recognised professional body.

What about your work?
Being an interpreter/translator is an ongoing process as you have to maintain contact with all your languages, which in my case are English, Italian and French. Interpreters charge fees on a per day basis. Translations are generally charged by the page in Italy although sometimes by words which works out at about £65-70 per 1,000 words.

What is the social life like?
Here in Rome there are clubs for the British, Canadian and Americans. Actually they tend to be mixed nationality as there are a lot of Italian husbands. It's not so easy for a newcomer to socialise with Italians who although open and welcoming are reserved. Playing sports is another good way to socialise. Also, there are two types of foreign communities, those *en passage* who are here for two or three years and those who live here permanently.

Is it pleasant living in Rome?
Yes, apart from July and August when it is very humid, the climate is very pleasant

and mild, especially in winter. The area around, particularly the hills are beautiful and in winter you can go skiing for the day at Terminillo and Campo Felice about one and half hour's drive away. The sea is also close and there are some lovely resorts such as Sperlonga, Circeo, Friggene, Santa Marinella.

Have you any advice for those thinking of going to work in Italy?
I would advise that you don't have too many romantic ideas about Italy, coming here to work is not like coming here on holiday when you are free from all cares. You need to have a pragmatic approach. If you don't already know the country and the language very well then I would recommend that you start by working here on a full-time basis because then the company posting you, or the employer recruiting you does all the paperwork and sometimes fixes up your accommodation as well. This way you get to know your way around the procedures so that it is all familiar when you come to do it for yourself and you feel less like an outsider.

MARIA MAKEPEACE

MARIA MAKEPEACE, A FREELANCE ARTIST and teacher, moved from the UK to Siena in 1988. In 1997 she moved to Florence. She is a qualified teacher of art, English and geography and has over 20 years' teaching experience. Despite being half Italian she did not learn to speak Italian properly until she arrived in Italy and has now made contact with the Italian side of her family who live in Tuscany. She has had over 30 exhibitions of her work in Italy. Her 'bread and butter work is Tuscan landscapes and she paints to commission including animal portraits (☎ 055-223819). She also writes poetry based on the history, traditions and/or culture of Tuscany. Her exhibitions have been very successful with a large part of her work going to clients abroad including the United States. We asked her:

Is it difficult to survive on painting alone?
It would be, but I do some teaching as well. For instance I have given private English lessons, and taught art in *elementari and scuola media* schools in extra-curricular classes paid for by the parents. I also taught at the *Università Populare* (a kind of Italian WEA) in Siena. Also, I have just recently done my first simultaneous translation.

How do you find the Italian bureaucracy
It is very irritating. For instance when I have to send one of my paintings to a client abroad there are forms to be filled out in triplicate and I have to take an actual painting (and they can be very big) to the Belle Arti inspector in the main national gallery for checking that I am not illegally exporting anything. The other thing you have to do is register for tax. Freelances have to register for *partita EVA* (VAT), but I am not generally earning enough for this. I am now also registered with the British Chamber of Commerce in Milan.

Another small niggle concerns publicity. Posters have to be stamped by the *comune* and each stamp costs money. I have been known to make myself a T-shirt instead of a poster and walk around Siena for a few days before an exhibition – wearing my publicity! Permits from the *Vigili Urbani* (Traffic Wardens) to transport exhibitions into central pedestrian areas are yet another bureaucratic nightmare – unless you know someone who knows the chief traffic warden.

How do you find social life and the Italians

In Siena I was living just outside the town in the countryside and met a lot of Italian country people. In Florence I tend to meet only English people. I am not a club person at all and the nature of my work is such that I need to be alone quite a lot of the time. I go to lectures at the British Institute here in Florence and use their wonderful library. I am also going to life-drawing evenings occasionally to keep my drawing 'in form'.

How do you find a place to exhibit?

You usually have to ask the *Comune* (town hall). Sometimes they will rent you space and sometimes it will be provided free. Another possibility is to 'pay with a picture', for example in hotels.

Have you any advice for anyone, particularly artists thinking of setting up in Italy?

Firstly, don't come to Florence thinking it is the art centre of the world. In one sense it is – for art from the past, but definitely not for modern art.

Another tip is about exporting. If you sell to foreigners make sure that you charge enough so as not to make a loss on the carriage abroad which can be very expensive if you go to *spedizionari* (specialised freight companies), especially if they have the local monopoly. You have to have special wooden crates for packing. You need a friendly carpenter to make the crates at a fraction of the price and then take them to the freight company's office yourself, having been to Belle Arti yourself with the picture first, so that it is ready packed.

You can save a lot of money by doing your own framing and publicity (see above). You need adaptability, imagination, staying power....and a knowledge of several languages, not just Italian, is useful; as is an interest in the history and cultural heritage of Italy.

JOHN MATTA

JOHN MATTA, ORIGINALLY FROM LONDON had an Italian-British father who ran a wine importing business (F.S. Matta Ltd) in the UK. In the 1960's his father bought into a Chianti vineyard and John began to shuttle back and forth between London and Italy which meant he could spend a total of four to five months a year there. He did a three year course in oenology at the Istituto Tecnico Agrario Umberto Primo, (a state-run college that specialises in oenology) located in Alba in Piemonte. He now runs the family vineyard, Castello Vicchiomaggio (75 acres) and produces, a Chianti Classico DOCG. As well as being a wine producer, he also exports worldwide, lets holiday apartments and owns a restaurant. He has been permanently resident in Italy since 1980. We asked him:

Obviously you had a head start, but how difficult is it to set up a business in Italy?
Setting up a business in Italy is definitely not as easy as the UK where you can buy an off the peg company one day and be trading the next. Here, you have to allow at least four months for all the processes to be completed. It is a big mistake to think you can do it all on your own. You should start by using one of the specialist companies that make their living from company start-ups. They charge a fee yes, but in the end it will save you a lot of time and be worth it. Also, unless you can communicate freely in Italian you cannot expect to make a success of business here.

What about foreigners in the wine business. Are there any British-run vineyards here?
I don't believe so, though there are a couple of Swiss and Germans and one American that I know of. Also, the big American company Kendall-Jackson from Napa Valley have taken over the vineyard of San Leonino which is a Chianti Classico.

What would your advice be to prospective wine-growers?
You need at least fifteen hectares (about 45 acres) if you want to bottle and market your own label. Less than 15 hectares would be a 'hobby vineyard and you could sell your grapes to the local wine co-operative. If one person wanted to grow, harvest and sell the grapes themselves then four hectares is manageable if you wanted to do the picking yourself (though there is always local help willing to come and pick for you).

Any final words of advice?
You must realise from the outset that Italy is a different country and that things are done quite differently here in a more time consuming way and there are procedures for everything. The UK is different from most European countries in this respect and it stems partly from the fact that Britain was never invaded. Napoleon invaded Italy and imposed the Code Napoleon which affects the laws and systems here. So if you are planning to come here and earn your living then think very carefully about it and the cultural adaptation it involves.

If you want to come here as a retiree, then things are quite different and it's much less of a big decision than coming here to start a business. Italians are so friendly and helpful and you can get by with conversational Italian.

ROGER WARWICK

ROGER WARWICK who is in his late forties has been based in Italy for about twenty years. He settled in Italy, after a period of taking extended holidays there, because he knew it better than other countries. He grew to like northern Italy and he preferred the climate to that of Britain. He was at one time manager of the duty-free facilities at Heathrow Airport and during his trips to Italy in the 1970's he taught English at private schools. In 1978 he and his Italian wife set up a business offering financial investigative services, which includes everything from assessing companies prior to merger or acquisition, to advising on counter industrial espionage tactics. Roger is also the regional secretary of the local Chamber of Commerce for Bologna and Emilia Romagna. He lives just outside Bologna on a modern development. We asked him:

Was it difficult to set up a business?

Yes it was. We are the only British-run organisation offering investigative services that has a licence from the local *prefetto* (magistrate). It is extremely difficult to obtain such a licence.

How do you find living and doing business in Italy compared with the UK?

Obviously I prefer it in Italy, or I wouldn't be here. Northern Italy is fine because it is efficient and things work well. I'm talking about the private sector; the public sector and the bureaucracy are Kafkaesque. I'm lucky enough to have found a niche and doing business here amongst normal people (i.e. not bureaucrats) is enjoyable, partly because a high standard of education is more widespread than in the UK. Italians are very good at pulling something out of the hat. When you ask an Italian engineer to produce something unusual or new he can do it. In Britain, it would be damned on the drawing board. On the other hand Italians are extremely bad at marketing their products whereas the British, French, Germans etc. are very good marketers. I think this is partly due to the poor image the Italians have abroad. English promoters use Englishness and French promoters Frenchness and the world recognises these as something chic. There is no similar regard for Italianness; in fact you'd be hard put to think of anything except *The Godfather* and stilletto murders. There is definitely scope for British experts in marketing techniques to promote Italian products in the UK.

The cost of living in Italy is greater than in the UK. In Bologna it is particularly high – the highest in Italy I believe, because there is no unemployment in this region and so there is no need to lower the prices. Bologna is one of the most pleasant towns in Italy. It is small enough to be human and big enough to be a city.

How do you find the social life and the Italians?

I live on a modern development of fifteen houses and all the couples there are Italian and of a similar age to us; much of our social life revolves around them. I speak fluent Italian which is essential. I know foreigners who have lived in Italy for twenty years and can only mumble a few words in Italian which severely limits the possibilities of making friends with Italians as hardly any of them speak English well enough to have an interesting conversation. The other part of my social life revolves around the events organised by the local Chamber of Commerce.

Have you any advice for those thinking of taking the plunge?

Forget your preconceptions about all Italians being gangsters and come to the north of Italy: realise you are going to be up against a bureaucracy like something out of Kafka's *The Trial*: learn to speak Italian.

APPENDIX 2

READING LIST

Buongiorno Italia! Coursebook, £10.99 plus three cassettes £6.99 each). A beginners' course in Italian comprising 20 lessons. The textbook, teacher's notes and cassettes can all be purchased individually from the BBC online shop: www.bbcshop.com.

A Concise History of Italy, Christopher Duggan, Mark Duggan, Cambridge University Press, 334 pages, £13.95 (US$19.95).

Excellent Cadavers: Alexander Stille, Vintage, £8.99 (US$15.00). The story of the mafia.

Getting it Right in Italy, William Ward, Bloomsbury (£9.99): a combination of insight into and practical advice on, all aspects of Italian life including money, family life, sex, politics and the economy, by a journalist and broadcaster who has made Italy his home for over ten years. Full of fascinating facts and figures in an easy access format. 390 pages.

The History of the Decline and Fall of the Roman Empire (Abridged), Edward Gibbon, David Womersley, Penguin Books, 848 pages, £9.99 (US$15.00).

A History of Contemporary Italy: Society and Politics 1943-1988, Paul Ginsborg, Penguin, £7.99 (US$14.95): Ginsborg's book charts the success of Italy's transformation from a war-torn country to the success story of the late 1980's and also traces the failed and repeated attempts at much-needed political reform. 425 pages.

The Honoured Society, Norman Lewis, Collins, £8.99: the journalist Norman Lewis writes absorbingly and authoritatively about the development of the Mafia's power and influence in Italy. 266 pages.

The Italians: Luigi Barzini, Penguin, £9.99 (US$14.00).

Lonely Planet produce a number of Italian guides, including Italy, Rome, Venice, Sicily, Tuscany and Walking in Italy. Lonely Planet phrasebooks are also a good source of the slang Italian that crops up in everyday life but never appears in traditional language courses. Lonely Planet books can be found in most bookshops and also ordered from their website www.lonelyplanet.com.

The New Italians: Charles Richards, Penguin, £8.99.

Rough Guides produce a number of Italian guides, including Italy, Rome, Tuscany and Umbria and Sardinia. Rough Guides can be found in most bookshops and also ordered from their website www.roughguides.com.

Touring in Wine Country: Northwest Italy: Maureen Ashley, Mitchell Beazley, £12.99 (US$19.95): an exploration of Northest Italy, the source of some of the country's finest wines, unveiling the secrets behind its esteemed winemaking traditions. 152 pages.

A Traveller's Wine Guide to Italy: Stephen Hobley, Aurum Press, £9.99: a wealth of practical information on Italian wine, some reflections on cultural and gastronomic points of interest in Italy, and some suggested itineraries for visiting wineries. 144 pages.

The above books can be obtained through the Italian Book Shop (7 Cecil Court, London WC2N 4EZ; ☎ 020-7240 1634; www.eurobooks.co.uk). Nearest tube Leicester Square. The majority of the books listed above can also be bought from online booksellers such as www.amazon.co.uk, www.amazon.com and www.bn.com who will deliver worldwide.

ALSO AVAILABLE:

Other titles in Vacation Work's Live & Work *series include:*

Live & Work in Australia & New Zealand (£10.99)

Live & Work in France (£10.99)

Live & Work in Germany (£10.99)

Live & Work in Italy (£10.99)

Live & Work in Japan (£10.99)

Live & Work in Russia & Eastern Europe (£10.99)

Live & Work in Saudi & The Gulf (£10.99)

Live & Work in Scandinavia (£10.99)

Live & Work in Scotland (£10.99)

Live & Work in Spain & Portugal (£10.99)

Live & Work in The USA & Canada (£10.99)

These books are available from good bookshops, the Website www.vacationwork.co.uk or direct from the publishers (plus p. & p. £1.50 (UK)/£2.50 (overseas):

Vacation Work, 9 Park End Street, Oxford OX1 1HJ
Tel: +44 (0)1865-241978   Fax +44 (0)1865-790885
E-mail info@vacationwork.co.uk

Vacation Work publish:

	Paperback	Hardback
Summer Jobs Abroad	£9.99	£15.95
Summer Jobs in Britain	£9.99	£15.95
Supplement to Summer Jobs in Britain and Abroad *published in May*	£6.00	–
Work Your Way Around the World	£12.95	–
Taking a Gap Year	£11.95	–
Taking a Career Break	£11.95	–
Working in Tourism – The UK, Europe & Beyond	£11.95	–
Kibbutz Volunteer	£10.99	–
Working on Cruise Ships	£10.99	–
Teaching English Abroad	£12.95	–
The Au Pair & Nanny's Guide to Working Abroad	£12.95	–
The Good Cook's Guide to Working Worldwide	£11.95	–
Working in Ski Resorts – Europe & North America	£10.99	–
Working with Animals – The UK, Europe & Worldwide	£11.95	–
Live & Work Abroad - a Guide for Modern Nomads	£11.95	–
Working with the Environment	£11.95	–
Health Professionals Abroad	£11.95	–
Accounting Jobs Worldwide	£11.95	–
The Directory of Jobs & Careers Abroad	£12.95	–
The International Directory of Voluntary Work	£12.95	–
Live & Work in Australia & New Zealand	£10.99	–
Live & Work in Belgium, The Netherlands & Luxembourg	£10.99	–
Live & Work in France	£10.99	–
Live & Work in Germany	£10.99	–
Live & Work in Italy	£10.99	–
Live & Work in Japan	£10.99	–
Live & Work in Russia & Eastern Europe	£10.99	–
Live & Work in Saudi & the Gulf	£10.99	–
Live & Work in Scandinavia	£10.99	–
Live & Work in Scotland	£10.99	–
Live & Work in Spain & Portugal	£10.99	–
Live & Work in the USA & Canada	£10.99	–
Drive USA	£10.99	–
Hand Made in Britain - The Visitors Guide	£10.99	–
Scottish Islands - The Western Isles	£12.95	–
Scottish Islands - Orkney & Shetland	£11.95	–
The Panamericana: On the Road through Mexico and Central America	£12.95	–
Travellers Survival Kit: Australia & New Zealand	£11.95	–
Travellers Survival Kit: Cuba	£10.99	–
Travellers Survival Kit: India	£10.99	–
Travellers Survival Kit: Lebanon	£10.99	–
Travellers Survival Kit: Madagascar, Mayotte & Comoros	£10.99	–
Travellers Survival Kit: Mauritius, Seychelles & Réunion	£10.99	–
Travellers Survival Kit: Mozambique	£10.99	–
Travellers Survival Kit: Oman & the Arabian Gulf	£11.95	–
Travellers Survival Kit: South Africa	£10.99	–
Travellers Survival Kit: South America	£15.95	–
Travellers Survival Kit: Sri Lanka	£10.99	–
Travellers Survival Kit: USA & Canada	£10.99	–

Distributors of:

Summer Jobs USA	£12.95	
Internships (On-the-Job Training Opportunities in the USA)	£18.95	–
How to Become a US Citizen	£11.95	–
World Volunteers	£10.99	–
Green Volunteers	£10.99	–

Plus 27 titles from Peterson's, the leading American academic publisher, on college education and careers in the USA. Separate catalogue available on request.

Vacation Work Publications, 9 Park End Street, Oxford OX1 1HJ
Tel 01865–241978   Fax 01865–790885

Visit us online for more information on our unrivalled range of titles for work, travel and gap years, readers' feedback and regular updates:

www.vacationwork.co.uk